VEGIO

SHORT EPICS

ITRL 15

MAFFEO VEGIO

✦ ✦ ✦

SHORT EPICS

EDITED AND TRANSLATED BY

MICHAEL C. J. PUTNAM

with James Hankins

THE I TATTI RENAISSANCE LIBRARY

HARVARD UNIVERSITY PRESS

CAMBRIDGE, MASSACHUSETTS

LONDON, ENGLAND

2004

Series design by Dean Bornstein

Library of Congress Cataloging-in-Publication Data

Vegio, Maffeo, 1406 or 7–1458.
[Poems. Selections]
Short epics / Maffeo Vegio ; edited and translated by Michael C. J. Putnam,
with James Hankins.
p. cm. — (The I Tatti Renaissance Library ; 15)
Text in English and Latin.
Includes bibliographical references (p.) and index.
Contents: Book XIII of the *Aeneid* — Astyanax — The golden fleece — Antoniad.
ISBN 0-674-01483-9 (alk. paper)
1. Vegio, Maffeo, 1406 or 7–1458 — Translations into English.
2. Epic poetry, Latin (Medieval and modern) — Translations into English.
3. Anthony, of Egypt, Saint, ca. 250–355 or 6 — Poetry.
4. Astyanax (Legendary character) — Poetry.
5. Aeneas (Legendary character) — Poetry.
6. Jason (Greek mythology) — Poetry.
I. Putnam, Michael C. J.   II. Hankins, James.   III. Title.   IV. Series.
PA8585.V3A253 2004
873'.04 — dc22   2003067725

101406

Contents

❦❧❦

Introduction

꧁ ꧂

Maffeo Vegio (Maphaeus Vegius) was born in 1407 in the Lombard town of Lodi, some thirty-five kilometers southeast of Milan.[1] He was educated at the University of Pavia, an easy distance to the west of his native city. It was there that, in the year 1428 as a twenty-one year old student of the law, he published the work which was to be, for his own time and beyond, his chief claim to fame as a poet, a *Supplement* to Virgil's *Aeneid*. This begins where Virgil finishes, with the death of Aeneas's rival, Turnus, and takes the story to his hero's final deification.

Over the course of his career Vegio wrote some fifty works of prose and poetry.[2] The present volume collects four early hexameter poems, his major ventures into the meter and content of epic, published over an eight year period: the *Supplement* (often called *Book XIII of the Aeneid*), which was followed by the brief *Astyanax* (1430), four short books on the *Golden Fleece* (1431), and, finally, the four-book *Antoniad* on the life of St. Antony of the Desert (1436/7). In the year that saw the publication of the *Astyanax*, Vegio wrote two other poetic works in an attempt to flatter his way into the circle of Duke Filippo Maria Visconti at Milan, *Convivium Deorum* ("Banquet of the Gods") and *Carmen Heroicum ad Philippum Mariam Anglum Ducem Mediolanensium* ("Heroic Poem Dedicated to Filippo Maria Visconti, Duke of Milan"). When these failed in their mission, he turned successfully to the papal court and to Pope Eugenius IV, to whom he may have been introduced by his friend and fellow humanist, Lorenzo Valla.[3] In 1436 he was appointed to the posts of abbreviator and then datary. When the pope returned to Rome in 1443, Vegio became a canon of the Basilica of San Pietro, an office he held until his death in 1458.

*   *   *

Let us turn first to the *Supplement*. The poem begins a moment after the *Aeneid* ends, with its victorious hero surrounded by the Latins suing for peace. After a speech over the body of Turnus that is at once an accusation and a noble-minded act of conciliation, Aeneas withdraws to the dwellings of the Trojans and offers due sacrifice to the gods. He addresses first his son, Iulus, and then the assembled Trojans, on the glorious days ahead, with war a thing of the past. He is, in Vegio's unprecedented comparison, like a mother hen who has warded off a predator hawk from her brood.[4] The Rutulians meanwhile bring Turnus's corpse inside the city of Latinus. He takes charge of the cortege and utters words that begin with an abstract meditation on the perils of power but continue and conclude with a further apostrophe to Turnus that dwells on his impetuosity and on the sorrows it provoked, but also on his courageous death. He sends the body, suitably accompanied, to his father, Daunus, in his ancestral town of Ardea.

Vegio now shifts the scene to Ardea itself which, while elsewhere the battle was reaching its climactic conclusion, suffered a terrible conflagration (the people are like ants whose sheltering tree has been axed or a tortoise helpless on its back as flames approach). Daunus, grief-stricken, greets his son's funeral procession with a discourse which is at once lamentation for the sorrows that Turnus's demise has brought him, a eulogy of his son's gracefulness now lost, and a meditation on the horror of death's universality.

Halfway through the poem we return to Latinus who dispatches a mission to Aeneas and exhorts his people to receive the victor with whole hearts. When the embassy reaches the Trojans, Drances delivers an oration which is at once a *laudatio* of Aeneas and a detailed censure of Turnus and his negative conduct. Aeneas's reply, though alluding to the savagery of Turnus, anticipates the wedding to come and the building of the city of Lavinium. All now turn to the burial of the dead and its accompanying lamen-

tations. On the next day Trojans and Latin envoys return to
Laurentum where they are greeted by Latinus whose words,
though they veil a further reference to Turnus's past mischief, an-
ticipate Aeneas's new role as his son-in-law, a role which the hero's
reply happily embraces: Latinus will be his new Anchises. They
enter the palace as the throng voices its approval, and, upon the
arrival of Lavinia, the marriage ceremony takes place to the chant-
ing of the wedding hymn. Aeneas sends for appropriate gifts and
all join in the festive banquet. Latinus, after admiring Iulus, con-
verses with Aeneas about past events, especially those which had
occurred on the site of Rome.

With the nine-day celebration concluded, Aeneas begins the
foundation of his city. When he beholds his new wife's hair
aflame, he prays that the omen portend peace, and Venus makes a
sudden epiphany to confirm his request and to tell of the future
greatness of the race (whose prowess the fire symbolizes) that will
spring from Lavinia and take its brilliant start with the kingship
of Aeneas. After the passage of three years, Venus approaches Ju-
piter to ask for assurance of Aeneas's promised immortality upon
his death. Father agrees with daughter who commands the river
Numicius to wash away from her son's body whatever is mortal so
that she can carry the eternal remnant to the stars above.

Vegio's *Supplement* is the first autonomous poetic treatment of
events which follow directly, in terms of time and space, upon the
concluding moments of the *Aeneid*. He draws his inspiration, as
we will see, from ancient sources, particularly from hints within
the story of the *Aeneid* and from the *Metamorphoses* of Ovid, who
gives a brief survey of events in Aeneas's life subsequent to the
death of Turnus and offers, in his description of Caesar's apotheo-
sis, a model for Vegio to follow in depicting the stellification of his
hero. But Vegio was not the first to offer a detailed handling of the
material he made use of in the *Supplement*. Elements of the same
subject matter also appear in the final segments of earlier medieval

versions of the *Aeneid* as a whole. Two of these retellings, which might have been available to him, deserve special mention.

The first is the *Roman d'Eneas*, an anonymous Anglo-Norman poem dating from 1155–60, written in Old French and consisting of more than ten thousand brisk octosyllabic lines.[5] The poem as a whole reuses the tale of the *Aeneid* to document a saga of chivalric fulfillment in a secular realm devoted not only to knightly endeavors but also to the pageantry of worldly power that accompanies their successes. In both plot-line and rhetoric of presentation it elaborates on what Virgil merely suggests. In the first category, for example, the author takes delight, as would also have his audience, in documenting at length Aeneas's liaison with Dido as well as another "history" that Virgil never touches upon, namely a passionate romance between Aeneas and Lavinia, called Lavine.[6] In the second, he also has in common with his Renaissance successor, Vegio, a love of declamatory speeches which are often built on Virgilian foundations.

If we look specifically at what follows upon the death of Turnus in the narrative of the *Roman*, we find that its author takes 342 lines to bring his poem to a conclusion. Of these 217 are devoted to emotional soliloquies by Aeneas and Lavine, delivered during the eight days that separate the moment of agreement on a wedding date from the actual event. The remaining verses deal much more compactly with the wedding and its accompanying feast, with the subsequent building of the city of Albe (Alba) and with Aeneas's accession to the kingship and happy reign. The poem concludes with a brief survey of the hero's heirs leading to Romulus.

The second retelling is the *Eneasroman* of the Flemish poet Heinrich von Veldeke, written a generation later (c. 1170–90) and some 3500 lines longer than its immediate model.[7] Dependent on both the Virgilian original and the *Roman*, Heinrich uses three times as many lines as the latter to detail events subsequent to the death of Turnus. There are notable differences in content and presentation. Immediately upon Aeneas's decapitation of his antagonist, the narrator spends 28 lines praising Turnus and describing the grief of his retinue. There follow a much abbreviated version of the *Roman's* two love laments and a more extensive description of preparations for the wedding and of the ceremony itself.

Heinrich breaks his poem's affirmative tone momentarily with a vignette describing the morose final moments of Amata.[8] But the somber mood soon gives way to the pomp and circumstance surrounding the marriage and to the elaborate largesse associated with it. Aeneas and his bride are crowned king and queen, and build the city of Alba. The poet then adds a summary list of those who inherited Aeneas's throne, from his son Aeneas Silvius to Rome's first emperor, Augustus. The *Eneasroman* proper comes to an end with a reminder of the coming of Christ during the reign of Augustus and of the fact that we live now, not subject to the pagan gods, to whom Aeneas sacrifices, but blessed by the salvation that Christ's death has assured. Heinrich concludes with an addendum on the twists of fate that occurred to him during the poem's production and with a bow to his French source and to the *Aeneid* itself.

Among the major modifications that Heinrich makes to the *Roman* are his allowance of the unspoken posthumous encomium of Turnus, which among other purposes serves to magnify the defeated hero's position as a worthy opponent of Aeneas, and the extension of time between announcement of the wedding and the ceremony itself from eight to fourteen days. This temporal expansion and the more extensive detail allotted to the magnificence of the festivities themselves allow him to dilate on Aeneas's role not only as a conquering hero, whose physical prowess led to the death of Turnus, but also, what events consequent to that victory prove, as a nobleman of rare spiritual worth, fit to be a monarch and the ancestor of a glorious race of kings.[9]

Vegio accomplishes many of the same goals as the author of the *Roman* and as Heinrich von Veldeke. As in the work of his predecessors, events that the reader of the *Aeneid* knows lie in the future are realized by Vegio in his narrative's present, often with the effect of satisfying expectations that are not met at the epic's brusque conclusion. We will have again regal meetings between Aeneas and Latinus, the marriage of the hero and Lavinia, and Vegio's own way of glorifying Aeneas at the end. But there are essential differences between Vegio and the two earlier writers. Some lie on the surface. The author of the *Roman* and Heinrich make use of their vernacular languages, rewriting and expanding a powerful story so as to appeal to later audiences in their own words, elevated but contemporary (and with the tale appropriately modified to suit a chivalric world). They are also retelling the whole tale, from idiosyncratic beginnings to novel, post-*Aeneadic* finales.

By returning to Latin as the language of his poem and by beginning where Virgil's epic leaves off, with at least no surface attempt to modify the sacred text itself, Vegio achieves several effects. He appeals to the classicizing instincts of his contemporaries and relies on the depth of their knowledge, both of Virgil, his language and poetry, and of Roman culture in general, to appreciate his accomplishment. At the same time he implicitly claims for himself the title of *Vergilius redivivus*. The *vitae* of Virgil, which Vegio would have known in both ancient and more expansive medieval versions, tell us that the poet had hoped to spend three more years putting final touches on his masterpiece and then to devote the remainder of his life to the study of philosophy, but that death intervened.[10] Vegio accepts the challenge the *vitae* propose, but instead of attempting the impossible task of polishing the work of genius before him — fleshing out the incomplete lines, say, or searching for the "supports" *(tibicines)*,[11] that the poet is said to have written in place of more permanent hexameters to keep his inspiration flowing, and somehow bettering them — Vegio takes a different approach.

He looks to what he surmises to be incompletions, or even infelicities, in the narrative itself, and sets out both to extend and to modify Virgil's text in ways which we perhaps are meant to imagine might be Virgil's own (such is the poem's illusion) but which are in fact more those of Vegio and of his own time. He does in fact rewrite the *Aeneid* but only from the prospect of his own continuation of it, without in any way altering the poem itself, and in ways that are different from those taken by the *Roman* and by Heinrich. For, although the narrative of the *Supplement* itself is strictly speaking novel, Vegio is nevertheless engaged in a continuous dialogue with his master text, and to a lesser degree with Ovid's *Metamorphoses*, that proves not only his great indebtedness to Virgil but also his latent but constant desire to alter his model hero, and therefore to change as well the model epic that describes him, in essential ways. To put it in a bald generality: if, for the author of the *Roman* and for Heinrich von Veldeke, Aeneas becomes the embodiment of the kingly hero of chivalric romance, for Vegio he must be made the emblem of Renaissance *virtù*, the combination of valor of body and excellence of mind which shapes the essence of the ideal Italian prince.

We must also test Vegio's approach, and response, to a different medieval tradition regarding the *Aeneid* which in this case has its root in late antiquity, namely the allegorical reading of the epic. This sees the story of Aeneas as emblematizing the journey of man bettering himself as life progresses and, anagogically, of the soul's quest for ethical perfection ending in its claim to a seat with the saints in heaven. This is an approach that begins with the *Expositio Virgilianae Continentiae* ("Explanation of the Content of Virgil") by Fulgentius, in the sixth century, is expanded in the middle ages, especially in the twelfth century *Commentum Super Sex Libros Eneidos Virgilii* ("Commentary on Six Books of Virgil's

Aeneid") of Bernardus Silvestris, and reaches its Renaissance acme in the *Disputationes Camaldulenses* ("Camaldolese Disputations") of Cristoforo Landino (1424–1498), written around 1475 and therefore some two generations after the appearance of the *Supplement*. There is one strand of received critical opinion that sees in Vegio's work another exemplification of this Christianizing of the epic, borne out particularly by its climactic conclusion in which Venus wafts aloft with the soul of Aeneas, to fix it in the stars.[12]

Let us look at the verses in question (623–30):

Tum Venus aerias descendit lapsa per auras
Laurentumque petit. Vicina Numicius undis
flumineis ibi currit in aequora harundine tectus.
Hunc corpus nati abluere et deferre sub undas,
quicquid erat mortale, iubet. Dehinc laeta recentem
felicemque animam secum super aera duxit,
immisitque Aenean astris, quem Iulia proles
indigitem appellat templisque imponit honores.

Then Venus slips sliding down the breezes of air and seeks Laurentum. There the Numicius, veiled in reed, courses with the ripples of his stream into the nearby sea. She commands him to wash away from her son's body whatever is mortal and to carry it beneath his waves. Then in happiness she conducted the fresh, blessed soul with her above the air, and fixed Aeneas among the stars. His Julian offspring entitle him Indiges and in his temples offer the honors of his cult.

Vegio is indebted here to two places in Ovid's *Metamorphoses*. The first, 14.597–608, is concerned with the same event:

. . . perque leves auras iunctis invecta columbis
litus adit Laurens, ubi tectus harundine serpit
in freta flumineis vicina Numicius undis.

hunc iubet Aeneae, quaecumque obnoxia morti,
abluere et tacito deferre sub aequora cursu.
corniger exsequitur Veneris mandata suisque,
quidquid in Aenea fuerat mortale, repurgat
et respersit aquis: pars optima restitit illi.
lustratum genetrix divino corpus odore
unxit et ambrosia cum dulci nectare mixta
contigit os fecitque deum; quem turba Quirini
nuncupat Indigitem temploque arisque recepit.

. . . carried through the nimble breezes by her harnessed
doves, [Venus] approaches the shore of Laurentum where
Numicius, shrouded by his reed, winds the waves of his
stream into the nearby sea. She orders him to wash away
from Aeneas whatever is beholden to death and to bear it in
silent course under the depths. The horned god obeys her
commands, and cleanses and sprinkles with his waters what-
ever was mortal in Aeneas. His best part remained. His
mother anointed the purified body with perfume of the
gods, and touched his face with ambrosia mixed with sweet
nectar and made him a god. The people of Quirinus call him
Indiges and have honored him both with a temple and with
altars.[13]

Venus is also the protagonist of the second passage from Ovid's
Metamorphoses which deals with the deification of Julius Caesar.
We begin, however, with Jupiter's pronouncement that the event
is decreed by fate. He addresses his daughter in conclusion
(15.840–48):

'. . . hanc animam interea caeso de corpore raptam
fac iubar, ut semper Capitolia nostra forumque
divus ab excelsa prospectet Iulius aede.'
Vix ea fatus erat, media cum sede senatus

constitit alma Venus nulli cernenda suique
Caesaris eripuit membris nec in aëra solvi
passa recentem animam caelestibus intulit astris,
dumque tulit, lumen capere atque ignescere sensit
emisitque sinu . . .

". . . meanwhile snatch this soul [of Caesar] from his mur-
dered body and make of it a heavenly radiance so that for-
ever the deified Julius can look from his lofty temple upon
our Capitolium and forum." Scarcely had he spoken when
nourishing Venus, seen by none, took her place in the midst
of the senate-house and snatched the fresh soul of her Cae-
sar from his limbs, and, not allowing it to be dissolved into
air, she brought it within the stars of heaven, and while she
carried it she felt it begin to glow and catch fire, and she re-
leased it from her bosom . . .

Vegio's allusions achieve several effects at once. By using Ovid
to cap Ovid, he grants to Aeneas the stellification that Ovid
withholds from him but allows to Julius Caesar.[14] But, by nesting
the heavenly ascent, borrowed from *Metamorphoses* 15, within the
description of the purification by the Numicius (or, elsewhere,
Numicus), which comes largely from Ovid's preceding book,
Vegio honors him with the catasterism which Ovid had reserved
for Caesar but then returns us immediately and forcefully to
Ovid's Aeneas, in the poem's final line, with verses 629–30 —
"quem Iulia proles / indigitem appellat templisque imponit
honores" — serving as careful reminder of *Metamorphoses* 14.607–8:
"quem turba Quirini / nuncupat Indigitem temploque arisque
recepit." Though Vegio steps beyond Ovid, while adopting and
adapting him, in dealing with the stellification of Aeneas, his act
of closure returns carefully back to Ovid's earlier immortalized but
still terrestrial Aeneas.[15]

Both Vegio and Ovid's lines, from book 14 as well as 15, in turn look back to two moments in the *Aeneid*. The first comes in book 1 when Jupiter comforts Venus, worried for her son and his future, by predicting (258–60):

'. . . cernes urbem et promissa Lavini
moenia, sublimemque feres ad sidera caeli
magnanimum Aenean . . .'

". . . you will behold the city and promised walls of Lavinium, and you will carry great-souled Aeneas to the stars of heaven . . ."

The second initiates the dialogue between Jupiter and Juno in book 12 that constitutes the reader's last glimpse of the Olympians. The god asks his consort (12.793–95):

'quae iam finis erit, coniunx? quid denique restat?
indigitem Aenean scis ipsa et scire fateris
deberi caelo fatisque ad sidera tolli . . .'

"What now, my wife, will be the end? What further remains? You yourself know, and confess to know, that Aeneas, as native god, is owed to heaven and is raised by fate to the stars . . ."

Therefore not only does Vegio look back to Ovid's more detailed treatment of Aeneas's fluvial purgation and borrow from the Latin poet's deification of Caesar for his own treatment of Aeneas's apotheosis, but he also turns back to Virgil's more succinct accounts of the same two events. Especially the rare word *indiges*, that initiates Vegio's final hexameter and is Virgil's brisk way of reminding the reader of the tradition of Aeneas's death, looks both to *Metamorphoses* 14.608 and to its only appearance in the *Aeneid* where it is also the first word in the line, in elision with the one that follows.[16]

We will return later to the dialogues of Venus and Juno with

Jupiter in connection with Vegio's modification of the *Aeneid*'s final moments. It is important to note here both the fact of Vegio's backward literary glance to Ovid and Virgil at the conclusion of his poem and its intensity. On the occasion when Vegio would be expected to add even an indirect Christian element to Aeneas's final progress not only is nothing forthcoming but his language is almost completely dependent on his great Roman predecessors. This is as if to say that it is in the classical literary background that his interest lay and that such should be the focus of attention for his contemporary readers as well.[17]

To be more specific, the circular return in Vegio's act of closure seems a sign on Vegio's part of unwillingness to allow interpretation of his poem to take the step toward anagogy. Just as he shuns the tradition of a romance Aeneas, so here too he avoids any step that would lead the reader toward any medieval, anagogical interpretation of the hero's life. There is no hint that the stellification of Aeneas's *anima* is the equivalent of his admission into the Christian heaven (the honor, for instance, that Dante pays the soul of Statius in the concluding cantos of *Purgatorio*). Vegio chooses not to have Aeneas, in however oblique a manner, suffer the change from paganism to Christianity. Nor does he craft for himself a parallel literary and ethical progress, one that would leave behind the hints in Virgil's story line, and Ovid's elaboration of them, on which he directly builds, for the intellectual and spiritual world of Christian allegory of which Dante's masterpiece, written in the first decades of the preceding century, is the capstone. There is no reference, in Aeneas's celestial transmutation, to God's eternal grace extended to his mortal soul and every possibility that Vegio wished us to see Aeneas's deification as the result of his notable achievements as ancestor of, and moral paradigm for, future Romans and their Renaissance descendents. In this respect, too, Vegio is inexorably classicizing.

There is no question, however, of Vegio's desire to present

Aeneas as the noblest of pagans, and accordingly worthy even of divinization. Writing some sixteen years later, in *De educatione liberorum* ("On the Education of Children") (1444), he remarks that Virgil "in the character of Aeneas wished to show a man endowed with every virtue, now in unfavorable circumstances, now in favorable ones"[18] and there is no reason to believe that his goal in the *Supplement* was any different. He accomplishes this by several methods. One patent means is by building up the character of Aeneas while at the same time denigrating Turnus.[19] Another is by playing on his audience's knowledge of the *Aeneid*, allusions to which saturate his text, so as to alter, in ways immediate and less apparent, both Virgil's emphases and the reader's expectations.[20]

Vegio's initial hexameters set the pattern. His first lines — "Turnus ut extremo devictus Marte profudit / effugientem animam" — by reference to the first line of *Aeneid* 12 — "Turnus ut infractos adverso Marte Latinos / defecisse videt" ("When Turnus sees the Latins broken and giving way, with the God of War against them")[21] — announce to the reader that we are about to witness in some form a replay of the final book of the *Aeneid*, and the remainder of his second and third verses — "medioque sub agmine victor / magnanimus stetit Aeneas, Mavortius hero" ("and amid the host stood great-souled Aeneas, War's victorious hero") — takes us briskly to the epic's conclusion — "stetit acer in armis / Aeneas volvens oculos dextramque repressit" ("Aeneas stood, fierce in his armor, his eyes darting, and held back his right hand").

Through the repetition of *stetit* we find ourselves again watching the victorious hero as he stands over Turnus. Now, however, the latter is in the form of a lifeless corpse, rather than a vanquished suppliant. The change of Turnus from living to dead, as we move from one poem to the other, is accompanied by an equally dramatic spiritual metamorphosis on the part of the conqueror. In altering *acer* into *magnanimus* Vegio moves from ferocity to magnanimity, from implicitly hostile energy to nobility, as the typifying characteristic of his hero. In so doing he carefully elides Virgil's troubling description of Aeneas, in the act of remembering his "savage grief" (*saevi . . . doloris*) and "set aflame by furies and terrifying in his wrath" (*furiis accensus et ira / terribilis*) as he prepares to kill, and "blazing" (*fervidus*) after he has performed the deed.[22]

Vegio, however, has pondered Virgil's words well, and by adopting them but distributing them to protagonists other than his central hero he relieves Aeneas of their moral onus, as instigators of his action, and places their burden elsewhere. Turnus now, not Aeneas, is the victim of *furiae* (47 and, implicitly, 340) and of *furor* (31, 146, 342). At 196 and 269 we hear of him *furentem* and at 428 his negative emotionality is generalized as *furens licentia*. The *odia* that Turnus imputes to Aeneas in his last words (12.938) Vegio distributes between the righteous animus of the gods (295) and Turnus's own negative hatred (342). Anger (*ira*), too, is given to the heavenly powers and their reaction to Turnus (29, 295, 429). At 294 the gods are *saeva* and at 295 *incensa*, as is Turnus (*incensus*) at 341. Likewise *dolor* is no longer a motivating force for Aeneas but is suffered by the Latins (5, 18) and by Daunus.[23]

When *magnanimus* Aeneas does come center stage at line 23 Vegio once more finesses a salient part of the conclusion of the *Aeneid*. The speech that the hero now delivers contains the material that we might expect a rational Aeneas to convey before he offers the death blow to Turnus (that he affronted the gods, broke the treaty and gave himself over to war's frenzy). The apostrophe to Turnus that Vegio places in the middle of his oration, by momentarily reenlivening his dead enemy, gives Aeneas a chance to put aside the final words of vendetta that Virgil's narrator allots him (12.947–49) immediately before he kills and to replace them with a reasoned, high-minded discussion of why Turnus deserved death.

A look at the lines which introduce the speech (23–24) will help make the point through allusion: "Tunc Turnum super adsistens placido ore profatur / Aeneas." Vegio would have us think back to *Aeneid* 10.490, one of the poem's famous incomplete hexameters: "quem Turnus super adsistens . . ." ("Then standing over him Turnus . . ."). We are at the moment when Turnus has just killed Pallas and is about to strip his sword-belt from him, an action which causes the narrator to exclaim on his overweening pride. As Aeneas replaces Turnus, and Turnus becomes the dead Pallas, Vegio fleshes out Virgil's line with the phrase *placido ore profatur*, imputing to Aeneas a post-killing calmness, and absence of arrogance, that Virgil denies Turnus. He further purges Aeneas of violence by having him, in the course of his speech, offer Pallas's baldric to his father, Evander, as a consolation for his loss. What in the *Aeneid* had been an emblem of hauteur for Turnus and the source of *dolor* and arouser of *ira* for Aeneas is cleansed by Vegio of its negative, activating elements, a process during which Aeneas also turns from victim of passion to statesmanlike source of authority.[24]

We spoke earlier of the dialogue between Juno and Jupiter in *Aeneid* 12 in relation to the tradition of Aeneas as *indiges*. It also serves as counterbalance to the dialogue between Jupiter and Venus in the first book, and both look to a future beyond the scope of Virgil's poem. Vegio recalls both interchanges in the dialogue between the king of the gods and his daughter with which he brings his poem to an end.[25] His purposes are several. For one it brings satisfaction to the reader by accomplishing in reality what the *Aeneid* only hints at, namely the deification of Aeneas. For another, it serves in a grand gesture further to eliminate the end of Virgil's epic, from the descent of Jupiter's Fury to disable Turnus to the latter's soul making its indignant way to the world of Shades. We leap, as it were, over the poem's intense conclusion into a story of the dead mourned and buried, treaties affirmed rather than broken, a marriage celebrated and the principal protagonist deified.

In this respect the opening lines are also anticipatory of the *Supplement* as a whole. Beginning at line 4 we read of the Latins as "astonished" (*obstupuere*) at Turnus's death, then as putting their shields down from their shoulders (*scutaque deponunt umeris*, 9); they are compared to the followers of a defeated bull who now submit themselves to the leadership of his victor. Vegio would have us think back to *Aeneid* 12.707–22 where first all the warriors "put down their armor from their shoulders" (*armaque deposuere umeris*), then Latinus stands awestruck (*stupet*) at the two combatants who are compared to two bulls battling over the lordship of a herd. Once more Vegio takes a moment before the end of the *Aeneid*, together with the simile through which Virgil characterizes it, and shows us its aftermath.[26] And once again we are not shown the death scene of Turnus, only what happens in its wake.[27]

Vegio's treatment of the figure of Latinus deserves special mention. He is relieved of all the blame that he places upon himself or is given by others in Virgil's poem.[28] For Vegio he becomes a replacement figure for Anchises, to serve now as Aeneas's new father.[29] One moment in Vegio's treatment stands out. It occurs during the wedding festivity of Lavinia and Aeneas, description of which is meant both to remind us of the banquet Dido puts on for Aeneas at the conclusion of *Aeneid* 1, and to give assurance that what now follows will not bring about suicidal passion but a future of marital bliss. Vegio interrupts his description of the course of events for eight lines (501–8) to tell of Latinus's affectionate reception of Iulus. Again Vegio's allusions set up a moment at the end of *Aeneid* 1 for comparison, this time with Dido's acceptance into her lap of Cupido in the disguise of Iulus. Dido's wretched future is ameliorated and transferred to Latinus who embraces Aeneas's real son and comments on his father's good fortune.[30]

However we interpret the poem it stands as a clear act of homage to Virgil and, to a far lesser degree, Ovid.[31] We have traced aspects of Vegio's intellectual allegiance to his model. Suffice it to say that the rhetoric of presentation is also beholden to the master poet, especially, and naturally, to the *Aeneid*. For instance, of the eight similes that dot the text several — the mother hen protecting her brood, the tortoise on its back, unable to escape an approaching fire — are of striking originiality, but all, to some degree, owe their inspiration to Virgil.

A word is in order on the history of the *Supplement*. Its popularity was such that it circulated widely in manuscript form during the fifteenth and early sixteenth centuries and was printed already by 1471 in Adam de Ambergau's edition of the *Aeneid* and for the next century was attached to several other editions.[32] It received a full commentary from Iodocus Badius Ascensius in 1501,[33] and was translated by Gavin Douglas as part of his Scottish version of the *Aeneid*, completed in 1513 but not printed until 1553. It was also appended to the first rendering of Virgil's epic into English by Thomas Phaer (1510–60) and Thomas Twyne (1543–1613). Phaer published a translation of the poem's first seven books in 1558 and at the time of his death had completed a translation of the next two, with all nine published posthumously in 1562. This was completed, with the addition of the last three books, and published in 1573, by Twyne, who in 1584 republished his translation with the addition of the *Supplement*.

The second hexameter work written by Vegio, whose source also lies in ancient myth, is *Astyanax* (1430), a concise retelling of the circumstances surrounding the death of Hector's son who, at least briefly, survived the downfall of Troy. Though the boy is mentioned twice in the *Aeneid*,[34] Vegio's main source for narrative material is not in Virgil but in the tragedies of Seneca, particularly the *Troades*.

This influence is exerted in two ways. First the plot line of Vegio's poem is largely drawn from Seneca's play.[35] Second, Vegio's penchant for set speeches, so prominent in the *Supplement*, is here even more apparent, abetted by the fact that his model, naturally enough, consists entirely of dialogue. Roughly two-thirds of the *Astyanax* is spoken, while one of the longer sections of narrative that intervene between speeches (236–50) is inspired by the messenger's speech at *Troades* 1068–1103, and at 189–90 Vegio puts into his narrative a version of the command which Ulysses utters at *Troades* 627–29.

To put the matter baldly: the speech of Agamemnon at 23–44 is based on words that Seneca gives to Ulysses, about or directed toward Andromacha (524–55, 605–22, 704); the subsequent speeches of Ulysses (47–80 and 157–178), draw, respectively, on lines 524–55, 568–72 and 634–41 in Seneca, for the first, 524–55 again, for the second.[36] The last third of the poem is largely devoted to three speeches by Andromacha, all equally dependent on Seneca for inspiration. The first, at 181–88, recalls *Troades* 556–67 and 594–97. The second, 192–224, is reminiscent of her words addressed to Ulysses at *Troades* 686–704 with elements drawn from Agamemnon's speech at *Troades* 271–80 while her address to Astyanax (216–24) is heavily dependent on the directive that she gives her son at *Troades* 705–17. Finally Andromacha's language at 260–308 looks not only to segments of the *Troades*, especially to the descriptions of the boy's mangled body and to Hecuba's final lament at 1165–77, but also to Seneca's *Phaedra* with its macabre detailing of Hippolytus's dismembered corpse.[37]

But Vegio's beloved Virgil is always present as a potent influence. On several occasions Seneca and Virgil overlap as sources.

For example, when Venus appears to Andromacha in the guise of Hector, her speech (136–41) serves as a double reminder to the reader, first, of the hero's appearance to Aeneas in a dream in the second book of the *Aeneid* (268–97) and of his words there,[38] but also of *Troades* 438–60 where Andromacha also tells of a parallel experience which likewise repeats his words (452–56). Moreover Andromacha's final speech, whose Senecan sources we have noted, is introduced, at 251, by a clear allusion to *Aeneid* 9. 474, where Rumor announces to the mother of Euryalus the death of her son, and as Andromacha's words commence, Vegio would have us recall the language that Virgil gives the distraught mother at *Aeneid* 9. 481–97.

But the force of Virgil often stands alone, and it permeates the whole. Vegio acknowledges this clearly in his opening verses, where the initial hexameter—"Musa, refer quae causa metum post diruta Troiae" ("Tell, O Muse, what occasioned the anxiety after the collapse of Troy's walls")—looks to Virgil's initial address to the goddess of inspiration (*Aeneid* 1.8)—"Musa, mihi causas memora, quo numine laeso . . ." ("Muse, recall for me the reasons why [Juno], her will thwarted . . .")—and his fourth and fifth lines, "tu, diva, canentem / Prosequere" ("Goddess, assist your singer") contain a bow to *Aeneid* 7.41–42, where Virgil again addresses the Muse, now at the commencement of his epic's second half: "tu vatem, tu, diva mone . . ." ("Do you, goddess, remind your bard . . .").

The same holds true for other aspects of Vegio's presentation. Let me offer two examples. At line 82, after establishing his narrative line in a (literally) dramatic fashion, through the speeches of Agamemnon and Ulysses, Vegio makes the only lengthy adaptation in his poem of epic convention. He shifts the action from earth to heaven, from human doings to the world of the gods, and to a dialogue between Jupiter and Venus. The *variatio* in genres is as effective as the twist in events is novel with Vegio. Nevertheless, it is only achieved with the help of Virgil. As he crafted the conversation between father and daughter, Vegio was thinking of the interchange, already mentioned in connection with the *Supplement*, between the same protagonists during the first book of the *Aeneid*, with their speeches in the same order.[39]

The result is to bring momentary relief from the exigencies of the story in progress. In Virgil's epic, Venus is reassured about the future happiness of Aeneas and the glory of Rome to come, whereas in the *Astyanax* the king of the gods is of no immediate help to his offspring in any attempt to rescue the doomed boy. He does assure her, however, that more positive events will occur in the future, and he accomplishes this by direct reference to Aeneas, to the power of the city his descendants will found and to their victory over Greece. So, even as Vegio carefully distinguishes his immediate plot line from that of the *Aeneid*, he also with equal finesse twice-over adopts Virgil for his own purposes, in his imitation of the speeches themselves and by alluding in his own poem to the ultimately positive turn of fate that Roman history will take, a positive turn which Jupiter reveals to his daughter in the first of the *Aeneid*'s great prophetic moments.[40]

Another bow to an epic convention which he had followed successfully in the *Supplement* is Vegio's use of simile. In this poem there are only two and again, as in the case of the Venus-Jupiter exchange, Virgil is in the background. The first occurs at 150–54 where Ulysses is compared to a wolf driven by hunger to attack a sheepfold. Vegio takes his inspiration from *Aeneid* 9.59–64 where Virgil uses a similar analogy for Turnus ranging angrily before the camp of the besieged Trojans.[41] Vegio gives to his wolf a stealthiness and innate savagery—he would snatch a nursing lamb from the tender udder of its mother—absent in Virgil yet neatly characterizing both the wiliness and cruelty of the Greek hero. The second we find at 228–34 where Astyanax, about to be ushered to his death by the Greek soldiery, is compared to a bird pursued by a hawk which at first buries its head in the earth to escape and then becomes the dying prey of its stronger foe. Once more a Virgilian simile is in the background, this time from *Aeneid* 12.749–57 as Aeneas, pursuing Turnus, is likened to a hunter-hound attacking a deer.[42] On this occasion, however, little more than the violent tracking of weaker by stronger member of the animal kingdom is in common. Beginning with the name of the hawk, *astur*, which does not appear in classical Latin, Vegio has fashioned a novel portrayal of a creature realizing its doom, attempting unsuccessfully to pretend it away, and finally succumbing.

One further Virgilian reminiscence will shed light on Vegio's practice. During the course of her second speech, Andromacha addresses to Ulysses a lesson on the restrained use of power (207–16). Immediately thereafter she turns to her son (217–18): "Astyanax, procede tuumque / Affare et dominum supplex humilis precare" ("Astyanax, step forward and in suppliant fashion address your master and pray the prayer of the humbled"). Vegio would have his reader think of *Aeneid* 12.930–31: "ille humilis supplex oculos dextramque precantem / protendens" ("he, a suppliant, eyes lowered and stretching forth his right hand in prayer"). We are at the moment, twenty lines before Virgil brings his epic to a violent conclusion, when Turnus, on his knees before his victorious enemy, prays Aeneas for pity and suggests that sparing his life is an option. Vegio is therefore asking us to imagine ourselves into a scenario parallel to that of the end of the *Aeneid*, with Turnus replaced by Astyanax and Aeneas by Ulysses. In other words we are at the moment in time that immediately precedes where the *Supplement* picks up after the killing of Turnus, a moment that the *Supplement* suppresses. Now, however, we have in place a helpless victim and a sly, ruthless tyrant just before the former is dragged off to his death. Would Vegio, writing two years after the publication of the *Supplement*, now have us rethink his approach to the conclusion of Virgil's epic? Are there characteristics less noble than magnanimity to be found in Aeneas as he performs his final deed, characteristics that Vegio might have us sense in the implacable Ulysses? Here again, then, Vegio both absorbs and remakes the classical tradition. There is no question of Vegio's dependence on his classical models, in the case of the *Astyanax* especially Seneca and Virgil. Yet his challenging merger of elements of epic and of tragic drama along with the novel variations he achieves on his Virgilian inheritance give this brief poem its own measure of originality.

The next year (1431) saw the publication of a more expansive hexameter work, *The Golden Fleece*. In a little over a thousand lines divided into four books, it tells the tale of the arrival of the Argonauts at Colchis, Medea's hesitation and then affirmation of her love for Jason, and the latter's surmounting, through the aid of her magic, the trials he must confront. Medea escapes her pursuing father's vengeance by dismembering her brother, Absyrtus, and forcing Aeëtes to pause and collect the parts which she has strewn on the water in his path. The final segment brings the heroes back safely to Greece, with their double set of spoils, the golden fleece and the barbarian princess.[43]

I will turn to Vegio's sources in a moment. First, we may speculate on what may have impelled him to turn to the myth of Medea after writing the *Astyanax*. One possible impetus may have been the plays of Seneca. We have traced briefly the influence of the philosopher's *Troades* on the *Astyanax*. It happens that, in the form of the manuscript tradition that would most likely have been available to Vegio, the *Medea* follows directly on the *Troades*. It is a plausible hypothesis, therefore, that Vegio turned again to Senecan drama for inspiration, in particular to the play that to him came next in sequence after the one most influential on his immediately preceding work.[44] We must remember that the *Argonautica* of Valerius Flaccus was apparently not known to Vegio[45] and that the

lengthiest narrative telling of the early part of the myth of Medea
that would have been available to Vegio from antiquity, Ovid's ver-
sion at the opening of the seventh book of his *Metamorphoses*,
lasted only a hundred and fifty verses. It is reasonable to suppose
that Vegio would consider himself staking out new turf in an ex-
panded rendering of the initial segments of Medea's tale, especially
since the playwright had already offered a full dramatic presenta-
tion of the final, tragic episodes of her career.

Vegio himself supplies supporting evidence for this hypothesis.
Seven lines before he concludes his poem, he gives Medea's father,
Aeëtes, this curse as his final words (4.246–47): "'At demum
maria et terras caelumque pererrans / exsul, egens, despecta, sua
se caede cruentet!'" ("And in the end, after she has roamed sea and
earth and sky as a fugitive, needy and despised, may she bloody
herself with slaughter of her own making!"). Vegio is thinking of
words Medea herself utters, near the beginning of Seneca's play
(20–21), as she curses her husband Jason, now absconding with a
new bride: "per urbes erret ignotas egens / exul pavens invisus
incerti laris . . ." ("May he wander through unknown cities, needy,
an exile, terror-stricken, hated, homeless . . ."). With this delib-
erate allusion Vegio, at his conclusion, recalls Seneca's opening
scene, one curse anticipating and reflecting the other.[46] By this
means he is telling the reader that, though he is the later author by
many centuries, he has seized the opportunity to put into verse
the earlier part of a narrative history, hitherto apparently untold
in any detail, whose bloody finale was dramatized by the Roman
author.

If we look for further connections between tragic drama, espe-
cially Seneca's *Medea*, and the *Golden Fleece*, it may not prove coin-
cidental that the initial divinities upon whom Seneca's protagonist
calls—Juno, Minerva, Oceanus, the Sun as Titan, and Hecate—
all play roles, some of them of his own invention, in Vegio's work,
as if their mention, too, had focused his imagination.[47] Further-

more, there is one character common to both the *Medea* and the *Golden Fleece* who is closely associated with tragic drama, namely the nurse. She figures prominently in Seneca's play and Vegio furthers the connection of his poem with Senecan and other tragedy by giving the second longest of his poem's many speeches to Minerva in the disguise of Medea's *nutrix* (2.206–44). Finally, we have the speeches themselves, for which, once again, we find a marked propensity on Vegio's part. Though this tendency is also present in the *Supplement*, and though the percentage of lines devoted to the spoken word is less than in the *Astyanax*,[48] nevertheless Vegio's close involvement with Senecan drama in the second and third of his hexameter works may have further fostered his ease at including speeches in an ostensibly third-person narrative framework.[49]

The major sources for Vegio's narrative are from the poetry of Ovid.[50] First chronologically is *Heroides* 12, a letter from Medea to Jason, one extensive "address" imagined as directed to Jason and conceived of as written on the eve of the tragic finale of her story.[51] Equally important is *Metamorphoses* 7, lines 1–158, especially Medea's soliloquy at 11–71. This monologue, taken together with the whole of *Heroides* 12, lies behind much of the matter of the three speeches which Vegio gives his protagonist (2.164–204, 3.126–55 and 231–50). Large segments of the end of Vegio's third book and the beginning of the fourth are built on Ovid's two accounts, in *Heroides* 12 and *Metamorphoses* 7, of the trials which Jason must surmount in order to gain possession of the fleece. Finally *Tristia* 3.9.5–34 details Medea's dismemberment of her brother Absyrtus in language Vegio well knew.[52]

The presence of Ovid is strongly felt in more limited manifestations. The ekphrasis that initiates Vegio's description of the palace of Aeëtes (1.164–78) is inspired by the ekphrastic opening of *Metamorphoses* 2, and many of its details are borrowed from the subsequent narrative in that same book, telling of the Sun's daily round.

Moreover, the simile at 4.103–6, which compares Jason's slaying of the earth-born brood to Cadmus's slaughter of the men born from his strewing of the dragon's teeth, draws on Ovid's telling of the latter tale at *Metamorphoses* 3.100–30.

But, as always with Vegio, it is the force of Virgil's poetry that his reader most strongly senses.[53] *Eclogues*, *Georgics* and *Aeneid* are all echoed on many occasions, but it is the latter poem which again exerts the greatest influence. Allusions to the epic's opening lines bracket Vegio's work. *Aeneid* 1.1 (*Arma virumque*) is echoed at *Golden Fleece* 4.214 (*arma virosque*) and Virgil's eighth line (*Musa . . . causas memora*) is reflected at Vegio's eighteenth (*memorate, deae . . . causas*).[54] And if, for instance, we look at some of the ways in which the first book of the *Aeneid* exerts imaginative influence on Vegio's text, we find that beginnings and endings also play a significant role. The commencement of the story line of *Aeneid* 1 is reflected in the speech of Aeolus which initiates Vegio's third book, and the banquet that concludes Virgil's initial book finds its parallel at the end of Vegio's opening book. In between we have an allusion to Aeneas's encounter with his mother (especially to lines 407–9) at *Golden Fleece* 2.255–66, where Medea chastises Minerva, and the sequence of events that culminates in Venus's beautifying of her son so as to charm Dido is reflected in a sweep of details at the opening of Vegio's same book — Venus, like Virgil's Juno, cataloguing the insults that have come her way, her enhancement of Jason's good looks, and her enlisting the aid of Cupido who here stands alone.[55]

On some occasions Virgil and Ovid combine as influences. Take *Golden Fleece* 3.190–91, for instance, where Medea's love is "qualis congestas, tacitus quibus incubat ignis, / aura solet rapida stipulas accendere flamma" ("like a breeze that is wont to set aflame with quick flash a heap of stubble in which the fire quietly broods"). Vegio is thinking of Ovid's analogy at *Metamorphoses* 7.79–81 where Medea's burgeoning passion is

ut . . . solet ventis alimenta adsumere, quaeque
parva sub inducta latuit scintilla favilla,
crescere et in veteres agitata resurgere vires . . .

just as a tiny spark, lurking beneath the ashes, is wont to
gain sustenance from gusts of wind, to grow and, fanned to
life, regain its former strength . . .

But he also has in mind the advice that the narrator of *Georgic* 1
gives his farmer (84–85): "saepe etiam sterilis incendere profuit
agros / atque levem stipulam crepitantibus urere flammis" ("Often
also it has proved effective to set barren fields afire and to burn
flimsy stubble with crackling flames").

On other, more numerous occasions Vegio borrows simulta-
neously from two works of Virgil. Take, for example, the simile at
3.222–25 where Jason and Chalciope, on their nocturnal way to
Medea, are likened to wolves:

ceu turba luporum,
quos inimica dies pallentis noctis in umbra
praedae avidos iubet ire, canum ne irrumpat euntes
custodumve invisa cohors . . .

like a pack of wolves, ravenous for prey, whom the hostile
light of day forces to go on their way during the twilight's
shade so that the hated throng of dogs or keepers not burst
in on their pursuit . . .

For the simile proper Vegio is thinking of *Aeneid* 2.355–58 where
Aeneas and his fellow Trojan warriors are compared to ravening
wolves whose hunger sends them in a dark mist searching for
food. But he also draws on two details from the *Georgics*. At
Georgic 1.130 we learn that, as part of his new dispensation, Jupiter
"ordered wolves to be predators" (*praedari . . . lupos iussit*) and at
3.357 we watch how, in the land of the Scythians, "the sun never

dispels the pale mists" (*sol pallentis haud umquam discutit umbras*). The added details are small but they enhance an already powerful analogy as Jason, a dashing hero in the eyes of Medea, becomes a robber, prepared not only to capture his booty but also ultimately to betray her as well.[56]

Equally subtle changes in emphasis can be found in other similes which have their primary source in Virgil. Let me offer two examples. At 2.43–47 Vegio crafts a simile comparing Medea, stricken by Cupido's arrow, to a doe fatally wounded by a hunter's poisoned arrow who no longer gives thought to food, "so much is her mind fixed upon the deadly wound" (*fixa sibi tantum letali in vulnere mens est*). He is drawing extensively on *Aeneid* 4.69–73, where Dido is also compared to an unwary deer fatally wounded, on this occasion, by an ignorant shepherd. However many the details that overlap, Vegio's emphasis on the mind of Medea is novel and adds a psychological dimension missing from his model. The same distinction holds true for another simile coming later in the book where Vegio compares Medea, attempting to cope with and mitigate her passion, to the Northwind's clearing away the rain and darkness that the Southwind has brought to the heavens (246–50). He is drawing on *Aeneid* 12.365–67 where Turnus, routing his enemies, is likened to the Northwind clearing the sky of clouds. But once more Vegio turns physical to metaphysical as he takes us into the processes of Medea's thoughts.[57]

In the *Golden Fleece*, as we found both in the *Supplement* and in the *Astyanax*, Vegio is also concerned with commenting vicariously on the end of the *Aeneid*. Primary evidence comes from a passage appropriately near Vegio's own conclusion as Medea, spurred on by the Fury Tisiphone, kills and dismembers her brother (4.197–206):

Sic fata atque avidum tepido sub pectore liquit
conceptaeque auxit dirum feritatis amorem.

Non secus ac, si forte acrem sit nactus in ima
valle canis dubiusne feram petat, ocius autem
hortatus doctique impulsus voce magistri
congrediturque audetque ingentem et colligit iram:
Tali impulsa igitur rursum Medea furore
corripit et ferrum germani in viscera condit
cervicemque secat medios et dividit artus
inque Tomitana fugiens tellure relinquit

With these words [Tisiphone] lodged in Medea's lukewarm breast a dire, passionate eagerness which she increased with a renewal of savagery. No differently than if in a deep valley a hound has chanced to encounter a fierce beast of the wild and is in doubt whether to pursue it, goaded by the urgent voice of his skilled trainer, he builds up a huge anger and rushes with daring to confront the foe: so Medea, spurred by such madness, rouses herself and buries her sword in her brother's entrails. She beheads him and divides up his limbs, and, as her flight continues, abandons them in the land of Tomis.

Vegio would have us first think (199–200), as he did at *Astyanax* 228–34, of the initial lines of the simile at *Aeneid* 12.749–55 where Aeneas tracking Turnus is compared to a hunter-hound on the trail of a deer. His compressed account of the epic's final reach then takes us to the end of that pursuit as, in its concluding lines, Aeneas addresses and then kills his suppliant foe (12.950): "Hoc dicens ferrum adverso sub pectore condit" ("After saying these words he buries his sword in the chest of his foe"). Anger and fury likewise figure in both scenes, as Aeneas kills Turnus and Medea her brother,[58] but Vegio makes one noteworthy alteration to his model. As Medea first readies herself to kill, she held back "and spared his throat" (*iuguloque pepercit*, 177).[59] It is only after the intervention of the Fury Tisiphone, risen from Hell, that rage takes full control of Medea and that the possibility of sparing gives way to final violence. Virgil's Aeneas is "set aflame by furies" (*furiis accensus*), roused to deadly action after a moment of hesitation brought on by Turnus's plea for *misericordia*. A primary difference between the two moments lies in the fact that the impetus for Aeneas's rage is self-generated, consequent to his sighting of the sword-belt of Pallas who had earlier been killed by Turnus and whose baldric he now wears. Medea, by contrast, acts only when Tisiphone takes matters into her own hands, exhorting her to savagery with a thirteen line speech!

The end of the *Aeneid* makes a less direct appearance a few lines later when Aeëtes, following in the wake of Medea as she scatters the body of her brother, is compared, in a powerful simile, to a tigress whose young have been stolen from her. If, in pursuit of her enemy, she comes upon any of her cubs, she pauses and in so doing allows the predator to escape. Her dilemma, to choose between revenge on her enemy or the saving of her young, is put by Vegio in terms that resonate with any reader pondering the interpretation of the *Aeneid*'s final lines. As Vegio puts it (4.228): "simul certant pietas materna furorque" ("rage and a mother's piety vie with each other"). Should Aeneas's piety toward his father, whose dictum about sparing the humbled any reader would remember, win out over his rage to avenge the killing of his protégé? For Virgil it does not, indeed could not.[60] Vegio, by contrast, again mitigates the force of his Virgilian inheritance. If in the case of Medea the intervention of Tisiphone places the blame for her final fury elsewhere than on her own inner demons, here, by making Aeëtes's practice of *pietas* both possible and practicable, he lets any propensity for a vendetta based on madness yield to a father's devotion to his son.

Finally, it is well also to look at a few of Vegio's own variations on what we might call "the Medea theme." Some concern matters of plot. No desire, for instance, to gain back his rightful property motivates Jason's aspirations for the golden fleece, only a yearning for fame from heroic accomplishments. Moreover the kindly reception given the Argonauts by king Aeëtes is original with Vegio. Likewise, the murder in former times of Phrixus by Aeëtes is a new twist to the tale and helps, for a moment at least beginning with the opening of book 3, change the reader's at first positive feelings for the Colchian king.[61]

As for the *dramatis personae*, the whole apparatus of divinity, though a bow to his epic inheritance, especially from Virgil, is largely of Vegio's own invention. We find Venus, motivated by her hatred of the Sun, initiating Medea's love for Jason with the help of her son Cupido. The Sun, in turn, wishes to quench the girl's passion and asks for help from Minerva who then brings Jupiter into the picture. Aeolus, who plays no part in earlier versions of the Argonaut myth, appeals to Juno for help in seeking vengeance against Aeëtes.[62] The appearance of Mars near the opening of book 4, though it resembles Virgil's portrayal of Neptune in *Aeneid* 1 and of Vulcan in his epic's eighth book, is novel as are the interventions of Oceanus and Tisiphone as the book progresses.[63] Finally we should mention the fourteen similes that enliven Vegio's work, here again a prominent bow to the epic tradition. We have already looked at several for their niceties of detail. But taken as a whole they form an impressive group and, however much Virgil may still be present in the background, display an inventiveness that complements Vegio's originality of narrative presentation, with its novelties of plot and its striking union of elements drawn from both epic and drama.

Perhaps by way of an initial poetic offering, Vegio addressed his next major work, the *Antoniad*, to Pope Eugenius IV in 1436/7, some five years after the completion of the *Golden Fleece*. In four books of slightly over five hundred hexameters, the poem centers on the major event in the life of St. Antony Abbot, his meeting with St. Paul the Hermit, another of the so-called desert fathers. Following his dedication to the Pope, Vegio summarizes the virtues of his hero and then shifts the scene to Heaven where God addresses the angels, now victorious after the struggle with their fallen brethren, Satan and his followers. God reflects on their prowess but turns his particular attention to the centenarian St. Antony who, together with his fellow monks, will serve as a crucial terrestrial source of good in the continuing battle with the Devil and his minions. It has come to His attention that Antony falsely considers himself the first of the desert fathers. God therefore dispatches the archangel Gabriel down to earth to send Antony to visit St. Paul, his fellow anchorite and elder by two decades.

At the start of the second book we discover ourselves in Hell with Satan addressing his comrades on the bitter lot they have brought upon themselves. Their present threat is from individuals with the moral quality of an Antony. Satan leaves Hell in order to tempt the saint on his journey. He assumes the form of a centaur and a pan but in neither guise is he successful against Antony, who curses Alexandria and its paganism. The opening of book 3 finds the journeying saint led by a wolf to the entrance of a cave that he realizes is Paul's hermitage. The older saint bars the way but, at the pleading of his visitor, grants him entry. As they talk at a fountain's edge, a crow brings a loaf of bread which they duly divide. At the start of the poem's final segment, Paul sends Antony to fetch a cloak which bishop Athanasius once gave him as a gift so that he can use it as a shroud. Antony obeys and as he returns he sees a vision of Paul ascending to heaven in glory. After wrapping the corpse in the cloak, Antony is aided in the burial of the saint by two lions which arrive miraculously from the desert. When the funeral days have passed, Antony returns to his comrades to recount his adventures.

Vegio's *Antoniad* is the first Christian Latin epic of the Renaissance, preceding by nearly a century Jacopo Sannazaro's *De Partu Virginis* (1526) and the contemporary *Christiad* (1535) of Marco Girolamo Vida.[64] We can only speculate about why he chose the life of St. Antony as a topic. The importance of all aspects of monasticism to the late middle ages need not be argued.[65] Moreover, depictions in art of two scenes which Vegio features, the temptations of St. Antony and the meeting of St. Antony and St. Paul, were popular both before and long after the date of his poem.[66] But there may be a deeper reason. As Vegio turned from a secular to a religious source of patronage, he moved, equally dramatically, from pagan to Christian literature for a subject. Since this change amounts to a spiritual conversion of sorts on his part, what better way to illustrate it than to retell, for an appreciative pope (himself an Augustinian hermit[67]) and a new audience, the story that stood behind what is probably the most famous conversion in post-Pauline Christian literature, namely that of St. Augustine. Its telling helps form what is, at least from an autobiographical point of view, the climax of the *Confessions*, in its eighth book. Augustine prepares the way for the momentous event by first describing the visit to his house of a certain Ponticianus who noticed that the future saint had been reading the epistles of St. Paul. This leads the guest, who is as amazed at this gap in the knowledge of his interlocutors as they are to hear his words, to tell the story of St. Antony (*Conf.* 8. 6).[68] Ponticianus continues, in Augustine's narrative, by relating a story which occurred when he and three friends had been in the service of the emperor at Trier. Two had gone off by themselves and discovered in the house of a local Christian a book containing the life of Antony. Upon reading it, one of the pair accepts the revelation that his own future should be modeled on the saint's ascetic career.

Augustine now leaves the story for a moment, having carefully prepared the reader for the climax which occurs in chapter 12. There he tells of hearing the voice of a neighboring child singing the words "Take it and read, take it and read" *(tolle lege, tolle lege)*. Augustine interprets the words as a miraculous sign that he should emulate the story of Antony who once chanced to enter church while the gospel was being read. The future saint, on listening to Christ's command, from the text of Matthew, to sell his belongings and follow Him, suffered an immediate conversion.[69] Augustine, following suit, opens the *Epistles* of St. Paul and reads words that cause a similar alteration in his own life.[70]

What we watch, as the eighth book of the *Confessions* evolves, is a marvelous interplay of books and lives leading toward the conversion of the writer.[71] The sequence takes the form of a brilliantly structured chiasmus. We begin with reference to the book, which Augustine had been reading, containing St. Paul's epistles and turn from there to mention of the life of St. Antony and to the force it exerted during an earlier act of conversion. Then, as the book nears its culmination and conclusion and we share in the writer's own experience, we first again hear of Antony, converted as he listens to the Gospel being read in church, an event Augustine presumably remembers from the narrative of Ponticianus (and the reader recalls that it was the life of Antony in book form that had caused the conversion of Ponticianus's friend). Finally the saint describes the actual moment of his own conversion, as he opens the book of the epistles of St. Paul, which he tells us in chapter 6 he had been studying, and reads the saint's words addressed to the Romans. Two earlier conversions, those of St. Antony himself and of the friend of Ponticianus who read the life of the hermit monk, lead inexorably to the decisive moment in Augustine's life. The *Vita Antonii*, in the form of a totemic book and in the details of the story it tells, thus plays as crucial a part as the epistles of St. Paul in the conversion of St. Augustine to Christianity. It no doubt would have appeared so to Maffeo Vegio.

A third person can be added to this impressive hierarchy, Francesco Petrarch. On April 26, 1336, he writes to his friend Francesco

Dionigi de' Roberti of Borgo San Sepolcro about an ascent he had made of Mt. Ventoux near Avignon.[72] Upon reaching the summit he chanced to open a copy, which he always carried with him, of the *Confessions* to 10.8.5: "Et eunt homines admirari alta montium et ingentes fluctus maris et latissimos lapsus fluminum et oceani ambitum et giros siderum, et relinquunt se ipsos" ("Yet men go out and gaze in astonishment at high mountains, the huge waves of the sea, the broad reaches of rivers, the ocean that encircles the world, or the stars in their courses. But they pay no attention to themselves"). The aptness to his own experience of the text on which he had happened leads Petrarch to a further meditation on the similarities of his situation both to that of Augustine, reading the words of Paul's epistle, and of Antony, hearing Christ's message in the gospel of Matthew. He concludes:

> Et sicut Antonius, his auditis, aliud non quaesivit, et sicut Augustinus, his lectis, ulterius non processit, sic et michi in paucis verbis que premisi, totius lectionis terminus fuit, in silentio cogitanti quanta mortalibus consilii esset inopia, qui, nobilissima sui parte neglecta, diffundantur in plurima et inanibus spectaculis evanescant, quod intus inveniri poterat, querentes extrinsecus . . . [73]

> And as Anthony, having heard this, sought nothing else, and as Augustine, having read the other passage, proceeded no further, the end of all my reading was the few words I have already set down. Silently I thought over how greatly mortal men lack counsel who, neglecting the noblest part of themselves in empty parading, look without for what can be found within . . .

Petrarch, too, suffers a type of conversion, just as had Augustine, from reading St. Paul, and as had Antony earlier, from hearing the Gospel. And just as Antony figured in Augustine's account of his own transfiguration, so he appears again in Petrarch's powerful description of the self-revelation that he experienced upon marveling at the mountain-top vista and upon reflecting on other words of Augustine that urge contemplation not of external beauty but of one's own inner self and its value. The author of the *Antoniad* would easily have known Petrarch's letters which in twenty-four volumes he allowed to be published in 1361, half a century before Vegio's birth.

St. Augustine, whose remains are buried in Pavia, would no doubt also have been a presence in Vegio's intellectual life from the beginning of his student days. Though there is no proof that he became an Augustinian himself, certainly Augustine and his mother, St. Monica, figure prominently in his writings upon the papacy's return to Rome (eight works are dedicated to one or both).[74] In 1455, three years before his death, Vegio built a chapel to the left of the main altar in the church of Sant' Agostino to honor St. Monica, whose remains had been brought from Ostia to Rome in 1430. It is there that Vegio's own body lies buried.

Paradoxically, it is not Evagrius' translation of the *Vita Antonii* that had the most impact on Vegio as he wrote the *Antoniad*. Its presence, to be sure, is felt from time to time, especially in the second book of Vegio's poem, which reflects Evagrius's chapters 5–13, telling of Antony's various encounters with the Devil and other demons. Far more influential was the *Vita Pauli* by St. Jerome (written 376–77).[75] Though nominally concerned with the life of the elder hermit, eleven of its eighteen chapters are devoted to the encounter between the two desert fathers. The last half of Vegio's second book and the whole of his third and fourth are largely versifications, in the expected dactylic hexameter, of the prose of Jerome.

There are overt references to Jerome's text also in Vegio's initial book, and one of these may suggest a less hypothetical reason than we have hitherto offered for Vegio's choice of the life of Antony for his verse-making. One pattern that we have found in Vegio's hexameter poetry is his apparent need either to bring someone else's earlier work to a completion that he senses to be lacking in the original — the case of the *Supplement* — or to fill in gaps in the telling of traditional myths inherited from the classical past. This is true for the *Astyanax* and the *Golden Fleece*. The first of these, as we have seen, is a fleshing out of details gleaned largely from Seneca's *Troades*. The second draws on the same playwright's *Medea* and on the account of her doings in the seventh book of Ovid's *Metamorphoses* but expands upon them in ways that Vegio would not have known from antiquity. The same is true for Jerome's *Vita Pauli*, and therefore, vicariously, for Vegio's absorption and elaboration of it.

Though Jerome, in his account of the *Vita Pauli*, is at pains to prove it a complement to the life as written by Athanasius and translated by Evagrius,[76] he also aims to supplement it as well, as witness the last two and half books of Vegio's *Antoniad*. One major addition to be found in *Antoniad* I is the idea, which Jerome mentions at *Vita Pauli* 7, that Antony remained at first unaware of the existence of Paul, and that he therefore considered himself the first of the desert fathers and the founder of the western eremitic tradition. The description of this ignorance and its results, including a seventy-five line speech, with no apparent precedents, by God the Father, takes up three-quarters of Vegio's first book, from line 48 to its conclusion.

The ignorance of Antony, touched on by Jerome and enlarged upon at length by Vegio, can be viewed against the background of the passage mentioned earlier from *Confessions* 8. 6, in which we first hear the story of Antony in the narrative. Augustine there puts stress not on the story of Antony's conversion but on the ignorance of himself and his friends, in the eyes of Ponticianus, about the existence of the desert father. Ponticianus, according to

Augustine, goes on to tell of the practice of monasticism at Milan itself:

> inde sermo devolutus est ad monasteriorum greges, et mores suaveolentiae tuae, et ubera deserta heremi, quorum nos nihil sciebamus. Et erat monasterium Mediolanii, plenum bonis fratribus, extra urbis moenia, sub Ambrosio nutritore, et non noveramus.

> After this he went on to tell us of the groups of monks in the monasteries, of their way of life that savours of your sweetness, and of the fruitful wastes of the desert. All of this was new to us. There was a monastery at Milan also, outside the walls, full of good brethren under the care of Ambrose, but we knew nothing of this either.

That Augustine's discovery of Antony has a parallel in Jerome's discussion of how Antony himself learned of the existence of Paul is suggested in the language Vegio uses to describe the latter moment. At *Antoniad* 1.51–2 Vegio has Antony, ignorant of the more ancient saint, speak of his belief in himself as "the first elder to dwell in the desert's breadth" (*vastae . . . parentem / cultoremque heremi primum*) while Ponticianus, mediated by Augustine's brilliance, can describe the paradoxical "fruitful deserts of the wilderness" (*ubera deserta heremi*) of which the saint had hitherto remained unaware.

Vegio, in *Antoniad* 1, elaborates on the divine intervention which sends Antony on his way to Paul (Jerome speaks only of the fact that the existence of Paul and his goodness was "revealed" to Antony "while he lay at rest during night").[77] Vegio's use of the *Confessions*, in the process of emphasizing God's role in changing ignorance to knowledge, is a further way of linking the series of examples and imitations connected with conversion that we have been tracing—of Antony with the Gospel of Matthew, of Ponticianus and his friends with the *Vita Antonii*, of Augustine with the Epistle of St. Paul to the Romans, and, finally, as we bring matters full circle, of Petrarch with the *Confessions* themselves.

Whatever the variety of his sources, the stamp of Vegio's originality is visible throughout the piece. His penchant for epideictic oratory is powerfully demonstrated in the speeches of God and Satan, in Books I and II respectively, and the descent of Gabriel from heaven initiates this topos in western letters.[78] But what remains most striking is the admixture of pagan Latin literature with the essentially Christian content. For example, twelve similes complement the text, many of them with ancestors in ancient letters. Several stand out for the connections they draw particularly, and appropriately, with epic. In the first book, God, admiring his cohorts of angels, is compared to a Greek or Trojan hero marshalling his forces (132–36).[79] Toward the end of Book III (102–4) Antony and Paul, in conversation, are likened to old soldiers reminiscing. And, as the poem nears its conclusion, the soul of Paul, escorted to heaven by crowds of applauding angels, is paralleled to "the sons of Romulus" in victory, celebrating a triumph on the Capitolium. Vegio never lets his reader lose sight either of his legacy from Rome or of his inheritance, as poet, especially from Greek and Latin epic.

Once again, in ways both general and specific, the influence of Virgil permeates Vegio's text. For the meeting between Antony and Paul and for the latter's death, the reader schooled in the *Aeneid* remembers Aeneas's descent into the Underworld, in the epic's sixth book, to visit with his father Anchises as well as the father's passing at the conclusion of Book III. Let me offer two out of many possible examples with a strong Virgilian presence, where pagan and Christian elements interpenetrate. The first occurs at 4.81–84 where Antony, having witnessed Paul's apotheosis and now rushing to return to the saint's cave, is compared first to a bird, then to a man in a dream carried through a vast void:

> Instar avis volitantis iter, ceu quando sopora
> Nos somni placidam capimus sub nocte quietem,
> Et nunc sistere, nunc agiles attollere plantas,
> Et passim longum ferri per inane videmur.

> . . . like a bird on the wing: such is the moment when during the drowsy night we claim our rest in sleep's calm, now we seem to stop still, now to lift our nimble feet, now to be born along hither and yon through a vast void.

The first brief simile comes from St. Jerome (ch. 15). The second is inspired by the extraordinary last simile of the *Aeneid*:[80]

> ac velut in somnis, oculos ubi languida pressit
> nocte quies, nequiquam avidos extendere cursus
> velle videmur et in mediis conatibus aegri
> succidimus; non lingua valet, non corpore notae
> sufficient vires nec vox aut verba sequuntur:
> sic Turno, quacumque viam virtute petivit,
> successum dea dira negat.

> As in dreams, when by night languid sleep weighs down the eye, we seem to desire in vain to pursue our eager course and in the midst of the endeavor fainting we fail; the tongue has no strength, the body does not provide its usual power; neither voice nor words follow: thus, wherever he valiantly sought escape, the dread goddess denied Turnus success.

Virgil, describing through metaphor Turnus's failing response to the pursuit of Aeneas, is himself altering and expanding a simile from Homer's *Iliad* (22.199–200) where Achilles and Hector, the one giving chase, the other fleeing, are compared to two people in a dream who are incapable, the one, of capturing his prey, the other, of escaping. Among Virgil's most brilliant variations of

Homer is the addition of the word *videmur* ("we seem") which has the effect of uniting writer and readers—all of us—with Turnus so as to share his helplessness. Particularly by his echo of *videmur*, Vegio both shows himself aware of Virgil's genius at its most moving and rings his own change by drawing us in to share the trance-like response of the saint, who seems now to stand still, now to move, now to be active, now passive, as he hurries to the side of his dead friend.

My second example of how Vegio combines pagan and Christian in his use of allusion is offered by the poem's final three lines, 4.131–33:

> Tunc, ubi clara sequens tenebras Aurora fugavit,
> Discedit: cupidusque domum sociosque revisit,
> Caelestemque hominem, facta et caelestia narrat.

> Then, when the subsequent morn's bright dawn had put the darkness to flight, he departs and eagerly returns to his home and comrades, and tells them of the godlike man and his godlike deeds.

The first of these hexameters ends with a bow to *Aeneid* 3.521— "Iamque rubescebat stellis Aurora fugatis" ("And now Aurora reddens with the stars put to flight")—while the second alludes to 6.899, three lines before Virgil finishes the first half of his epic— "ille viam secat ad navis sociosque revisit" ("[Aeneas] speeds the way to his ships and returns to his comrades"). The ultimate line, however, is a paraphrase of the last sentence in the final paragraph of which Vegio made use, in Jerome's *Vita Pauli* (ch. 16). He thus brings his own poem to an end not only by reference to his major sources but to concluding moments in them, drawing, therefore, on both content and structure as he creates his own small masterpiece.[81]

* * *

I am most grateful to Virginia Brown and John Van Sickle for casting a careful eye on the translations. Emma Buckley, Christopher Celenza, Preston Edwards and Benjamin Low have helped in a variety of ways. Kenneth Gaulin, as always, provided unwavering support and a setting *sine qua non*. I dedicate the book to Polly Chatfield, who has been there from the start.

NOTES

1. For details on Vegio's life and works see Minoia; Raffaele; Brinton, pp. 5–34; Vignati; Sottili; and the introductions to the editions by Schneider, pp. 14–17, and Glei-Köhler, pp. 8–11. (Full citations may be found in the Bibliography.)

2. For convenient lists of Vegio's writings see Raffaele, pp. 83–85, with the précis that follows; Brinton, pp. 145–46.

3. Eugenius IV, pope from 1431 to 1447, lived in exile in Florence and elsewhere from May 1434 to September 1443.

4. Possible Christological associations in the simile, suggesting an equation between Christ and Aeneas, are to be found already in the commentary of Ascensius. See, most recently, Tudeau-Clayton, pp. 521–22, with notes 51–53.

5. For the text see, ed. J. J. Salverda de Grave, *Eneas: Roman du XIIe siècle*, 2 vols. (Paris, 1925–29) and, for an English version, *Eneas: A Twelfth-Century French Romance*, tr. J. A. Yunck (New York, 1974).

6. Creusa speaks to Aeneas at *Aeneid* 2.783 of his future *regia coniunx*, and in Book VI Aeneas is told of her twice, in obscure terms by the Sibyl (93) and then at 764 where Anchises first names her to his son (*Lavinia coniunx*). Though fated to be Aeneas's consort (7.72, 314, 359), she is often connected in the epic's last six books with Turnus (see 12.17, 64, 80 and 194) who renounces her near the end of his final words (12.937: *tua est Lavinia coniunx*: "Lavinia is your wife"). Virgil never makes mention of any amatory connection between Aeneas and his future wife. Vegio therefore offers one of his more dramatic shocks to a reader of the

Aeneid by saying that his hero "paused enchanted" (*stupefactus inhaesit*, 470) at his first sight of Lavinia.

The passage recalls the language of *Aeneid* 1.613–14, where Dido first catches sight of Aeneas, and of 6.451–53, where Aeneas sees Dido in the Underworld. By replacing Dido with Lavinia, Vegio turns the destructive aspects of Aeneas's earlier relationship, as developed by Virgil, into the calm creativity of the hero's marriage and settlement in Latium.

7. For the text, with a translation into modern German, see *Heinrich von Veldeke: Eneasroman*, ed. L. Ettmüller (Stuttgart, 1986). There is a recent translation by R. W. Fisher: *Heinrich von Veldeke: Eneas*, Australian and New Zealand Studies in German Language and Literature, no. 17 (Bern, 1992), with a detailed comparison of Veldeke's work with the *Roman d'Eneas*. For a briefer comparison see Yunck (cited in note 5 above), pp. 46–52.

On the *Roman d'Eneas* and Heinrich von Veldeke's *Eneasroman*, see further J. Monfrin, "Les *translations* vernaculaires de Virgile au Moyen Âge," in *Lectures Médiévales de Virgile*. Collection de l'École française de Rome, 80 (Rome, 1985), pp. 189–249; N. Henkel, "Vergil's *Aeneis* und die mittelalterlichen *Eneas-Romane*," in Claudio Leonardi and Birger Munk Olsen, eds., *The Classical Tradition in the Middle Ages and the Renaissance: Proceedings of the First European Science Foundation Workshop on the Reception of Classical Texts* (Spoleto, 1995), pp. 123–41.

8. Heinrich adopts his lines from *Aeneid* 12.593–613 where Amata commits suicide at what she believes to be the death of Turnus, exclaiming that she is the cause of the evils that have occurred. Heinrich's queen, by contrast, curses both her husband and daughter before dying a natural death.

9. In this light it is no accident that he compresses to some forty lines (12705–44) his depiction of Aeneas's lovesickness, after the death of Turnus and before his marriage, a subject to which the author of the *Roman* allots four times as many verses (9922–10090).

10. *Vita Donati* 35 in Colin Hardie, ed., *Vitae Vergilianae Antiquae* (Oxford, 1966).

11. *Vita Donati* 24.

12. See in particular Brinton, pp. 2 and 24–26; Allen, p. 141; Bono, pp. 44–45 and cf. pp. 173–74.

Aside from the pertinent passages in Virgil and Ovid dealing with the aftermath of Aeneas's death, we find in the poets that Tibullus (2.5.43–44) would place him, as *Indiges,* in heaven (*caelo*) whereas Horace in a late ode (4.7.15) puts him in the Underworld. Prose writers contemporary with Virgil, Livy (1.2.6) and Dionysius of Halicarnassus (1.64), debate the matter (see also the brief reference in Dio 1 [= Zonaras 7.1]). Compare also Dido's curse at *Aeneid* 4.619–20. For further details, see Julia T. Dyson, *King of the Wood: The Sacrificial Victim in Virgil's Aeneid* (Norman, Oklahoma, 2001), pp. 51–60.

13. Quirinus is appropriately used here as the name of the deified Romulus. *Indiges* means something like "native god."

14. Only Tibullus, among ancient authors, grants this honor to Aeneas (see note 12 above).

15. Vegio brings closure to his "completion" of the *Aeneid* via allusion to Ovid's own act of continuing the narrative of Aeneas's tale up to its conclusion with his death. But the pattern of allusiveness to Ovid in Vegio's final lines, a pattern that leads from *Metamorphoses* 14 to 15 and then back to 14, is a further indication of Vegio's unwillingness to progress, in whatever manner, beyond Virgil and Ovid, a step which might have taken the form of a Christian twist to the hero's catasterism. Instead we return to the Numicius and to Aeneas as noble Roman, further ennobled as *indiges*.

16. Virgil's only other use of the word, this time in the plural, is at *Georgic* 1.498.

17. One of Vegio's few alterations is to replace Ovid's *turba Quirini* with *Iulia proles* as if to associate the Roman populace more closely with Caesar and Augustus than with Romulus.

18. *De educatione liberorum et eorum claribus moris libri sex*, ed. M. Fanning (Washington, D.C., 1933), 2.18, quoted by Brinton, p. 27, and Kallendorf, *In Praise of Aeneas*, pp. 102, and idem, *Virgil and the Myth of Venice*, pp. 52–53, whose translation I use. Four years later (1448) in *De perseverantia religionis* (published in an edition of Paris, 1511) he expands on the topic of

Aeneas's life as moral model in more fully allegorical terms. See Brinton, pp. 27–9 and Kallendorf, "Maffeo Vegio's Book XIII," pp. 49–50.

19. The most obvious path which Vegio follows for the defamation of Turnus is simply to have the poem's protagonists point out his faults in speech after speech. Of the five orations found in the first half of the poem, three, by Aeneas, Latinus and Daunus, are delivered over the hero's corpse and exclaim as often on his faults as on his virtues (cf. also the speech of Drances at 331–73). For observations on the *Supplement* as a *laudatio* of Aeneas and a *vituperatio* of Turnus, see Hijmans, passim. Vegio never implicates Juno, as Virgil does from the beginning of his epic to near its conclusion, with negative aspects of the *Aeneid*'s plot. (The only hints that Juno may have harbored unfriendly feelings toward the Trojans come at lines 611 and 620 where her assent to the Trojans' newfound happiness and to Aeneas's deification assumes some less than positive feelings on her part toward them in the past.) Turnus stands alone as villain.

Buckley (p. 4) rightly sees the two halves of the *Supplement* as in general illustrating "the 'tragic' *Iliad* . . . superseded by the 'comedic' *Odyssey*." In this regard, Vegio may have arranged the three speeches over the corpse of Turnus which demarcate his "Iliadic" first half as a reminder of the three speeches of Andromache, Hecuba and Helen at the funeral of Hector which bring the *Iliad* to its memorable conclusion.

The epideictic quality of Vegio's speeches taken as a whole is the essential topic of Kallendorf, *In Praise of Aeneas*.

20. To recent readers, the very intensity by which Vegio marks the goodness of Aeneas and the faults of Turnus throughout his poem is a sign of his latent dissatisfaction with certain aspects of Virgil's text and especially with his portrayal of the irrational violence of the hero in the epic's last moments. See in particular Kallendorf, *In Praise of Aeneas*, pp. 127–28; idem, "Historicizing the Harvard School," pp. 397–98; Putnam, pp. 334–35; Thomas, pp. 279–84; Buckley, passim. On Vegio and the ending of the *Aeneid*, see further note 58 below.

21. Most of Vegio's bows to Virgil are to be found in the footnoted citations of Schneider's edition. Buckley, pp. 3–4, points out that *Supplement* 2 looks to the epic's final line (952) and that Vegio refers to *Aen.* 12.1–2 at *Supp.* 304–5 to demarcate nearly the opening of his poem's second half.

1

For a discussion of Vegio as part of a more general survey of the influence of Virgil on Renaissance literature see Zabughin, 1:281–87 with notes. Zabughin makes due reference to the other Renaissance attempt to "supplement" the *Aeneid* by Vegio's slightly older contemporary, Pier Candido Decembrio (1392–1477). Decembrio's text is quoted by Schneider, pp. 136–38. (Raffaele, pp. 20–25, and Schneider, pp. 17–18, offer comparisons between the two texts.)

22. *Aen.* 12.945–47 and 951.

23. We learn this first in the words of Latinus (180) and the narrator (180), then from Daunus himself (253, 257, 287, 298).

24. In a similar way Vegio also clears away the violence of Aeneas's actions subsequent to the death of Pallas by changing the phrase *inimico pectore fatur* (he speaks from his hostile heart, 10.556) to *amico pectore fatur* (he speaks from his friendly heart, 376) as Aeneas receives the Latin envoys.

25. The preceding dialogue between Venus and her son also plays a role in the aspects of the *Supplement* that rehabilitate Aeneas. The careful recollection of *Aeneid* 2.589–93 at *Supplement* 550–51 reminds us that we have come a long way from Aeneas's soliloquy of rage against Helen, followed by his mother's calming intervention, to a moment when Aeneas's care centers on an omen of his wife's hair catching fire and his mother can respond with a prediction of his happy rule and subsequent deification. Not only does Vegio change the parallel omen in *Aeneid* 7 (with *Supplement* 540–42 cf. *Aen.* 7.72–80) from negative to positive, from anticipation of war to prediction of enduring peace, he takes his hero out of one of his most unsettling contexts and establishes him as concerned ruler of a stable people.

26. See also Thomas, pp. 281–82.

27. Lines 21–22: *foedusque precari / pacis* ("they solicit the compact of peace"), take us even further back into *Aeneid* 12, to 242–43: *foedusque precantur / infectum* ("they pray that the compact be undone"). The breaking of one treaty, that leads to renewed war, in the *Aeneid*, is answered in the *Supplement* by the confirmation of another and the peace that ensues.

28. See, e.g. *Aeneid* 11.354–56 and 468–72, and 12.29–31 and 657–58. Vegio's Latinus puts all blame on Turnus (see 161–70).

29. The connection is made by direct mention of Anchises (e.g. at 117, 346, 446, and 484) or by allusion (e.g., with 419 cf. *Aen.* 8.162–63, and with 424 cf. *Aen.* 6.687).

30. Vegio suppresses mention of Dido at one of the few places where she might tactfully have been brought into his poem, an adjacent passage in which Aeneas offers gifts to Latinus and Lavinia (478–89). Cf. *Aen.* 1.643–56.

31. For Vegio's bows to Ovid see also the citations collected by Schneider. The most extensive allusions are those which we have traced him making to *Metamorphoses* 14 and 15 in his poem's concluding lines. Vegio also borrows prominently from *Metamorphoses* 14.573–80 for his description of the metamorphosis of Ardea into a heron at 234–38.

32. On the text and its history, see Schneider, pp. 24–41, the review of Schneider by Kallendorf in *Renaissance Quarterly* 49 (1987): 95–96, and the supplementary list of manuscripts by Kallendorf and Brown (q.v.). Their diffusion is traced by G. Mambelli, *Gli annali delle edizioni virgiliane.* Biblioteca di bibliografia italiana 27 (Florence, 1954).

33. Or Josse Bode (1462–1535); his commentary on the *Supplement* of Maffeo Vegio was first published by Theilmann Kerver for the printers Jean Petit and Johann of Koblenz (Paris, 1500/01) in *Aeneis cum commentariis Servii, Beroaldi, Donati, Badii et Vegii* (which despite the title does not contain a commentary by Vegio, but rather Bodes's commentary on Vegio's *Supplement*).

34. *Aen.* 2.457, 3.489. Ovid's brief mention of Astyanax is at *Metamorphoses* 13.415–17.

35. Two story lines interweave in the tragedy. One centers on the necessity for Astyanax's death and its implementation through the wiles of Ulysses practised against Andromacha, Hector's widow. The second, which Vegio ignores, is the death of Polyxena, Priam's daughter, sacrificed in mock marriage to the shade of Achilles.

36. Vegio's initial line deliberately recalls the first line of Ulysses's speech which also incorporates the speech of Calchas at *Troades* 365–70.

37. Vegio was thinking particularly of *Phaedra* 1105–14 (the messenger is speaking), 1168–90 (Phaedra) and 1256–70 (Theseus).

38. Vegio would have us ponder especially 281–86 and 289–95.

39. Venus speaks first (86–103) followed by her father (105–121) as in the *Aeneid* (Venus, 229–53; Jupiter, 257–97).

40. The verbal echoes between the two sets of speeches are frequent, especially in their initial lines.

41. The echo of *insidiatus ovili*, concluding the initial line of Virgil's comparison, in *insidiatur ovili* at exactly the same position in Vegio's initial hexameter, is Vegio's way of urging the reader to make a correlation.

42. The line preceding Virgil's simile (*insequitur trepidique pedem pede fervidus urget: Aen.* 12.748) is adopted, and adapted, by Vegio in the first line of his simile (*cum volucrem insequitur curvis trepidam unguibus urgens:* 229).

43. The notion of this double booty is Ovid's (*Metamorphoses* 7. 156–57). Seneca combines the two at *Medea* 361–62 and 982–84.

44. In the so-called "A" class of manuscripts, *Troades* and *Medea* are adjacent. In the rarer, but more authoritative, "E" class the *Phoenissae* intervenes between *Troades* and *Medea*. For details see the entry "Tragedies" by R. J. Tarrant under "Seneca the Younger" in *Texts and Transmission*, ed. L. D. Reynolds (Oxford, 1983), pp. 378–81. Vegio's knowledge, not to say use, of Seneca's play would be a reason for his not giving the same title to his own work.

45. See *Vellus Aureum*, ed. Glei and Köhler, pp. 20–21. Of the *Argonautika* of Apollonius of Rhodes Vegio apparently knew, or at least used, only the initial catalogue of heroes (1.18–227). See the comparison in Glei-Köhler, pp. 21–27.

46. That her father's final curse upon her anticipates the later "Medea-Tragödie" is noted by Glei-Köhler, p. 145, n. 25.

47. The last line of Vegio's poem (4.252) contains the word *coniuge*, and the first of Seneca's play *coniugales*; his line 249 refers to the helmsman

Tiphys who is named directly by Seneca in his line 3. Of other parallels we might note the descriptions of Absyrtus at *Medea* 130–31 (*inclitum regni decus / raptum*) and at *Vellus Aureum* 4.236–38 (*nostri inclita regni / . . . spes . . . / . . . rapuit*).

48. In the *Vellus Aureum* 410 lines out of 1009 are devoted to speeches.

49. There are all told twenty-nine speeches, clustered largely in the last three books.

50. See also Glei-Köhler, pp. 27–29 (on the *Metamorphoses* as providing the poem's "Makrostructur").

51. See *P. Ovidii Nasonis: Heroidum Epistula XII: Medea Iasoni*, ed. F. Bessone (Florence, 1997), especially pp. 23–41, for the relationship with *Metamorphoses* 7 and for the intimations of dread times to come in Medea's final words. Though the form of Ovid's work is nominally a letter, it presents itself in effect as a spoken monologue addressed *in absentia* by one lover to another.

52. Ovid's poem, written in exile at Tomis on the Black Sea, is largely an attempt to connect the etymology of the town with Greek τέμνειν (to cut). Medea's dissection of her brother as well as the location of the event lend appropriate support to his hypothesis.

53. See Glei-Köhler, pp. 29–34, for a detailed list of parallels between Vegio's narrative and the *Aeneid*.

54. We have already seen Vegio's use of the same line in the initial hexameter of the *Astyanax*.

55. In *Aeneid* 1 Cupido displaces Iulus (Ascanius) but keeps his appearance.

56. See the words of Aeëtes at 4.243. In many respects Vegio's Jason is an anti-hero, especially by comparison to his Aeneas. Though he has his moment of glory, it is brought about by the help of Medea whose theatrics and the response to them by her father bring the poem to its final, ghastly climax.

57. See Glei-Köhler, p. 93, n. 15.

58. Forms of *ira* end *Aeneid* 12.946 and *Vellus Aureum* 4.202, and we remember that Aeneas, earlier in the same line, is *furiis accensus*. On the

ambiguity of the *ferrum . . . condit* (*Aen.* 12.950) see most recently S. James, "Establishing Rome with the Sword: *Condere* in the *Aeneid*," *American Journal of Philology* 116 (1995): 623–37. The use of the verb *condere* in the antepenultimate line of the poem and in the fifth hexameter from its beginning (*Aen.* 1.5, in the phrase *dum conderet urbem*, "until [Aeneas] should found his city") is a crucial item in Virgil's carefully plotted lexical correspondences between the beginning and the end of his epic. He brings about closure not by the easy narrative satisfactions that Vegio elaborates in the *Supplement* but by the more challenging, and troubling, rhetorical means of repetition, first, in the iteration of *condere* that highlights its ambiguity, second, in giving the language of angry Juno, that follows soon upon the first appearance of *condere*, to angry Aeneas in the poem's final lines.

59. Any reader pondering the morality of Aeneas's actions at the end of his epic must weigh in his thoughts the command Aeneas's father addresses to him, as the progenitor of Romans to come, to remember, when acting from a position of military power (6.853): "parcere subiectis et debellare superbos" ("to spare the humbled and war down the proud"). It is not coincidental that Vegio uses a form of *parcere* at the moment when Medea contemplates offering mercy to her helpless brother.

60. We know that Turnus will die, even though for the moment of Aeneas's pause Virgil would seem to make clemency a possibility. What Virgil leaves the reader of the *Aeneid* to ponder is not so much the whys and wherefores of Aeneas's quasi-fated necessity to kill but the rage and fury with which he does the deed.

61. The character of Aeëtes is largely modeled on benign father figures in the *Aeneid*, such as Latinus and Evander, and on Dido when still possessed of her regality.

62. Several ironies are in play here. Vegio models Aeolus on the figure of Juno in *Aeneid* 1, going to him for aid in destroying the Trojans. He thus not only reverses Virgil's narrative situation but also is guilty of what might be called anachronism through allusion, by referring to an event well in the future at the time of the exploits of the Argonauts (on the lat-

ter point see Glei-Köhler, p. 97, n. 3). Perhaps Vegio would also have us think of how belated his own text is in relation to Virgil's epic.

63. Vegio allows himself occasional flashes of wit. The figure of the Sun god and the depiction of his daily course is, as we have seen, drawn in a certain measure from the second book of Ovid's *Metamorphoses*. Nowhere, however, does Ovid have him end his day, as does Vegio, resting on a grassy seat playing a shepherd's pipe (1.177–78). The fact that the last phrase *modulatur avena* (he makes music on a rustic pipe), is Virgilian (*Ecl.* 10.51) or pseudo-Virgilian (*Ille ego qui quondam gracili modulatus avena*), does not detract from the charm of Vegio's vignette of the Sun god as Apollo the pastoralist.

64. The *Antoniad* is mentioned in passing by Zabughin, 2:179–80, as one of the predecessors of these better known works.

65. Biographies of St. Paul and St. Antony are included, as numbers 15 and 21, in the so-called *Legenda Aurea* of Jacobus de Voragine, the Genoese Dominican who made his collection of lives of the saints around 1260. See *Iacopo da Varazze: Legenda Aurea*, ed. G. Maggioni (Florence, 1998), pp. 141–42, 155–60.

66. See M. Rochelle, *Post-Biblical Saints Art Index* (Jefferson, North Carolina, 1994) under Antony Abbot and Paul the Hermit, and, for a brief overview, J. Seznec, "The Temptation of St. Anthony in Art," *Magazine of Art*, 40 (1947): 86–93. The most well-known depictions of the scene of meeting are perhaps those of Sassetta, now in the Washington National Gallery of Art and dating some three or four years after the composition of Maffeo's poem (1440), and of Velazquez (1634) which shows St. Paul in prayer, with St. Antony watching as the crow descends with the loaf in its beak. The fifteenth century saw a plethora of representations of the temptations, by, e.g., Bosch, Cranach the Elder, and Lucas Van Leyden. Both scenes are portrayed by Matthias Grünewald as part of the famous Isenheim Altarpiece at Colmar (1515). For further detail see also H. Trebbin, *Sankt Antonius: Kult und Kunst* (Frankfurt, 1994), especially pp. 9–40.

67. For a detailed life, see Joseph Gill, S. J., *Eugenius IV: Pope of Christian Union* (Westminster, Maryland, 1961). As a young man Eugene had lived

in a house of Augustinian hermits in Venice; on his deathbed he is said to have regretted ever leaving his monastery.

68. The life of St. Antony, who lived c. 251–356, had been written in Greek, c. 357, by Bishop Athanasius of Alexandria (c. 296–373). It was translated into Latin by Evagrius (c. 320–c. 394), Bishop of Antioch. He was a close friend of St. Jerome, who devoted to him ch. 125 of *De Viris Illustribus* (written 392–3), where the translation is mentioned. If it is a correct presumption that it was Evagrius's Latin translation of the *Vita Antonii* that was read by Ponticianus's friend, then it would have had to be available some time before the conversion of Augustine (354–430) which took place in 386.

69. The Gospel of Matthew 19:21. The event is described, and the sentence from Matthew quoted, in ch. 2 of Evagrius's translation of the *Vita Antonii*.

70. Epistle of Paul to the Romans 13:13–14.

71. The language of the two conversion scenes, which show several parallels, is anticipated by the eagerness with which Augustine "grabs" (*arripui*) the writings of Paul at the opening of *Conf.* 7. 21 (cf. the uses of *arripere* at 8.6 and 12). I owe the earlier reference to Christopher Johnson.

72. *Ad Familiares* 4.1.

73. *Ad Familiares* 4.1.27.

74. On Vegio's religious writings see Charles Trinkaus, *In Our Image and Likeness: Humanity and Divinity in Italian Humanist Thought* (Chicago and London, 1970), pp. 648 and 844, n. 103.

75. For the text of the *Vita Pauli Primi Eremitae* (=*BHL* 6596) see *Studies in the Text Tradition of St. Jerome's Vitae Patrum*, ed. W. A. Oldfather (Urbana, Illinois, 1943), pp. 36–42, reprinted from vol. 48 of *Sanctorum Patrum Opuscula Selecta*, ed. H. Hurter (Innsbruck, 1885–97). Since there is no mention of Paul the Hermit in Athanasius's life of Antony, it is a reasonable conjecture that the episodes that conclude Jerome's *Vita* were invented by him.

76. At the start (*Vita Pauli* 1) of his work Jerome makes it clear that he wants it to be part of the biographical tradition, both Greek (Atha-

nasius) and Latin (Evagrius). He will only be filling in omissions rather than relying on his own inventiveness (*quia res omissa erat, quam fretus ingenio*).

77. *Vita Pauli* 7 (*illi per noctem quiescenti revelatum est*).

78. See Greene, pp. 107–12. There is apparently no parallel to the oration Vegio gives Satan in classical or post-classical Latin liturature, though we might compare the speeches that Claudian puts in the mouths of Allecto and Megaera in *In Rufinum* (1.45–65 and 86–115, respectively), or the description of hell, and concomitant speeches, in *De Raptu Proserpinae* (1.32–116). For Renaissance parallels we have Vida's *Christiad* 167–223 (Satan at a council of his followers), or, still later, the speech of Satan/Pluto in Tasso's *Gerusalemme Liberata* (4.65–136). The papal secretary and humanist Leonardo Dati includes a speech from Satan to the prophet Mohammed in his short epic or epyllion, *Carmen ad Nicolaum Papam V in Thurcum Mahomet* (1453/54), lines 15–62; the text is in James Hankins, *Humanism and Platonism in the Italian Renaissance* (Rome, 2003), pp. 375–383.

79. Throughout the poem angels are called *divi*, not *angeli*.

80. *Aen.* 12.908–14.

81. As with the preceding hexameter poems of Vegio, not only do the other works of Virgil share in shaping his imagination but so do many further authors as well. Ovid, as before, is a regular influence (for a particularly beautiful example compare *Antoniad* 3.11 with Ovid *Metamorphoses* 11.596). Even Homer, however vicariously, may have played a part. The opening book of the *Odyssey*, with the details of the hero's travails leading to a council of the gods and the dispatching of Hermes to Odysseus on Calypso's isle, could well have served as a structuring model for the description of Antony's trials and accomplishments preceding God's gathering of the heavenly hosts and the sending of Gabriel to rouse the saint to action. This last episode is paralleled in Jupiter's mission of Mercury, in *Aeneid* 4, to remind the hero of his fated destiny to journey on to Italy.

SHORT EPICS

AENEIDOS LIBER XIII

Turnus ut extremo devictus Marte profudit
effugientem animam medioque sub agmine victor
magnanimus stetit Aeneas, Mavortius heros,
obstupuere omnes gemitumque dedere Latini,
5 et durum ex alto revomentes corde dolorem
concussis cecidere animis, ceu frondibus ingens
silva solet lapsis boreali impulsa tumultu.
Tum tela infigunt terrae, et mucronibus haerent,
scutaque deponunt umeris, et proelia damnant,
10 insanumque horrent optati Martis amorem.
Nec frenum nec colla pati captiva recusant
et veniam orare et requiem finemque malorum.
Sicut acerba duo quando in certamina tauri
concurrant largo miscentes sanguine pugnam
15 cuique suum pecus inclinat, sin cesserit uni
palma duci, mox quae victo pecora ante favebant
nunc sese imperio subdunt victoris et ultro,
quamquam animum dolor altus habet, parere fatentur,
non aliter Rutuli, licet ingens maeror adhausit
20 pectora pulsa metu caesi ducis, inclita malunt
arma sequi et Phrygium Aeneam foedusque precari
pacis et aeternam rebus belloque quietem.
    Tunc Turnum super adsistens placido ore profatur
Aeneas: "Quae tanta animo dementia crevit,
25 ut Teucros superum monitis summique Tonantis
imperio huc vectos patereris, Daunia proles,
Italia et pactis nequicquam expellere tectis?
Disce Iovem revereri et iussa facessere divum.
Magnum etiam capit ira Iovem, memoresque malorum

BOOK XIII OF THE AENEID

When Turnus, beaten in the final bout of war, poured forth his fleeting life, and amid the host stood great-souled Aeneas, War's victorious hero, all the Latins, benumbed, uttered a moan and, venting harsh sorrow from the core of their beings, gave way in despair. Their minds were buffeted, as happens when a mighty grove is stricken by the north wind's swirl, and its leaves fall. Then they stab their spears into the ground and slump on sword hilts. They lower shields from shoulders, and curse the conflict, shuddering at the crazed passion for Mars they once desired. They do not refuse to brook either the reins or neck-yokes of the captured, and pray for pardon, for peace, and for an end to evil. So it is when two bulls charge towards one another, into the bitterness of strife, mingling their struggles with a slather of gore—his herd champions each. But should the palm of success fall to the lot of one lord, soon the cattle, which before offered allegiance to the vanquished, now humble themselves to the victor's sway and, though deep sorrow grips their spirits, they willingly profess their submission: so the Rutuli, though vast grief engulfs their hearts and fear assails them at the slaughter of their lord, prefer to follow famous arms, and Aeneas of Troy. They solicit the compact of peace and enduring quiet in place of the affairs of war.

Then, bestriding Turnus from above, Aeneas speaks from serene lips: "What was this vast madness that ripened in your mind, offspring of Daunus, so that you futilely presumed to drive out of Italy, and of the dwellings that were their due, the Trojans who had journeyed here at the behest of the gods above and at the command of the Thunderer on high? Learn to honor Jove and to fulfill the dictates of the gods. Anger grips even mighty Jove and

30   sollicitat vindicta deos. En ultima tanti
     meta furoris adest, quo contra iura fidemque
     Iliacam rupto turbasti foedere gentem.
     Ecce suprema dies aliis exempla sub aevum
     venturum missura, Iovem ne temnere frustra
35   fas sit et indignos bellorum accendere motus.
     Nunc armis laetare tuis! Heu, nobile corpus,
     Turne, iaces. At non tibi erit Lavinia parvo,
     nec dextra tamen Aeneae cecidisse pudebit.
     Nunc, Rutuli, hinc auferte ducem vestrum; arma virumque
40   largior atque omnem deflendae mortis honorem.
     Sed quae Pallantis fuerant ingentia baltei
     pondera, transmittam Euandro, ut solacia caeso
     haud levia hoste ferat Turnoque exultet adempto.
     Vos memores tamen, Ausonii, melioribus uti
45   discite bellorum auspiciis. Ego sidera iuro:
     Numquam acies, numquam arma libens in proelia movi,
     sed vestris actus furiis defendere toto
     optavi, et licuit, Troianas robore partes."
        Nec fatus plura Aeneas se laetus ad altos
50   vertebat muros et Troia tecta petebat.
     Una ipsum Teucrorum omnis conversa iuventus
     exultans sequitur, volucresque per arva pedum vi
     quadrupedes citat, incusans acri ore Latinos
     ignavosque vocans. Strepit altus plausibus aether.
55   Et quamvis inhumata rogis dare corpora surgat
     ingens cura animo sociosque imponere flammis,
     maius opus tamen Aeneas sub pectore volvens
     primum aris meritos superum mandabat honores.
     Tum pingues patrio iugulant ex more iuvencos
60   immittuntque sues niveasque in templa bidentes
     purpuream effuso pulsantes sanguine terram.
     Viscera diripiunt et caesum in frusta trucidant

4

retribution stirs the gods who remember evil-doings. See, now at   30
last the end is at hand of your wild madness through which,
affronting proper right and trust, you brought trouble on the Tro-
jan race by breaking the treaty. Take note, your last days will serve
as warning to others in time to come that it is wrong in vain to
scorn Jove's ordinance and set aflame the worthless frenzy of war
on war. Take joy, now, in your weapons! I grieve for you lying   35
there, Turnus, a noble corpse. But Lavinia will not be yours at a
small cost, and no shame will come to you from having perished at
Aeneas's right hand. Rutulians, it is time to bear forth hence your
lord. Weapons and corpse I bestow, along with every honor due to
a death worthy of lamentation. But the baldric's heavy weight,   40
once Pallas's, I will convey to Evander that he might feel some
strength of consolation in the slaughter of the foe, and revel in
Turnus's demise. Do you, Italians, yet learn through remembrance
to employ more worthy excuses for venturing on war. I myself take   45
an oath on the stars: it was never my pleasure to thrust my sol-
diery, never my own weapons, into battle, but, driven by your
madness and with due mandate, I chose with all my strength to
safeguard the interests of Troy."

  Saying no more Aeneas gladly turned toward the lofty palisade
and sought the Trojan tents. In jubilation all the Trojan youths   50
bent to follow together with him, and with forceful feet spur their
swift horses through the fields, assailing the Latins with biting
words and proclaiming them cowards. The lofty heavens resounds
with their cheers. And although intense concern looms in his   55
mind to place the unburied bodies of his comrades on their pyres
and ignite the fires, nevertheless, in prudence attentive to a more
solemn task, Aeneas first ordered appropriate honors on the altars
of the gods. Then, after the manner of their forefathers, they sac-
rifice fattened bullocks, and into the shrines herd hogs and snow-   60
white sheep which splash the crimsoned earth with gushing blood.
They slay and skin each animal, wrench forth its entrails, butcher

5

denudantque gregem, et flammis verubusque remittunt.
Tum vina effundunt pateris et dona Lyaei
65 accumulant. Plenis venerantur lancibus aras.
Tura ignes adolent; onerata altaria fumant.
Tum plausus per tecta movent magnumque Tonantem
extollunt Veneremque et te, Saturnia Iuno,
  —iam placidam et meliorem ingenti laude fatentur—
70 Mavortemque ipsum. Tum cetera turba deorum
in medium affertur summis cum vocibus altos
perlata ad caelos.
                      Ante omnes mitior unus
Aeneas duplices mittebat ad aethera palmas,
et puerum pauca ore dabat complexus Iulum:
75 "Nate, in quo spes una patris, per tanta viarum
quem variis actus fatis discrimina duxi,
ecce inventa quies, ecce illa extrema malorum
aerumnis factura modum acceptissima semper
atque optata dies, quam dura in bella vocatus
80 saepe tibi diis auspicibus meminisse futuram
iam memini. Nunc te, quam primum aurora rubebit
crastina, sublimem Rutulorum ad moenia mittam."
Dehinc sese ad gentem Iliacam volvebat amico
continuans vultu et placida sic voce locutus:
85 "O socii, per dura et densa pericula vecti,
per tantos bellorum aestus duplicesque furores
armorum, per totque hiemes, per quicquid acerbum,
horrendum, grave, triste, ingens, et quicquid iniquum,
infaustum et crudele foret, convertite mentem
90 in melius! Iam finis adest: Hic meta laborum
stabit, et optatam Latia cum gente quietem
iungemus. Dabit inde mihi Lavinia coniunx
bello acri defensa Italo cum sanguine mixtam
Troianam transferre aeterna in saecula gentem.

the carcass into morsels and give them over to spits and to the flames. Then they heap up the gifts of Bacchus and pour out wine from bowls. They do homage to the altars with brimming platters. 65 Fires burn incense, the laden platforms smoke. Then jubilation spreads through the homes and exalts the mighty Thunderer, and Venus, and you, Saturn's Juno—with the might of their praise they declare her now serene and of more kindly mien—and Mars himself. Then the remaining company of divinities, summoned to 70 the ceremony, is raised to the lofty heavens with bravo after bravo.

Peerless Aeneas, excelling all in gentleness, lifted both hands toward the sky and, embracing young Iulus, briefly spoke: "My son, 75 alone the hope of his father, whom I, driven by the vicissitudes of fate, guided through the vast crises of our wanderings, behold, we have discovered rest. Behold the day, finale of our evils, making an end to our trials, the day ever yearned for and most welcome. As I was summoned into war's cruelty, I now recollect that I often re- 80 minded you that this day would come to pass under auspicious gods. As soon as tomorrow's dawn glows red, it will be time for me to send you in glory to the Rutulian ramparts." Then, turning with friendly glance toward the crowd of Trojans, he continued thus in serene tones: "O comrades, who have traveled through 85 cruel, constant dangers, through massive surges of war and the re- doubled madness of fighting, through a siege of tempests, through whatever harsh, dread, oppressive, piteous, threatening might come our way, whatever unjust, accursed and savage, turn your thoughts to better things! Now the conclusion is at hand. Here 90 will be the end-goal of our trials. With the Latin race we will es- tablish the peace for which we have yearned. Thence will my wife Lavinia, sheltered through the bitter war, grant me to transmit the destiny of the Trojan race, commingled with Italian blood, into all

95   Unum oro, socii, Ausonios communibus aeque
ferte animis, et vos socerum observate Latinum!
Sceptrum idem sublime geret; sententia mentem
haec habet; at bello vos et praestantibus armis
discite me et pietate sequi. Quae gloria nobis
100   cesserit, in promptu est; sed caelum et sidera testor:
Qui vos tantorum eripui de clade malorum
idem ego sub maiora potens vos praemia ducam."
     Talibus orabat, variosque in pectore casus
praeteritos volvens partamque labore quietem
105   haud parvo nimium ardenti exundabat amore
in Teucros, gravibus tandem evasisse periclis
exultans. Velut exiguis cum ex aethere gyrans
incubuit pullis et magno turbine milvus
insiliens avido ore furit stragemque minatur,
110   tum cristata ales concusso pectore mater
consurgit misero natorum exterrita casu,
rostrum acuit totisque petit conatibus hostem
et multa expulsum vi tandem cedere cogit,
dehinc perturbatos crocitans exquirit et omnes
115   attonitos cogit pro caris anxia natis
et tanto ereptos gaudet superesse periclo,
non secus Anchisa genitus mulcebat amicis
Troianos dictis, antiquum corde timorem
flagrantisque agitans curas et gaudia longis
120   tandem parta malis, et quae perferre molestum
ante fuit, meminisse iuvat. Verum altior idem
ingenti et clara Aeneas supereminet omnes
virtute excellens, et pro tot numina donis
exorat summisque Iovem cum laudibus effert.
125   Interea Rutuli magnum et miserabile funus
exanimumque ducem tulerant sub tecta frequentes
correpti maerore animos largumque pluentes

8

ages to come. I ask one thing, comrades: treat the Italians justly 95
with kindred minds and grant respect to our father-in-law,
Latinus. He will wield the glorious scepter. This my mind has de-
creed. But, as warriors, learn to emulate me, both in the excellence
of your soldiering and in your piety. The glory that has accrued to
us is plain to see. But I will call the heavens and the stars to wit- 100
ness: I, who have rescued you from the calamity of such great
evils, will myself, in power, guide you to still greater rewards."

Such was his prayer. As he pondered the diverse perils now
past and peace procured through dint of effort, he brimmed with a
blaze of warmth toward his beloved Trojans, jubilant at the formi- 105
dable dangers they have at last passed beyond. Just as when a
kite, circling from the heavens, has careened toward tiny nestlings
and, swooping down in a tremendous whirl, shrieks greedily and
threatens mayhem, then the wattled mother hen, heart shaken in 110
terror from the grievous peril to her young, rises up, whets her
beak and, assailing the foe with all her effort, finally compels him
to yield as she drives him out with full force. Then, cackling away,
worried for her young, she seeks out the bewildered brood and 115
herds the troubled throng, glad for their survival, snatched from
the brink of disaster. So the son of Anchises soothed the Trojans
with friendly words, going over and over in his heart his prior fear
and burning worries, as well as the joys at last brought forth from
a stretch of evils. He gains pleasure in the memory of what before 120
was a trial to withstand. Aeneas towers in stature, surpassing all
in the depth and renown of his goodness. He offers prayers of
thanksgiving to the gods for their profusion of gifts and extols Ju-
piter with the highest praise.

Meanwhile the amassed Rutulians had brought into the city the 125
lifeless body of their leader, majestic and worthy of sorrow, their

imbrem oculis; et iam lato clamore Latinum
defessum et varios agitantem pectore casus
130   complerant. Qui postquam altos crebrescere questus
et Turnum ingenti confossum vulnere vidit,
haud tenuit lacrimas; dehinc maestum leniter agmen
corripuit manibus verbisque silentia ponens.
Ceu spumantis apri quando per viscera dentes
135   fulmineos canis excepit praestantior omni
ex numero, tunc infausto perterrita casu
cetera turba fugit latrantum atque ore magistrum
circumstans querulo pavitat magnoque ululatu
infremit, at commota manu dominique iubentis
140   ore silet gemitumque premit seseque coercet,
haud aliter Rutuli suppressa voce quierunt.
142   Tum sic illacrimans rex alto e corde Latinus
145   incipit: "O fragilis ruitura superbia sceptri!
O furor, o nimium dominandi innata cupido,
mortales quo caeca vehis? Quo gloria tantis
inflatos effers animos quaesita periclis?
Quot tecum insidias, quot clades, quanta malorum
150   magnorum monimenta geris? Quot tela, quot enses
ante oculos, si cernis, habes! Heu, dulce venenum
et mundi letalis honos! Heu, tristia regni
munera, quae haud parvo constent, et grandia rerum
pondera, quae numquam placidam promittere pacem
155   nec requiem conferre queant! Heu, sortis acerbae
et miserae regale decus, magnoque timori
suppositos regum casus pacique negatos!
Quid, Turne, ingenti Ausoniam movisse tumultu
et dura Aeneadas turbasse in bella coactos,
160   quid iuvat et pactae violasse optata quietis
pignora? Quae tibi tanta animo impatientia venit,
ut Martem cum gente deum iussuque Tonantis

minds in the throes of grief, their eyes flooding over with weeping.
And now the intensity of their keening had filled Latinus, ex-
hausted and pondering many a danger. After he heard their deep   130
groans keep swelling and saw Turnus pierced through with a gi-
gantic wound, he did not hold back his tears. Then gently he took
charge of the cortege, calling for silence by gesture and by word.
As when a hound, better than all the pack, has taken in through
his vitals the blazing teeth of a frothing boar, then the remainder   135
of the baying troop, terrified by the unfortunate turn of fate, takes
flight and, all atremble, with a yelp encircles its keeper and barks,
howling away. Yet, responsive to its master's gesture and words of
command, it grows still, suppresses its groaning and regains con-   140
trol: in such a manner the Rutulians silence their talk.

Then tearfully, from his heart's depths, King Latinus begins: 142
"How precarious is the scepter's transient pride! O wildness, o na-   145
tive lust for overweening power, whither in your blindness do you
drag us mortals? Whither, Glory, wooed by a succession of haz-
ards, do you drive our swaggering minds? How many traps, how
many defeats, what boundless reminders of evil do you sport?
How many spears, how many swords do you behold, if you have   150
eyes to see? Alas, the entrancing poison and deadly worship of
worldly things! Alas, the dire duties of ruling power, steadfast at
great cost, and the fraught weightiness of affairs, which can never
pledge the calm of peace or bestow tranquillity! Alas, the bitter,   155
piteous lot that graces kings, the risks of royalty, jeopardized by
ample fear and bereft of peace! What pleasure was it, Turnus, to
have shaken Italy with mighty turmoil, to have provoked the fol-
lowers of Aeneas and driven them into war's cruelty? What plea-
sure also to have breached the longed-for trust in a peace for   160
which we had covenanted? What massive restlessness possessed
your mind to wage war with offspring of the gods who voyaged
hither at the command of the Thunderer, and of your own voli-

huc vecta gereres nostrisque expellere tectis
ultro instans velles et natae solvere foedus
165   pollicitae genero Aeneae et me bella negante
dura movere manu? Quae tanta insania mentem
implicuit? Quotiens te in saevi Martis euntem
agmina sublimemque in equo et radiantibus armis
corripui et pavitans cedentem in limine frustra
170   temptavi revocare et iter suspendere coeptum!
Inde ego quanta tuli, testantur moenia tectis
semirutis magnique albentes ossibus agri
et Latium toto defectum robore et ingens
exitium fluviique humana caede rubentes
175   et longi trepidique metus durique labores,
quos totiens senior per tanta pericula cepi.
At nunc, Turne, iaces! Ubinam tam magna iuventae
gloria et excellens animus? Quo splendidus altae
frontis honos? Quonam illa decens effugit imago?
180   Ah, quantas Dauno lacrimas acrisque dolores,
Turne, dabis! Quanto circumfluet Ardea fletu!
Sed non degeneri et pudibundo vulnere fossum
aspiciet; saltem hoc miserae solamen habebit
mortis, ut Aeneae Troiani exceperis ensem."
185   Haec fatus lacrimisque genas implevit abortis.
Tum sese ad turbam vertens miserabile corpus
attolli et caram maesti genitoris ad urbem
deferri atque pios fieri mandabat honores.
Mox circumfusi Rutuli lato agmine caesum
190   sublimem ingenti iuvenem posuere feretro,
multa super Teucrum raptorum insignia secum
et galeas et equos ensesque et tela ferentes.
Post currus Phrygia sudantes caede sequuntur.
It lacrimans et ducit equum docta arte Metiscus
195   rorantem et fletu madidum, qui vexerat ante

tion willingly to assail and expel them from our abodes, to sunder
the promised pledge of my daughter to my son-in-law Aeneas and,
against my stated wish, rouse cruel war with your hand? What   165
grand insanity entangled your wits? How often did I rebuke you,
lofty on your steed, your weapons aglimmer as you marched to-
ward fierce Mars's troops, and, in my fright, on the threshold
vainly attempt to call you back and to halt the course that you had
begun? What ordeals I have since withstood our walls, houses   170
half-collapsed, attest, and broad fields glistening white with bones,
Latium deprived of all its manhood, devastation everywhere,
streams crimsoned with human slaughter, the long and trembling
fear, the harsh trials which I, though aged, so often experienced   175
through such great perils. And now, Turnus, you lie in state!
Where is your youth in all its grandeur, your loftiness of mind?
Whither the glistening glory of your lofty brow? Whither has fled
that sign of grace? Ah, what weeping, Turnus, what bitter sorrows
will you bring to Daunus! With what a stream of tears will Ardea   180
flow! Yet it will not behold you pierced, in shame, by an ignoble
wound. At least it will have this solace for the sadness of your
death: you received the sword of Aeneas of Troy."

These were Latinus's words, as tears welled up and drenched   185
his cheeks. Then, facing the multitude, he gave orders that the pit-
eous corpse be shouldered, conveyed to the sad father's beloved
city and offered proper solemnity. Quickly hurrying around, the
Rutulians in a mass raised the body of the youth high on an   190
enormous bier, bringing along with them as well the trappings
plundered from the Trojans—helmets and horses, swords and
spears. Behind follow chariots oozing with Phrygian gore. Weep-
ing, Metiscus makes his way and expertly leads Turnus's horse, be-
dewed with a flow of tears, who in time past had carried him in   195

13

victorem Turnum atque hostili strage furentem.
Hinc alii versa arma gerunt. Tum cetera pubes
flens sequitur largisque umectat pectora guttis.
Et iam fessi ibant per muta silentia noctis
200   caedentes sese, gressumque in tecta Latinus
flexerat ingenti turbatus funere mentem;
una omnes lacrimas matres puerique senesque
fundebant maestam implentes mugitibus urbem.
    Inscius at tantos Daunus superesse dolores
205   et natum extremo consumptum Marte superbam
effudisse animam largisque ad moenia duci
cum lacrimis alios gemitus curasque fovebat.
Namque ex diversa caderent dum parte Latini
et calido Turnus foedaret sanguine terram,
210   urbem ingens flamma et muros invaserat altos,
fumabatque rutis miseri patris Ardea tectis
et tota in cinerem vergebat, et astra favillae
altivolae implebant, nec spes plus ulla salutis,
sive quidem sic diis placitum est, seu praescia Turni
215   signum ut fata darent horrendo Marte perempti.
Extemplo concussi animos et tristia cives
pectora caedentes miserandae sortis iniquum
deflebant casum longoque ex ordine matres
atque avidos totis fugiebant viribus ignes.
220   Ac veluti cum nigra cohors posuere sub alta
arbore et in fixa radice cubilia longo
formicae instantes operi, sin dura securis
incumbat versoque infringat culmine parvas
saeva casas, mox certatim sese agmine fuso
225   corripiunt maestaeque fuga trepidaeque feruntur;
et velut ignitum testudo eversa calorem
cum sensit, luctata diu pedibusque renitens
caudam agitansque caputque acri vi cedere temptat,

victory, raging amid the carnage of the enemy. Others on their way
carry their weapons reversed. The rest of the youth follow behind,
weeping, soaking their chests with a rain of tear-drops. And now,
smiting themselves, they made their exhausted way through the
night's unresponsive silence, and Latinus, his thoughts afflicted by   200
the huge cortege, bent his steps toward the palace. All the mothers
with the children and the elders shed tears and filled the gloomy
city with their groans.

But Daunus, unaware of the intense sorrows in store — that his
son, destroyed in Mars's final conflict, had breathed forth his   205
proud spirit and, amid a flow of tears, was being accompanied to-
ward the walls — was anxious about other griefs and troubles. For
while elsewhere the Latins were suffering defeat and Turnus with
his warm blood was soiling the earth, an enormous conflagration
had swept through the city and its lofty walls, and Ardea, with the   210
smoking palace of his poor father collapsed in ruin, was sinking
completely to embers. The ash, flying heavenward, was suffusing
the stars. There was no further hope of salvation, whether such in-
deed was the pleasure of the gods, or whether the foreknowing
fates were offering a token of Turnus's extinction in the fright of   215
war. Forthwith the townsfolk together with the matrons in long
array, their spirits shaken, smiting their sad breasts began to be-
wail the unjust misfortune of their sad fate while with all their
might they were fleeing the ravenous flames. As when a black
squadron of ants, struggling over their lengthy task, have posi-   220
tioned their abodes in a firmly planted root beneath a lofty tree: if
a cruel ax applies its force and, breaking the towering crest, sav-
agely shatters their tiny dwellings, immediately they vie with each
other in sallying forth, the whole army in a rush, and, mournful
and terrified, they are propelled along in flight; and as when a tor-   225
toise, overturned on its back and feeling the heat of a fire, sweating
strains and struggles with its feet while, waving its tail and head in
a violent effort, in agitation it makes attempt after attempt to

aestuat et multa insudans conamina miscet,
230   haud aliter miseri per tanta incendia cives
iactabant sese et confusa mente ferebant.
    Ante omnes senio confectus ad aethera voces
fundebat querulas Daunus superosque vocabat.
Tum vero e mediis visa est consurgere flammis
235   percussisque ales volitare per aera pennis
indicium nomenque urbis versae Ardea servans,
et cui sublimes stabant in moenibus arces,
mutata effusis nunc circumlabitur alis.
Attoniti novitate omnes monitisque deorum
240   haud parvis deiecti umeros atque ora tenebant.
At Daunus patriae ardenti concussus amore
eversae duros gemitus sub corde premebat.
Haec inter magno volitans praenuntia motu
Fama ruit latisque animos clamoribus implet
245   adventare novum magno cum milite funus
et Turnum exanimem et letali vulnere victum.
Mox exciti omnes nigras duxere frequentes
incensas ex more faces: ardentibus agri
collucent flammis. Dehinc se venientibus addunt.
250   Quos postquam toto videre ex agmine matres,
percussis vocem palmis ad sidera tollunt.
    At Daunus, cari ut patuerunt funera nati,
substitit, et demum ingenti correpta dolore
ora movens medium sese furibundus in agmen
255   proripuit Turnumque super prostratus et haerens,
quam primum affari potuit, sic edidit ore:
"Nate, patris dolor et fessae miseranda senectae
rapta quies, quo me, tantis iactate periclis,
duxisti, et saevis tandem devicte sub armis?
260   Quo tua me praestans animi constantia vexit?
Hic clarae virtutis honos et gloria sceptri?

move away, similarly the poor citizens, their minds in turmoil, 230
were betaking themselves helter-skelter through the thick of the
blaze.

In the presence of everyone Daunus, undone by old age, was
pouring forth words of woe to the heavens, and appealing to the
gods above. Then it was that a bird was seen to rise up from
the midst of the conflagration and, beating its wings, fly through
the air, in metamorphosis keeping the identity and the name of 235
Ardea.[1] That which had stood as soaring turrets upon walls glides
now, in altered state, with outspread wings. All were astonished by
the miracle and by such grand warnings from the gods; their dis-
couragement was evident in the droop of their shoulders and 240
faces. But Daunus, though overcome by ardent affection for his
ruined land, suppressed bitter groans within his heart. In the
midst of these events, Rumor descends in headlong rush and fills
their minds with extended lamentation, heralding that a squadron
of soldiers in a death-march was at hand, and that Turnus had 245
breathed his last, overwhelmed by a mortal wound. Soon every-
one, in a troubled mass, carried black torches, set afire as custom
had it — the fields glowed with burning flames — and merged with
those approaching. After the matrons had sighted them in massed 250
rank, they strike their hands and wail toward the stars.

But Daunus, when the cortege of his beloved son came into full
view, stood motionless. Then, his face wrenched with spasms of
deep grief, in frenzy he cast himself into the midst of the array,
and clinging prostrate to Turnus, as soon as he could find voice, 255
spoke these words over him: "My son, your father's sorrow and
the calm of his weary age now wretchedly snatched away, where
have you, harassed by dangers of such magnitude and vanquished
at the last by ferocity of arms, where have you led me? Where has
your surpassing steadfastness of mind conveyed me? Is this the re- 260
spect due virtue's fame, is this the esteem that power gains? Is this

Hoc magni decus imperii? Talesne triumphos,
nate, refers? Haec illa quies promissa parenti
afflicto totiens, haec meta optata laborum?
265   Heu miserum! Quam praecipites labentia casus
exagitant, quanto vertuntur saecula motu!
Qui iam sublimes referebas clarus honores,
et magnus toto in Latio, quem Troes in armis
horrendum et trepidi totiens sensere furentem,
270   nunc, mi Turne, iaces, miserandum et flebile corpus!
Iam mutum et sine voce caput, quo pulchrior alter
non fuit in tota Ausonia nec gratior ullus
eloquio nec quis sumptis ingentior armis.
Nate, ubi forma nitens niveaque in fronte serenus
275   ille decor laetusque oculorum aspectus et altae
egregius cervicis honos? His gloria Martis
contigit hospitiis? Tali rediture paratu
discedens voluisti avidis te credere bellis?
Heu mortem invisam, quae sola ultricibus armis
280   elatos frenas animos, communia toti
genti sceptra tenens aeternaque foedera servans,
quae magnos parvosque teris, quae fortibus aequas
imbelles populisque duces seniumque iuventae!
Heu mortem obscuram! Quae causa indigna coegit
285   eripere atque meum crudeli vulnere natum
afficere? O felix tam grato caedis Amata
successu laetare tuae; quae tanta dolorum
fugisti monimenta gravisque immania casus
pondera! Quid misero genitori plura paratis,
290   o superi? Natum rapuistis et Ardea flammis
consumpta in cinerem versa est; nunc aethera pennis
verberat. Ah me, Turne, tua plus caede cruento.
Deerat adhuc sors ista patris suprema senectae.
At vero quem saeva premunt et numina torquent,

the glory of great empire that you procure for me, my son, are
such its triumphs? Is this that calm pledged your father in his
many moments of distress, is this the end of my sufferings for
which I pined? Miserable me! How precipitate are the misfortunes   265
which the gliding ages prompt, in what a vortex do they unfold
their course! You who in your fame claimed exalted honors,
mighty throughout all of Latium, whose fearfulness in arms and
whose rage the trembling Trojans felt time upon time, now, O
Turnus mine, you lie, a body to pity and lament, a silent, voiceless   270
head. No other in all Italy was more handsome, none more grace-
ful of speech or a more imposing presence, with armor donned.
Where, my son, is your beauty's gleam, that calm charm on snow-
white brow, your eyes' happy glance and long neck's sterling look?   275
Was Mars's acclaim realized at the cost of lodging with death? As
you set forth, did you yearn to commit yourself to greedy fighting
only soon to make your return in such a procession? Alas, hateful
death, who alone reins in spirits carried away by vengeful arms,
who holds all humanity in omnipotent grasp and whose covenants   280
endure forever! You grind down both the grand and the lowly, you
bring hero level with coward, lords with rabble, young with old.
Alas, dark death, what shameful reason drove you to snatch away
my son and to assail him with savage wound? Ah, fortunate   285
Amata, take joy in the welcome advent of your death. What re-
minders of suffering you have escaped, what huge burdens of mis-
fortune's weight! What more, gods above, are you contriving for a
father who is sick at heart? You have seized my son, and Ardea,   290
devoured by flames and turned to ash, now batters the sky with
wings. Ah, Turnus, how I further torture myself from your
slaughter! For your father the final destiny of old age still remains
to come. But the poor creature whom the gods, kindled by hatred

295 illum incensa odiis atque acrem concita in iram
funditus evertunt miserum. Sic fata rotant res."
　　Dixerat, et multa illacrimans largo ora rigabat
perfusa imbre trahens duros e corde dolores,
qualis ubi incubuit validis Iovis unguibus ales
300 et parvum effuso divulsit sanguine fetum,
cerva videns miseri tristatur funere nati.
　　Postera lux latum splendore impleverat orbem;
tunc pater infractos fatali Marte Latinus
defecisse videns Italos totamque potenti
305 cedere fortunam Aeneae, bellique tumultum
ingentisque animo curas et foedera volvens
conubii promissa suae nataeque hymenaeos
praestantes vocat electos ex agmine toto
mille viros, qui Dardanium comitentur ad urbem
310 spectatum virtute ducem, iungitque togatos
multa oratores memorans, et euntibus ultro
imperat, ut quando auspiciis monitisque deorum
Troianam miscere Italo cum sanguine gentem
expediat, placido intersint animoque revisant
315 Aeneadasque vehant alta intra moenia laeti.
　　Interea ipse urbem labefactam et vulgus inerme
componit solidatque animos requiemque futuram
spondet et aeternam ventura in saecula pacem.
Inde iubet meritos turba plaudente triumphos
320 sublimesque domus fieri regalis honores;
atque alacris monet, unanimes ut fronte serena
occurrant genero venienti et pectore toto
excipiant gentem Iliacam partaeque quietis
gaudia et optatae diffundant pacis amores.
325 　　Iamque instructa cohors Teucrorum castra subibat
cincta comas ramis oleae pacemque rogabat.
Quam bonus Aeneas ad se intra regia duci

20

and driven by anger's violence, fiercely hound and torture, him 295
they utterly ruin. Thus the fates revolve man's affairs."

Words at an end, he drenched his cheeks with a flood of tears,
drawing forth woeful sorrows from his heart: as, when Jupiter's ea-
gle has swooped down with mighty talons and has torn apart her
small fawn, its blood gushing, the doe looks on, in sorrow at the 300
death of her youngling.

The morrow's light had filled the broad earth with its gleam.
Then father Latinus, beholding the Italians broken and faltering
from the fate of Mars and fortune's full favor yielding to Aeneas's
power, and pondering the upheavals of the fight, the enormity of 305
his agonies as well as his commitment to the marriage treaty and
the wedding of his daughter, summons from the host a thousand
men, chosen for their excellence, to serve as entourage to the city
for the Trojan chief, whose quality was clear to all. He joins with 310
them togaed speakers, under full instructions, and further com-
mands them, in parting, that, since it seemed meet, in face of the
cautionary omens from the gods, for the Trojan people to com-
mingle with Italian blood, they should share in the proceedings,
with calm minds seek out Aeneas and his followers, and convey
them joyfully within the lofty walls. 315

Meanwhile he himself firms up the stricken city and its de-
fenseless citizenry, strengthens their spirits with the promise of
harmony in the future and of enduring peace as the generations
pass. Then, with the people's acclaim, he orders the celebration of
triumphs deserved and the bedecking of the royal palace with au-
gust tributes. In eagerness he urges them, with hearts united and 320
brows untroubled, to greet his approaching son-in-law, enthusias-
tically receive the Trojan people and broadcast their joy at calm re-
stored and their delight in the realization of peace.

And now in formation the embassy, their locks encircled with 325
sprigs of olive, was entering the camp of the Trojans, to sue for
peace. Noble Aeneas commands that they be conveyed to him

tecta iubet causamque viae laeto ore requirit.
Tunc senior sic incipiens ardentia Drances
330   verba movet nimium erepti pro funere Turni
exultans: "O Troianae dux inclite gentis,
gloria spesque Phrygum, quo nec pietate nec armis
maior in orbe fuit, victi obtestamur et omnes
iuramus divos divasque, invitus in unum
335   conflatum vidit Latium et temerata Latinus
foedera, nec Phrygios umquam turbavit honores.
Quin natae, quando superum sic vota ferebant,
conubia et generum magno te optabat amore.
Sed quicquid tanto armorum flagrante tumultu
340   tantorum furiisque operum atque laboribus actum est,
id rapidus Turni et stimulis incensus iniquis
correptusque odiis furor attulit; ille negantes
invitasque dedit Latias in proelia gentes.
Illum omnis conversa cohors poscebat, ut armis
345   cederet et magnum sineret succedere pactis
conubiis Anchisiaden. Inde optimus ambas
iungebat palmas defessa aetate Latinus
confectus nimioque ardentem Marte rogabat.
Nec nostrae potuere preces inflectere durum
350   nec divum portenta animum, quin acrius ignem
spumabat ferus ore vomens bellumque ciebat.
At vero dignum invenit pro talibus ausis
exitium, qui te tandem victore momordit
nigrantem prostratus humum. Nunc improbus aedes
355   Tartareas visurus eat quaeratque sub imo
nunc alias Acheronte acies aliosque hymenaeos.
Tu melior succede bonis Laurentibus heres.
In te omnis domus et fessi inclinata Latini
spes iacet. Unum omnes Itali super aurea mittunt
360   sidera et ingentem bello et caelestibus armis

within the royal dwelling and with happy voice asks the reason for
their journey. Then aged Drances, with too palpable pleasure at
the loss and death of Turnus, begins his passionate speech: "O fa- 330
mous leader of the Trojan people, the Phrygians' pride and prom-
ise, unsurpassed in the world for loyalty and courage, in our defeat
we call to witness, and swear an oath to every god and goddess,
that Latinus watched as Latium, against his will, bonded together
in scorn of its treaties, nor did he ever pose objection to paying the 335
Trojans their honors due. In fact, since divine ordinance so di-
rected, with great fervor he anticipated the wedding of his daugh-
ter to you, his son-in-law. But whatever was fomented by the wild
fractiousness of fighting and the sheer, insane effort in the under- 340
taking, the headstrong madness of Turnus, lashed to flame with-
out just cause and seized by hate, brought upon us. He consigned
the Latin peoples into battle, while reluctant and averse. All the
soldiery addressed him with the plea that he withdraw from arms
and that he allow the mighty son of Anchises to implement the 345
contract of marriage. Likewise peerless Latinus, though tired and
weakened by age, joined hands in prayer and pleaded with Turnus,
as he burned with Mars's intense flame. Nor could our entreaties
bend his obdurance, nor heaven's omens his intent. No, he spewed 350
forth fire more fiercely from his mouth and, foaming beast-like,
lent impetus to the fight. And yet he faced a doom worthy of such
daring as, stretched before you, his conqueror, he gnawed at last
the darkening earth. Now let the villain go to see the lodgings of
Tartarus. Now in the depths of Acheron let him scout out other 355
battle formations, other marriages. Do you, the superior heir, ac-
cept your legacy of Laurentum. The hope of exhausted Latinus
and of his whole clan rests, turned toward you. You alone all the
Italians send soaring beyond the golden stars, and you, armed by
the immortals, they revere for might in battle. Their blazoning ut- 360

extollunt, et vera canunt praeconia voces.
Te gravium veneranda patrum consultaque turba
invalidique aetate senes, te laeta iuventus
et cupidae matres, pueri innuptaeque puellae
365 unanimes aequo ore volunt Turnumque sub armis
exultant cecidisse tuis; te tota precatur
Ausonia et claris praestantem laudibus effert.
In te unum conversi oculi. Pater ipse Latinus
iam senior sola haec longaevae munera vitae,
370 quod natam tibi iungat, habet, generique nepotes
Troianos Italo admixtos in saecula mittat.
Ergo age, magne, veni, Teucrorum ductor, et altos
ingredere et celebres cape quos spondemus honores."
Finierat cunctique eadem simul ore fremebant.
375 Quos pius Aeneas hilari cum fronte receptos
prosequitur paucis et amico pectore fatur:
"Nec vos nec placida solitum sub pace Latinum
arguerim, verum infesti violentia Turni
tantum opus, haud dubito, et tanti discrimina Martis
380 concivit, iuvenili autem plus laudis amore.
Quicquid id est tamen, Ausonii, nil pacta recuso
conubia et sanctam firmato foedere pacem
iungere. Rex idem imperium et veneranda tenebit
sceptra socer, statuentque mei mihi moenia Teucri,
385 et nomen natae urbis erit, sacrosque penates
adiciam. Vos communes in saecula leges
concordique pares animo mittetis amores.
Interea, quod restat adhuc, imponite flammis
corpora, quae duri miseranda insania belli
390 eripuit! Dehinc nos, quam primum crastina surget
clara dies, laeti Laurentia tecta petemus."
Dixerat, et tanto affatu conversa tenebant
ora simul stupefacti omnes et apertius ingens

24

terance chants the truth. All with one mind and with one voice
yearn for you, you, the throng of fathers, solemn in their wisdom,
old men numb with age, joyous youth and anxious mothers, boys
and chaste girls. They glory that Turnus fell to your force. All Italy   365
offers you prayer and exalts your excellence with resounding
praise. Toward you alone our eyes are turned. Father Latinus him-
self in his old age has only these duties after life's lengthy span—
to unite his daughter with you, and to impart to the ages his de-   370
scendants, Trojans blended with the Italian race. Come then, great
leader of the Trojans, make your entrance to claim your bounty of
promised honors."

When he had drawn to an end, all united in a roar of approval.
Noble Aeneas, after he had received them with happy counte-   375
nance, returns their greetings in brief words of friendship: "I
would point no finger at you or Latinus, whose wont is the calm
of peace. Rather it is the savagery of the reprobate Turnus, even
more than his youthful craving for praise, that, I have no doubt,
instigated this chain of happenings, these crises that aroused   380
Mars. Nevertheless, whatever the case, Ausonians, in no way do I
stand opposed to the wedding contract and the peace made holy
by assured compact. The king, my father-in-law, will claim for
himself the scepter's authority and respect. My Trojans in their
turn will establish walls for me—a city to bear your daughter's
name—and I will add Penates[2] to bless their dwellings. Your leg-   385
acy to the ages will be the mutuality of laws and warmth shared
with hearts at one. Meanwhile on their pyres place the pitiable
dead (we still have that task) whom the ruthless ferocity of war
snatched from us. Then, as soon as tomorrow's bright gleam is
risen, with spirits rejoicing we'll repair to our homes at Lauren-   390
tum."

When his words had come to an end, the whole audience to-
gether held its gaze turned toward him, openly in awe of his utter-

mirantes pietatis opus. Mox robore vasto
395   congestas statuere pyras ignemque repostis
civibus immisere; altum super aethera fumus
evolat, atque atris caelum sublime tenebris
conditur. Innumeras ex omni rure trucidant
delectas pecudes et nigros terga iuvencos
400   immittuntque rogis. Latos incendia campos
denudant. Fremit impulsus clamoribus aer.

    Iamque sequens clarum extulerat lux aurea Phoebum;
tunc Teucri Ausoniique omnes mixto agmine laeti
consedere in equis et gressum ad tecta movebant
405   Laurenti atque altis erectam moenibus urbem,
ante omnes pius Aeneas, post ordine Drances
multa duci senior memorans, dehinc unica proles
Ascanius multumque animi maturus Aletes
et gravis Ilioneus Mnestheusque acerque Serestus,
410   Sergestus fortisque Gyas fortisque Cloanthus;
post alii mixtimque Itali Teucrique sequuntur.

    Interea effusi stabant per moenia cives
primorumque manus alacres imbelleque vulgus
Troianam cupido expectantes pectore turbam.
415   Et iam adventabant, placida quos fronte Latinus
occurrens magna excepit comitante caterva.
At postquam medio venientem ex agmine vidit
Dardanium Aenean, vera haud illusit imago;
namque omnes super excellens atque altior ibat
420   et late regalem oculis spargebat honorem
sidereis. Tunc quam primum data copia fandi est
et voces capere optatasque adiungere dextras,
incipit et prior affatur sic ore Latinus:
"Venisti tandem, cupidum nec fixa fefellit
425   spes animum, lux Troianae clarissima gentis,
magnorum quem iussa deum tot casibus actum

26

ance and astonished at this majestic instance of his piety. Forth-
with they raised funeral piles, heaped up with huge beams, placed   395
upon them the bodies of their countrymen and set the fires.
Smoke billows over the lofty heavens, and the reaches of the sky
are buried in dusky night. They slaughter countless herds of sheep
and black-backed cattle, chosen from the country round about,
and set them on the pyres. Flames char wide swathes of field. The   400
firmament resounds with the storm of lamentation.

And now the new day's golden light had lifted up the Sun's
brilliance. Trojans and Italians mingled together in joyous assem-
blage, and, mounting their steeds, headed toward the houses and
high-built walls of the city of Laurentum. In front of all was noble   405
Aeneas, after him in line the aged Drances, who recalled many a
memory for the leader, then Ascanius, only child to his father,
Aletes, venerable and sage, august Ilioneus, Mnestheus, sharp-
willed Serestus, Sergestus, brave Gyas, and brave Cloanthus. The   410
rest, Italians and Trojans intermingled, followed in the rear.

Meanwhile the citizen body streamed into position along the
walls, the eager corps of leaders together with the common people
unused to war, awaiting the Trojan throng with eager hearts. And
now, all anxiety allayed, Latinus and his large entourage received   415
them in welcome as they made their arrival. And after he glimpsed
Trojan Aeneas approaching in the midst of his retinue, his true
appearance in no way disappointed. As he made his way he far
surpassed all, in stature and in the princely charm that radiated
from his star-bright eyes. As soon as the opportunity came for   420
talk, to exchange words after the clasping of hands they had long
anticipated, Latinus is the first to begin to speak: "You have
reached us, at last, nor did the hope to which we clung deceive our
yearning mind, most lustrous light of the Trojan race, whom the   425
behests of the great gods, in spite of many misfortunes, purposed

Italia et nostris voluerunt sistere tectis,
quamquam humana furens nimis ausa licentia sanctas
turbarit leges et divum exciverit iras,
430   quin etiam invitum totiens meque arma negantem
crediderit duri perferre pericula Martis.
Factum etenim, sed nec parvo: sat numina iustas
indignata animis misere ultricia poenas.
Nunc age, magne Phrygum ductor, quando omnis origo
435   seditionis abest et tanti criminis auctor,
conubiis succede et promissis hymenaeis.
Sunt mihi regna, manent erectis oppida muris.
Sola autem fessae spes unica nata senectae:
Te generum et natum tempus complector in omne."
440   Quem contra bonus Aeneas: "Rex maxime, nullam
te causam armorum et tanti movisse tumultus
crediderim sacrae cupientem foedera pacis;
et si qua est, pone hanc animo, precor, optime, curam.
Nunc adsum et patrem et socerum te laetus in omnis
445   accipio casus. Magni mihi surget imago
Anchisae et rursum ardebo genitoris amore."
    Talibus orabant inter se et tecta subibant
regia. Tum studio effusae matresque nurusque
longaevique patres stabant iuvenumque cohortes
450   pulchra revisentes Troianae corpora gentis.
Ante omnes magnum Aenean cupidoque notabant
altum animo genus et praestantem frontis honorem
quaesitamque alacres pacem atque optata quietis
munera laudabant. Ceu quando longus et ingens
455   ignavos tenuit resolutis nubibus imber
agricolas curvumque diu requievit aratrum,
tunc, si clarus equos spatioso lumine Titan
laxet et aurato caelum splendore serenet,
laetitia exundant et sese hortantur agrestes,

to settle in Italy, in our dwellings, even though human lawlessness
in a bout of fury deranged the sanctity of rule and aroused the
wrath of heaven. Indeed time and again it consigned me, also, to
suffer the menace of Mars's grimness, against my will and shun-   430
ning recourse to arms. This indeed occurred, but at no small cost:
suffice it that the heavenly powers, roiled in mind and vengeful,
have unleashed punishment. Since the source of rebellion and the
begetter of such mischief has ceased to be, now is the time, mighty   435
leader of the Trojans, to enter upon the marriage compact and
promised wedding. I too have a kingdom, my towns survive with
walls still standing. But my only daughter is the single hope of my
weary old age. I embrace you as son and son-in-law for all time to
come."

Good Aeneas responds: "Mightiest of kings, it was not my be-   440
lief that you, in your desire for peace's holy bonds, would have
provoked such a clash of arms! If any worry remains, worthiest of
men, put it from your mind, I pray. Now I am in your presence
and I joyfully claim you as father-in-law and father, whatever the
future may have in store. A vision of mighty Anchises will well up   445
within me and once again I will burn with love for a father."

After such reassurance for each other, they entered the royal
palace. Thereupon mothers and daughters, rushing forth in their
eagerness, aged fathers and companies of the young, stood survey-
ing the handsome figures of the Trojan race. They are anxious be-   450
fore all to behold mighty Aeneas, his renowned heritage, the pre-
eminent grace of his features. They are swift to praise the goal of
peace and the coveted gift of quiet. Imagine a time when a massive
downpour without let-up held the now idle farmers in its grip,
while the clouds unburdened themselves and the curved plough   455
found respite for many a day, then, should the bright Sun give rein
to his horses along their broad track and soothe the heavens with
his gilded gleam, the happy country folk surge abroad and urge

460 non secus Ausonii tam laeto in tempore rerum
composuere animos. Et iam rex alta Latinus
atria regalisque aditus intrarat et una
optimus Aeneas, sequitur quem pulcher Iulus,
dehinc Itali mixtique Phryges. Tum splendida lato
465 applausu et laeto completur regia coetu.
Haec inter matrum innumera nuruumque caterva
in medium comitata venit Lavinia virgo
sidereos deiecta oculos; quam Troius heros
virtute et forma ingentem, mirabile dictu,
470 ut vidit, primo aspectu stupefactus inhaesit
et secum Turni casus miseratus acerbos,
qui haud parva spe ductus ovans in proelia tantos
civisset motus durisque arsisset in armis.
Tum vero aeterno iunguntur foedera nexu
475 conubii et multa cum laude canunt hymenaeum
et laetam vocem per regia tecta volutant.
Dehinc plausus fremitusque altum super aera mittunt.
    At fidum interea Aeneas affatur Achatem,
vadat et Andromachae quondam data munera, vestes
480 intextas auro ferat et, quod saepe solebat,
dum res Troianae stabant, circumdare collo,
auratum gemmis circumsaeptumque monile,
praeterea magnum cratera, in pignus amoris
quem Priamus patri Anchisae donaverat olim.
485 Nec mora, iussa sequens pulcherrima portat Achates
munera. Tunc socer ingentem cratera Latinus
donatum capit, at coniunx Lavinia vestes
atque monile decens. Placido dehinc pectore sese
demulcent variisque trahunt sermonibus horas.
490   Et iam tarda epulas fugientis tempora lucis
poscebant; mox regali convivia luxu
effundunt latosque alta intra tecta paratus.

themselves on: so the Italians brought calm to their spirits in such 460
a happy time. And now King Latinus had advanced through the
royal entrance-way into the lofty hall together with Aeneas in all
his nobility, followed by beautiful Iulus and then the Italians and
Trojans, mingled as a group. At once the glittering palace was
filled with the happy gathering and its extended applause. While 465
this was happening the maiden Lavinia entered their midst, ac-
companied by a full entourage of mothers and daughters, her glis-
tening eyes cast down. When the Trojan hero first beheld her
grandeur of soul and body — a wonder in the telling —, he paused
enchanted at the sight, and to himself pitied the bitter chain of 470
sufferings endured by Turnus. (Carried away by expectations too
great, in his zeal he had occasioned huge assaults in battle and
burned for the cruelty of arms.) And so the marriage compacts are
joined in enduring bond. They chant the wedding hymn in an
outpouring of praise and send the sound of joy rippling through 475
the royal residence. They fling roars of applause beyond heaven's
heights.

Meanwhile Aeneas requests faithful Achates to make his way
and retrieve gifts once presented him by Andromache — raiment
threaded with gold, and a gilded necklace crusted with jewels with 480
which she was wont to adorn her neck while Troy yet stood. There
was also a magnificent mixing-bowl which Priam had once be-
stowed on father Anchises as a token of affection. In quick com-
pliance Achates returns with these loveliest of presents. Latinus 485
accepts the mixing-bowl as his son-in-law's gift, the graceful bride
Lavinia, the raiment and necklace. Then they offer each other
friendship's gentle refreshment and stretch out the hours with var-
ied conversation.

And now the unhurried passing of departing day called for the 490
banquet. Forthwith inside the lofty palace they heap high the royal

Convenere omnes strato discumbere in ostro
deliciis iussi et dapibus se inferre futuris.
495   Dat manibus cristallus aquas, mensisque reponunt
flaventem Cererem. Tum laeta fronte ministri
innumeri magno distinguunt ordine curas:
Pars dapibus reficit mensas, pars pocula miscet
craterasque replet, nunc hac, nunc volvitur illac
500   turba frequens varios miscetque per atria motus.
    At puerum pater immotis spectabat Iulum
luminibus vultum admirans moresque Latinus
et graviter puerili ex ore cadentia verba
maturumque animum ante annos, et multa rogabat
505   permixtas referens voces. Dehinc oscula figens
dulcia complexum manibus vinctumque fovebat,
et nimium exultans felicem et munere divum
donatum Aeneam pro tali prole ferebat.
    Postquam epulis compressa fames, traducere longam
510   incipiunt fando et labentem fallere noctem,
nunc duros Troiae casus gentesque Pelasgas,
nunc fera Laurentis memorantes proelia pugnae,
quo primum diffusae acies, quo tela vicissim
pulsa loco, qui primus ovans invaserit agmen
515   fulmineumque ardens in equo madefecerit ensem.
Praecipue Tros Aeneas seniorque Latinus
magnorum heroum Latiique antiqua potentis
gesta recensebant fugientemque horrida nati
arma sui Saturnum Italis latuisse sub oris;
520   hinc Latium dixisse genusque in montibus altis
composuisse vagum legesque et iura dedisse
et Bacchi et frugum cultus; dehinc tecta secutum
esse paterna Iovem, utque Electra Atlantide cretus
Iasio Idaeas caeso Phrygiae isset ad urbes
525   Dardanus, et Corytho multa cum gente profectus;

board with lavish display and a wealth of appointments. Everyone, invited to partake in the delightful feast to come, streamed together to recline on coverlets of purple. Glass crystal furnishes water for their hands. On the table they place blond Ceres's bread. Then the corps of smiling servants in grand parade divide their tasks: some restock the banquet tables, some mix the wine and refill goblets and bowl, the busy troop turns now here, now there, and performs a medley of functions throughout the halls.

But father Latinus fixed his gaze intently on young Iulus, marveling at his attractiveness and behavior, at the adult discourse that flowed from his youthful lips, at his mind mature beyond its years. He asked him about many things, moving from topic to topic. Then Latinus offered him gentle kisses as he clung to him fondly in warm embrace. In his gladness he gave thought to Aeneas's good fortune, vouchsafed such an offspring by the benison of heaven.

After their hunger was satisfied by the repast, they begin by conversation to pretend away the long passage of the night—now recalling to mind Troy's bitter demise and the Grecian tribes, now the savage conflicts of the Laurentine war, where the first battle lines were drawn, where weapons in turn on turn were hurled, who first in fervor plunged into the marshaled foe and with gusto slathered his flashing sword with equine blood. Above all Aeneas of Troy and aged Latinus recounted the exploits of mighty heroes from a time gone by, of Latin power, of how Saturn was hidden away on Italy's shores to escape his son's hostile pursuit, whence he entitled it "Hiding Land,"[3] how he brought order to the race that roamed the high hills, codified for them rights and laws, and the cultivation of wine and crops, how afterward Jupiter entered his father's dwelling, how Dardanus, sprung from Electra, daughter of Atlas, after the death of Iasius set out from Cortona with a large following and made his way to the cities of the Troad under Ida, and how, taking pride in his father Jupiter and his gift, had chosen

495

500

505

510

515

520

525

utque insignem aquilam dono et Iove patre superbus
Hectoreae gentis signum, illustresque tulisset
primus avum titulos, Troianae stirpis origo.
    Talibus atque aliis inter se longa trahebant
530   tempora. Tum fremitus laetaeque per atria voces
alta volant, strepitu ingenti tectum omne repletur.
Dant lucem flammae et lato splendore coruscant.
Consurgunt Phryges, et cithara resonante sequuntur
Ausonii et plausum ingeminant seque agmine toto
535   permiscent variantque pedes raptimque feruntur.
    Et iam festa novem largo conubia luxu
attigerant celebrata dies; tum maximus heros
Aeneas urbem curvo signabat aratro
fundabatque domos et amictas aggere fossas.
540   Ecce autem, fatu haud parvum, diffundere flammam
ingentem et fulgore levem et se nubibus altis
miscentem e summo Lavinia vertice visa est.
Obstipuit pater Aeneas duplicesque tetendit
ad caelum cum voce manus: "Si, Iuppiter, umquam
545   gens monitis Troiana tuis terraque marique
paruit imperiisque libens, si, numina, vestras
si metui coluique aras, per si quid agendum est,
quod restat, placidam felici afferte quietem
augurio et firmate malisque imponite finem!"
550   Talia iactantem circumstitit aurea mater
se Venerem confessa almo et sic edidit ore:
"Nate, animo pone hanc curam et meliora capesse
signa deum gaudensque bonis succede futuris.
Nunc tibi parta quies, nunc meta extrema laborum,
555   nunc tandem optatam componunt saecula pacem.
Nec flammam ad caelos perlatam e vertice carae
coniugis horresce; at constantem dirige mentem.
Namque erit illa, tuum celebri quae sanguine nomen

the stalwart eagle as emblem for the race of Hector, he, the
founder of the Trojan race and inaugurator of its forefathers' re-
nowned honors.

With such and other topics they stretched out night's length.
Then shouts of joy rush rumbling through the lofty halls, and a 530
mighty roar fills the whole palace. Torches bring their light and
glisten with expansive glow. The Trojans jump to their feet, the
Latins follow, as the cithara resounds. The applause intensifies as
they merge together into a single assembly, vary the rhythms of
their dance and yield to the frolic. 535

And now the celebration of the wedding festivity, in a spectacle
of abundance, had extended nine days. Then Aeneas, greatest of
heroes, with the curved plough outlined his city, established
houses and trenches surrounded by an embankment. But look,
memorable to tell: Lavinia, from the crown of her head, seemed to 540
pour forth a huge flame, nimble in its brightness and soaring into
the clouds above. Father Aeneas, astonished at the magnificence of
the image, stretched forth both his hands to heaven and spoke: "If
ever, Jupiter, the Trojan people willingly respected your portents
and your mandates, both on land and on sea, if I, heavenly pow- 545
ers, revered and worshipped your altars, by whatever else in the
offing remains to be effected, afford us, confirm for us, peace's hal-
cyon time, bring our evils to a close."

While he was thus exclaiming, his golden mother embraced 550
him. Declaring herself Venus, she spoke these kindly words: "My
son, put this worry from your mind, lay claim to the gods' more
propitious omens, and, glad at heart, enter upon your auspicious
future. Now peace is granted to you, now at last is the end of your
sufferings. Finally, now, the ages accept the covenant of peace long 555
craved. Have no fear of the flame carried to the heavens from the
crown of your dear wife's head. Stand firm, with mind assured.
For she it will be who enhances your line's repute with glorious

35

Troianosque auctura duces ad sidera mittat.
560 Haec tibi magnanimos sublimi prole nepotes
conferet, egregiis qui totum laudibus orbem
complebunt totumque sua virtute potentes
sub iuga victoresque trahent, quos gloria summo
Oceanum transgressa ingens aequabit Olympo;
565 quos tandem post innumera atque illustria rerum
gesta deos factura vehet super aethera virtus.
Hanc flammam ventura tuae praeconia gentis
designant; hoc Omnipotens e culmine signum
sidereo dedit. At tantarum in munere laudum,
570 quam statuis, dicas a nomine coniugis urbem.
Praeterea sacros Troia ex ardente penates
ereptos compone nova intra moenia et altos
infer ad aeternum mansuros tempus honores.
Hi, tibi mira feram, tanto urbis amore trahentur,
575 ut vecti ad sedes alias loca prima Lavini
sponte sua repetant iterumque iterumque reversi.
O felix, quem tanta manent! Dehinc pace tenebis
sub placida gentem Iliacam. Post fessus et aevo
confectus tandem Elysias socer ibit ad umbras.
580 Succedes sceptro atque Italis dominabere leges
communes Teucrisque ferens. Tum laetus ad altum
te mittes caelum. Sic stat sententia divum."
Dixit, et inde leves fugiens se vexit in auras.
Aeneas tanto stupefactam nomine mentem
585 percussus divae peragit mandata parentis.
Et iam compositos felici in pace regebat
Dardanidas. Et iam decedens sceptra Latinus
liquerat, et pius Aeneas successerat, omnem
Ausoniam lataque potens dicione tenebat.
590 Iam paribus Phryges atque Itali se moribus ultro
et socia ingenti firmabant pectora amore

offspring and exalts the heroes of Troy to the stars. She will be-
queath you high-souled descendants with august progeny, whose   560
extraordinary praise will fill earth's whole orb, which in its en-
tirety, victors through the power of their courage, they will draw
under the yoke. Their glorious grandeur, surpassing the bounds of
Ocean, will find its measure in the heights of Olympus. Nobility,
their source of godhead, in the wake of countless valorous deeds   565
accomplished, will lead them beyond the heavens. This flame her-
alds the signal achievements of your race; the Almighty has fur-
nished this token from his starry precincts. As gesture for such ac-
claim to be yours, give the city you are founding your wife's name. 570
Furthermore arrange within the new walls the blessed Penates,
snatched from the flames of Troy, and tender them distinguished
honors to endure for all time. I will tell you something extraordi-
nary: they are captivated by such affection for the city that, though
displaced to other posts, of their own will they seek Lavinium,   575
their original settlement, returning to it again and yet again.
Blessed by fortune, great things await you! In the time ahead you
will rule the Trojan people in the calm of peace. In due course
your father-in-law, tired and undone with age, will depart for the
shades of Elysium. You will succeed to the throne, your rule will   580
establish laws shared by Italians and Trojans. Then, rejoicing, you
will yourself ascend to the lofty heavens. So have the gods de-
creed." Words finished, she took her leave in flight to the sprightly
breezes.

　　Aeneas, his mind stunned in amazement at such fame, carried
out the commands of his goddess mother. And so he reigned over   585
the Trojans, united in the blessings of peace. Then, when holy
Aeneas had succeeded to the throne after Latinus's departure in
death, his power held broad sway over all of Italy. It was a time
when Trojans and Italians willingly strengthened the bonds of   590
their alliance through the sharing of customs and through deepen-

concordique aequas miscebant foedere leges.
Tum medio Venus exultans se immisit Olympo
ante Iovem et complexa pedes sic ore locuta est:
595   "Omnipotens genitor, qui solus ab aethere summo
cuncta moves, qui res hominum curasque recenses,
dum Teucros traheret fortuna inimica, recordor,
spondebas finem aerumnis rebusque salutem.
Nec tua me promissa, pater, sententia fallit;
600   namque omnes gaudere sacra tris pace per annos
viderunt Italae nullo discrimine partes.
Verum ad siderei missurum culmina caeli
pollicitus magnum Aenean meritumque ferebas
illaturum astris. Quid nunc sub pectore versas?
605   Iamque optat matura polos Aeneia virtus."
     Olli hominum sator atque deum dedit oscula ab alto
pectore verba ferens: "Quantum, Cytherea, potentem
Aeneam Aeneadasque omnes infessus amavi
et terra et pelago et per tanta pericula vectos,
610   nosti, et saepe equidem indolui commotus amore,
nata, tuo, tandemque malis Iunone secunda
imposui finem. Nunc stat sententia menti,
qua ductorem alto Phrygium succedere caelo
institui, et firma est; numeroque inferre deorum
615   constat, et id concedo libens. Tu, si quid in ipso
mortale est, adime, atque astris ingentibus adde.
Quin si alios sua habet virtus, qui laude perenni
accingant sese et gestis praestantibus orbem
exornent, illos rursum super aethera mittam."
620   Assensere omnes superi nec regia Iuno
abnuit, at magnum Aenean suadebat ad ipsum
efferri caelum et voces addebat amicas.
     Tum Venus aerias descendit lapsa per auras
Laurentumque petit. Vicina Numicius undis

ing affection; harmony through equality of law was their united agreement. Then a rejoicing Venus made her way into the presence of Jupiter at the center of Olympus, embraced his feet and spoke: "Almighty sire, who from heaven's zenith solely guide the 595 affairs of all and scan man's enterprises and his cares, it is my memory that, when ill-fortune held the Trojans in its grip, you promised them security and an end to trouble. Your judgment's pledge never failed me, father. Everyone has seen the whole of Italy, with no exceptions take delight in three years of holy peace. 600 You also gave solemn assurance that you would convey noble Aeneas to the peak of the glittering heavens and make his worth known to the stars. What now are you pondering in your heart? Already Aeneas's virtue in its fullness lays claim to the celestial pole." 605

The father of men and gods kissed her and from his inmost heart spoke: "From my very words, goddess of Cythera, you knew how much I have always loved stalwart Aeneas and all his followers, as they fared through such great perils whether on land or on sea, and, touched by your love, my child, indeed I grieved for them time and again. At last with Juno's approval I put an end to their 610 woes. My mind's decree, my determination that the Trojan leader should enter the lofty heavens, stands steady. To accept him within the congress of the gods is the decision. It is one I gladly grant. Yours the task to erase what might remain mortal in him, 615 and to engage him to the mighty stars. Also, if others possess his excellence, who encompass themselves with immortal praise and embellish the world through outstanding feats, I will convey them in turn beyond the Aether." All the gods granted approval. Nor 620 did royal Juno demur. To complement her words of friendship, she urged that Aeneas be borne to heaven itself.

Then Venus slips sliding down the breezes of air and seeks Laurentum. There the Numicius, veiled in reed, courses with the

625 flumineis ibi currit in aequora harundine tectus.
    Hunc corpus nati abluere et deferre sub undas,
    quicquid erat mortale, iubet. Dehinc laeta recentem
    felicemque animam secum super aera duxit,
    immisitque Aenean astris, quem Iulia proles
630 indigitem appellat templisque imponit honores.

PAPIAE VI. IDUS OCTOBRIAS MCCCCXXVIII

ripples of his stream into the nearby sea. She commands him to   625
wash away from her son's body whatever is mortal and to carry it
beneath his waves. Then in happiness she conducted the fresh,
blessed soul with her above the air, and fixed Aeneas among the
stars. His Julian offspring entitle him Indiges[4] and in his temples
decree the honors of his cult.   630

PAVIA, OCTOBER 10, 1428

ASTYANAX

[Carmen dedicatorium]

Maphaeus Vegius Laudensis Marchetto suo salutem.

Accipe quem scripsi nuper, Marchette, libellum,
  et nostro aeternum munere nomen habe.
Nunc te uenturi memorabunt laude nepotes
  et dicent: Musis hic quoque dignus erat.
5 Lugendum nati exitium matrisque dolorem
  fataque Spartanae gentis iniqua leges.
Haec cecini; at nostras placido percurre tabellas
  lumine, et ut facili cetera mente soles.

ASTYANAX

[Dedicatory Poem]

Maffeo Vegio of Lodi, good health to his Marchetto.[1]

Receive, Marchetto, the little book which I recently wrote, and
gain an undying name by means of our gift. Now your descen-
dants to come will keep your memory fresh with praise, and will
say: this [volume] was also worthy of the Muses.

Here you will read of a son's death, cause for mourning, of the   5
grief of a mother, and of the unjust decrees of the people of
Greece. This was my song. But do survey my work with gentle
eye, as in other matters is the wont of your indulgent disposition.

Astyanax

Musa, refer quae causa metum post diruta Troiae
moenia et extremas clades incussit Achiuis
principibus. Cur certa omnis penderet inulto
Astyanacte salus Danaum? Tu, diua, canentem
5   prosequere. Hectorei dicam crudelia nati
funera et afflictae planctus lamentaque matris.
    Exciderant saeuis euersaque Pergama flammis
funditus, et superum lacrimas motura iacebant,
Ilium humo sparsum tota, miserabile Teucris
10   supplicium, tumidas Graium satiauerat iras.
Ipse parens, post tot natorum fata suorum,
Laomedontiades Asiae regnator, ad imas
ense Neoptolemi caesus descenderat umbras.
Hic finis bellorum et iam tendebat utrasque
15   iungebatque manus laeta omnis Achaica pubes.
Dona ferens aris et diuos laude canebat,
optatos uisura lares, uisura penates,
et dulcis natos nuptasque patresque, simulque
expectatam armis requiem patriaeque salutem.
20   Tum uarios uoluens casus metuensque futuri,
Argolicos proceres maior cogebat Atrides,
utque alto stabat solio, sic edidit ore:
'Victores Danaï, quorum res numina laetas
respiciunt — neque enim nostrae sine numine eunt res —
25   iam tandem decimo Phrygios superauimus anno.
Iam tandem ad patrias fessi remeabimus urbes.
At uos, si qua manet magnorum certa laborum
affectata quies (parua est mora), state Pelasgi;
ne celerate oro. Meritas Neptunia poenas
30   satque superque luit, fateor, sat Troia cadentes

Astyanax

Tell, o Muse, what occasioned the anxiety and the final rampage of
the Achaean princes after the collapse of Troy's walls. Why did all
certainty of safety for the Greeks hang on scatheless Astyanax?
Goddess, assist your singer. I will relate the cruel death of Hec- 5
tor's son, the wails and groans of his wretched mother.

Troy had collapsed, razed to its foundations by savage flames,
and its fallen state brought tears to the eyes of the gods. Ilium, laid
low its length and breadth, pitiable punishment for the Trojans,
had glutted the arrogant anger of the Greeks. The father himself, 10
offspring of Laomedon, ruler of Asia, after the demise of so many
of his children, had made his descent to the nether shades, slaugh-
tered by the blade of Neoptolemus. This was the last of the war-
ring, and now the Greek youth, rejoicing all, stretched their hands
forth to embrace one another. They praised the gods with song as 15
they brought gifts to their altars, soon to see their homes, soon to
see the hearth-gods for whom they had yearned, and their sweet
children, their wives and fathers, as well as to experience well-
earned rest from battle and salvation for their homeland.

Then, pondering the twists of fortune and wary of what lay 20
ahead, the elder son of Atreus gathered together the Argive
princes and, standing by his lofty throne, he thus held forth: "O
Greeks, conquerors on whose deeds the gods look with a joyous
eye — no deeds of ours succeed with gods averse —, now, at last, in
the tenth year we have overwhelmed the Trojans. Now, at last, ex- 25
hausted though we be, we will make our way back to the cities of
our fathers. Nevertheless, you Greeks, though a sure time of peace
after mighty efforts remains your aspiration, pause for a brief mo-
ment. I ask of you, do not yield to haste. I admit that Neptune's
Troy enough and more than enough has paid the penalties it de- 30

deflevit, sparsos proprioque in sanguine ciues.
Verum et nunc uestras intenti aduertite mentes.
Nondum adeo cecidere Phryges, nondum omnis adempta est
spes Teucris: superest Priami de gente superba
35   Astyanax, qui si fortes maturior annos
attigerit, quantum exitium clademque Mycenis
portendat, quae fata mihi, neu credite! Calchas
ista canit. Vos consulite et Calchanta uocate.
Ille quidem, siue id senior dum Troia labaret
40   clam mandauit auus, seu fidae fraude parentis,
in tutum cessit. Sed quaeso promitte totas
ingenii uires. Tentanda est mater et astu
fallenda atque dolis, latitantem ut conscia natum
exhibeat. Vos nunc uestris succurrite rebus.'
45   Dixerat; arrectae mentes regumque ducumque.
Quem sic effari iussus Laertius heros
prosequitur: 'Dux o nostrae fidissime gentis
non indigna refers. Equidem me scire fatebor:
Quid Calchanta uocem? Nostra hunc si ignauia seruet
50   haud paruo uenturum, Argis iam cernere quanta
caede fluant riui uideor, iam dorica in enses
castra coacta alto resonare ad sidera planctu.
Quod potius precor auertant neque numina firment.
Ecce animum subit et nimium me terret imago
55   Hectoris, egregio cuius de sanguine natum
Astyanacta—animis an degenerare paternis
crediderim? Non sic animi neque mentis egens sum.
    'Nos fracti moneant Troes, nos Dardana tellus
edoceat tot quondam opibus, tot uiribus ingens,
60   nunc aequata solo, cui laetitiaeque dolorique
una eademque dies fuerit; breuis hora uetustum

served, enough has Troy mourned its fallen citizens, drenched in
their own blood. But give me now your careful attention. Not yet
have the Trojans fully succumbed, not yet has all hope been
wrenched from the offspring of Teucer. From the proud race of
Priam there remains Astyanax. Were he to attain the full strength   35
of years, you cannot believe what ruin and disaster he would fore-
bode for Mycenae, what doom for me! It is Calchas who chants
these prophecies. Take counsel and summon Calchas. The boy has
escaped to safety, whether this had been his aged grandfather's se-
cret command, while Troy was collapsing, or whether it results
from the treachery of a mother we had trusted. But I ask of you: 40
exert your wit's full force. His mother must be put to the test and
be tricked by the cleverness of our wiles so that she reveal her
knowledge of her son's refuge. Now is the time to advance your
own affairs."

His words sharpened the thoughts of princes and dukes alike.   45
At command the hero son of Laertes offers him this word in re-
sponse: "O most trusted leader of our people, you bring to our at-
tention matters worthy of concern. Indeed I will confess that I al-
ready realize this: why should I summon Calchas? If our lack of
initiative were to keep safe and sound him who will return as our
bane, I seem to behold now with what slaughter the streams at
Argos might flow, now the Greek camp, forced against the thrust   50
of swords, resounding with deep lamentation toward the stars.
May the gods instead, so I pray, turn this aside and grant it no ap-
proval. See how the image of Hector slips into my thoughts and
redoubles my fear, Hector from whose illustrious blood Astyanax   55
is sprung! Or am I to believe that his courage falls short of his fa-
ther's? I am not so lacking in intelligence.

"The Trojans, their spirits broken, should serve as warning to
us, the Dardan land should be our teacher. Once mighty in re-
sources, mighty in strength, now leveled to the ground, to whom   60
one and the same day brought both happiness and woe, a brief,

postremo imperium rapuit. Nos stamus eodem
quo Troia ipsa loco steterat, timor omnibus idem.
At uos si sapitis, Danai, si cura futuri
65   ulla sedet generis, Priami delete nepotem,
efficite et prorsus Troianum euertite nomen.
Nec puerum ulcisci tenerumque haurire cruorem
turpe putent: et me pietas tangitque mouetque.
Plus tamen argiuae matres gnatique nurusque
70   stringunt me pietate. Subit patria inclyta mentem,
Telemachus meus ante omnes atque optima coniunx
et carus genitor, quorum hic in funera crescit.
Ipse ego (quod reliquum est), si lingua aut pectore uobis
umquam profuerim, nunc has aperire latebras
75   polliceor. Prudentem huius quodcumque profari est
compellam genitricem arte occultumque fateri.
Quippe animos dudum didici simulataque matrum
consilia incassumque annexas uincere fraudes.
Si placet haec uestraeque manet sententia menti,
80   en adsum, mandate; libens ego iussa capessam.'
Finierat, cunctique eadem assensere frementes.
     Viderat et parui sortem Astyanactis iniquam
alma Venus miserata, oculos suffudit abortis
sidereos lacrimis. Tum magni ante ora parentis
85   constitit, has maesto referens e pectore uoces:
'Mene tuo, genitor, solam indignaris amore?
Quid potui meruisse? Phrygum quae tanta meorum
excidia et Graiae gentis commenta dolosque
euersamque urbem uidi, indoluique uidendo!
90   Solane sollicitis et tristibus anxia curis
semper ero? Miserere pater! Solatia natae
da non magna tuae. Ceciderunt Pergama et ipsi
Priamidae efflarunt misero de corpore uitam.
Id factum est; quae fata uolunt patienter et aequo

final hour snatched away the power of its ancient rule. We stand
in the same situation in which Troy itself stood. The same fear
possesses all of us. But if you are wise, my Greeks, if you cherish
any worry for your race to come, wipe out Priam's grandson, see 65
the matter through and once and for all obliterate the name of
Troy. Let people not pronounce it base to seek vengeance on ten-
der youth and quaff his blood. I, too, am touched and moved by
piety. Nevertheless I am duty-bound more by piety toward Greek
mothers, sons and daughters. The repute of my fatherland claims 70
my thoughts, my Telemachus before all, and my best of wives, and
my dear father. Astyanax's growth spells their doom. For the rest,
if ever my eloquence or my courage were of service to you, now I
myself promise to uncover his lair. With my artfulness I will force 75
his mother, wise though she be, to tell what she can and to reveal
the hidden. You would know that for some time now I have
learned to get the better of enmities, of the plots and pretenses of
matrons, of deceits added in vain. If these ideas please you and
still accord with our understanding, well, then I am yours. Com-
mand away! Gladly will I claim my orders." After he finished, all 80
agreed to his words with a roar of approval.

Kindly Venus had been watching, and as she felt pity for the
unjust lot of young Astyanax, tears welled up and suffused her
star-gleaming eyes. Then she stood face to face before her majestic
father, uttering these words of sorrow from her heart: "Do you, 85
father, consider me alone unworthy of your love? How could I
have deserved this? What ruination of my Trojans have I seen,
what treachery and deceit on the part of the Greek people! I have
watched my city overturned, and have grieved at the sight. Am I 90
alone always to be troubled by bitter tribulations and cares? Have
mercy, father mine! Grant some small solace to your daughter.
Troy has fallen and Priam's sons themselves have breathed forth
life from their pitiable bodies. What's done is done. It behooves us

95   ferre animo praestat. Sed te, rex maxime caeli,
      unum oro, concede unum. Satus Hectore forti
      restat adhuc magnae Astyanax spes unica Troiae,
      in quem nunc rapitur nondum exsaturata iuuentus
      Graiorum, puerique caput depectus Ulixes
100   insidias struit et miserae scelera atra parenti.
      Nunc illum e tantis potius defende periclis,
      qui solus Priami de tota gente supersit.
      Serua illum, precor, atque malis nunc eripe tantis.'
          Olli hominum diuumque parens haec pectore ab alto
105   verba dedit: 'Quid me totiens, Cytherea, fatigas,
      ardentis agitans curas? Quid, nata, querelis
      inflecti ueterum non exoranda sororum
      iura putas stabilisque aeterno foedere leges?
      Qui finis Priamum et patriam natosque manebat
110   nunc idem Astyanacta manet, neque uertere duris
      quae fatis placuere meum est; si uertere possem
      et Priamum patriamque et natos stare uideres.
      Non tamen Iliacas omnino extinguere uires
      decretum est. Tuus Aeneas seruabitur, unde
115   magni opibusque animisque duces nascentur et armis
      qui tandem domitas cogent parere Mycenas,
      quorum ingens toti nomen dominabitur orbi.
      Illum ego post multos pelagi terraeque labores
      sublimem ad caelum mittam et diuum numero addam.
120   Hic erit unde tuos solari, nata, dolores,
      et tristes Troum casus releuare licebit.'
          Talibus inter se, sed non contenta quiescit
      mens diuae, demumque leues perlabitur auras,
      conata Hectoreae rursum succurrere proli,

to suffer the will of fate in patience and in calm. But I ask one fa-   95
vor of you, most glorious king of the heavens, grant me one thing.
Astyanax, scion of bold Hector, still survives, the single hope of
mighty Troy. The youth of Greece, still unglutted, is now roused
against him and the schemer Ulysses is contriving plots against the
boy's survival and dark crimes for his poor mother. Rather, protect   100
him now from such dangers, he who alone survives from the
whole race of Priam. Save him, I beseech you, and snatch him
now from this spate of evils."

These are the words that the father of men and of gods replied
to her from the depths of his heart: "Goddess of Cythera, why do   105
you weary me time after time with your burning cares? My daugh-
ter, what gives you the notion that the unyielding mandates of the
sister-crones and laws steadied by ever-enduring compact can grow
compliant to your complaints? The same end that awaited Priam,
his fatherland and his sons, now awaits Astyanax. It is not mine to   110
subvert what seemed appropriate to the iron Fates. If I were capa-
ble of subversion, you would behold Priam, his land and sons, sur-
viving. Nevertheless, it is not the Fates' decree completely to ex-
punge the strength of Troy. Your Aeneas will be saved. From him
will be born dynamic leaders, mighty in resource and in courage   115
for arms, who will at last compel obedience from a tamed
Mycenae, whose grand repute will lord it over the whole earth. Af-
ter his course of trials on land and sea I myself will speed him
aloft to the heavens, and will join him to the number of the gods.
This, my child, will be the source of consolation for your sorrows.   120
From this you will gain respite from the Trojans' woeful misfor-
tunes."

So they conversed, but the restive mind of the goddess remains
ill at ease. And after a spell she glides through the nimble breezes,
her purpose yet again to offer help to Hector's offspring. She seeks
out the region of Ida; there, after she recognized the once tremen-

125   Idaeamque petit regionem; ibi maxima quondam
        moenia Dardanidum postquam cognouit et urbem
        euulsam, lacrimas grauiter perculsa profudit.
          Tempus erat quo noctem oriens aurora fugabat.
        Tunc Venus effigiem, fuerat quae tempore uitae,
130   Hectoris induitur, non ut ferus arma mouere,
        aut, quando in medios horrendum insurgeret hostes,
        magnanimus turmas Danaum terrere solebat.
        Fit maestus fletuque madens, fit pallidus Hector,
        et fossum ostendens pectus squalentiaque ora,
135   atque his Andromachen per somnum affatur et ultro
        compellat uerbis: 'Surge, o carissima coniunx,
        o coniunx, dum uita fuit, tecum arripe natum
        communem et nostro serua atque reconde sepulcro.
        Nullus enim tota locus est qui restet in urbe:
140   Consumpsere omnem miseranda incendia Troiam.
        Hunc tibi commendo; hic patriae nostrae una salus est.'
        Nec plura. Illa altis sese uelocior astris
        intulit. At tanto Andromache perterrita uisu
        nequicquam complexa uirum, tamen omnia cari
145   coniugis exequitur dicta et mandata facessit.
          Interea aduentans scelerum fabricator Ulixes
        nectebat fraudes animo, quo cingere matrem,
        quo capere eloquio posset. Quae exordia primum
        sumeret, huc animum meditans mutabat et illuc.
150   Non secus ac quando lupus insidiatur ouili,
        quem ieiuna fames cogit, tacito auia gressu
        arua legit, secumque dolos et tristia uersat
        fata quibus tenero lactentem ex ubere foetum
        eripiat, sic Laertiades dux ibat, in omnis
155   se uoluens curas. Cui postquam copia cessit,
        alloquitur tali defessam uoce parentem:

dous fortifications of the Trojans and the city torn from its roots, 125
in deep affliction she streamed with tears.

It was the time when rising dawn was routing the night. At that
moment Venus clothes herself in the likeness of great-souled Hec-
tor, but not as he had been at that time in his life when he was 130
wont fiercely to ready his weapons or, looming up, an object of
dread, into the midst of the foe to bring terror to the Greek
squadrons. She becomes Hector pale as death, Hector woebegone,
sodden from weeping. You could see the gash on his chest and his
blood-crusted features. Without a moment's pause she addresses 135
the sleeping Andromache with these urgent words: "Arise, dear
wife, dearest of wives, while you still have life, and clasp to your-
self the son we share. Save him and hide him in my tomb. No
other spot remains in the whole of the city. Grief-breeding flames 140
have devoured all of Troy. I place him in your care. He alone can
save our fatherland." With no further word she betook herself
with all speed to the stars above. Andromache, terrified by such a
sight, and seeking in vain to embrace her husband, nevertheless
follows to the letter the words of her dear consort and executes his
commands. 145

Meanwhile Ulysses, artificer of wickedness, makes his ap-
proach, in his mind weaving webs of deception so that his elo-
quence can besiege and capture the mother. As he ponders the
effect of his initial words, he changes his thoughts now in this di-
rection, now in that. The moment is not unlike when a wolf, 150
driven by hunger's fast, lies in ambush before a sheepfold. With si-
lent tread he skirts the pathless fields and ponders within himself
the wiles and bitter doom by which he might snatch a suckling
lamb from the tender udders: thus the leader, son of Laertes,
made his way, meditating to himself on all possible concerns. Af- 155
ter the chance came his way, he thus addresses the weary mother:
"If the gods had wished me to live my life according to my own

'Si me dii propriis uoluissent uiuere uotis,
non equidem dirae sortis tibi nuncius essem.
Iussa sequens Danaum uenio. Cum Teucria primum
160   urbs bello peteretur et aequora adire uetarent
humano donec placati sanguine uenti,
filia tunc sacras Agamemnonis imbuit aras.
Nunc eadem Calchas redituros fata manere
praedicit, rursum Graios caesoque piandas
165   Astyanacte rates. Tu quem rex gentis Achiuae
sorte tulit, casum non aspernare. Pelasgi
in te omnes conuersi orant. Ostende ubi natus.
Sic finem impones armis, sic tutior Argos
laetitia explebit requies. Venturus hic Hector
170   iam formidatur Danais longeque timetur.
Occultum huc reddas pignus. Quid turbida frontem
obducis, torquens oculos? An fallere Ulixem
feminea arte putas? Verum cogeris et ipsum,
quamquam inuita, dabis. Nunc summo ex aggere bustum
175   Hectoreum euellam prorsus, perque aera mittam
dispersos cineres, et saltem triste paterni
supplicium exsoluent manes poenaeque dolebunt
quas fugiet natus. Sed tandem hunc in medium affer.'
    Sic fatus stetit; illa tremens altumque repressit
180   quo potuit gemitum, dehinc talia reddidit ore:
'O utinam mea, nate, quies, mea gaudia quondam,
o utinam superesses! Et post omnia tantum
solamen matris miserae, his te, nate, lacertis
complecti atque tuo aspectu me pascere possem.
185   At cecidisti et tu in mediis nunc ignibus ardes,
forsitan aut nihil absumpto de corpore restat.
Gaudete, o Grai; sum uestrae nuncia mater

desires, I would certainly not be serving as messenger to you of a dread turn of fate. I come in obedience to the commands of the Greeks. When first the city of Teucer was our goal in war and the seas forbade our setting forth until the winds had been assuaged   160
with human blood, then the daughter of Agamemnon dyed the holy altars red. Calchas now prophesies that the same fortune again awaits the Greeks as they prepare for return and that their ships must be expiated by the killing of Astyanax. You, whom a   165
lord of the Greek people has gained by lot, do not treat lightly this turn of events. All the men of Greece appeal to you in prayer. Show us the whereabouts of your son. In this way you will put an end to war, in this way a time of assured peace will fill Argos with joy. This future Hector is now an object of fear and of great dread for the Greeks. Give us here back the child you have hidden. Why   170
do you knit your troubled brow and roll your eyes? Do you expect to deceive Ulysses with a woman's wiles? Nevertheless you will yield to compulsion and, though unwilling, give over the boy. Now it will be my sure purpose to tear open the top of Hector's burial mound and to send his ashes scattered through the air, and at least   175
the father's ghost will pay a grim penalty and will bemoan the punishment that the son will avoid. So, I ask you, bring him into our midst"

He stopped with these words. Trembling, she stifled a deep groan as best she could. Then she spoke thus in response: "O my   180
son, once my source of repose, once my joy, would that you had survived, o my son. After all that has happened, the only source of solace for his grief-stricken mother, with these arms I would be able to embrace you and to take nourishment from your sight. But you have fallen and you now burn in the midst of the flames, or   185
perhaps nothing remains from the body that they have consumed. Rejoice, o Greeks. I, his mother, am the messenger of your happiness: my son has died and surrendered his life."

laetitiae: periit natus uitamque reliquit.'
    His dictis incensa magis ducis ira, ruebant
190   iam famuli in tumulum moniti. Tum regia uirgo
Dulichii stetit ante pedes herois et ambas
intendens palmas, 'Tantum precor,' inquit, 'Ulixe,
si qua animum mollit pietas, auerte dolorem
Hectora iactari ut uideam; miserere measque
195   sume preces. Prohibe infandum scelus. En tibi natum
reddam, at tu melior dirae illum surripe morti:
Et natum et matrem seruabis. Hic est mihi sola
afflictae requies, maestae hic mihi sola uoluptas.
Per spes Telemachi, per castam coniugem, ego te
200   per seniorem oro genitorem: si tibi cura est
ulla domus quae te rediturum optatque manetque,
huic inopi succurre. Et commiserere parenti
et precibus moueare piis, si prona potentem
te fata euexere. Negas an parcere uictis?
205   Vicistis porro, [o] Danai, Troiaeque superbas
euertistis opes; iacet Ilium opus diuorum.
Verum agite et, quantum liceat, sperate secundos
caelicolas, laetis nimium neu fidite rebus.
Saepe etiam damno felix uictoria cessit.
210   Discite nunc miseros tutari, discite lapsos
erigere, et misereri inopum fractosque iuuare.
Fata rotant homines: quanto quisque altior hostem
oppressit sceptroque potens dominatur et omnes
exterret populos, animis tanto addere magnis
215   frena decet dubiam rerumque agnoscere sortem:
Nota loquor. Nunc e patrio descende sepulcro,
Astyanax parue. Astyanax, procede tuumque
affare et dominum supplex humilisque precare;
pone animos ueteres, proh auorum nomina, et altum
220   Troianae genus urbis et inclyta moenia cedant.

The fire of the chieftain's anger was fanned by her words. Following his command slaves now rush toward the funeral mound. Then the royal princess stood before the feet of the Dulichian hero and, stretching forth both hands, says: "I pray only for this, Ulysses, if any piety can soften your heart: only prevent the sorrow that would be mine were I to see Hector strewn abroad. Take pity and accept my prayers. Put a stop to this unspeakable crime. Watch now: I will give my son to you. Only please, in your nobility snatch him from dread death. You will have preserved son and mother. He is the only relief of my distress, he my only pleasure amid sadness. By your expectations for Telemachus, by your chaste wife, by your aged sire, I beseech you, if you have devotion for any dwelling place that in yearning awaits your return: grant your help to mine, now destitute. Take pity on a mother, bend to my holy prayer, if a favorable destiny has raised you to power. Do you refuse to spare the conquered? This is now certain, o Greeks: You have conquered and have overthrown Troy with its haughty wealth. Ilium, handiwork of the gods, lies in ruins. But pay heed. Place your hopes, as much as may be, on the favor of the gods; do not put too much trust in prosperity. Often a victory that comes with fortune's blessing has given place to loss. Learn now to protect the downtrodden, learn to raise up the fallen, to pity the beggared and sustain the broken. Fate turns mankind on its wheel. To whatever extent anyone in his pride has harried his foe and, once in power, has played the overlord, scepter in hand, and brought terror to all mankind, to the same degree it befits him to rein in the force of his strength and take note that our lot is ever uncertain. I speak from experience. Now, Astyanax my child, make your way down from your father's tomb. Astyanax, step forward and in suppliant fashion address your master and pray the prayer of the humbled. By the names of our ancestors, put aside your ancient animus and let the distinguished lineage of the city of Troy and the famous walls be a thing of the past. Why are your cheeks

57

Quid lacrimis maduere genae? Patriam exue mentem,
abice auos et disce pati. Quid brachia collo
innectis nostro? Quid matrem iterumque iterumque,
nate, uocas, frustra ingeminans? Heu heu miseram me!'
225   Talia iactabat lacrimans. Cui turba trementem
Astyanacta ducis iussu gremioque parentis
tutantem se nequicquam auxiliumque petentem
complexu e medio traxit. Velut astur inermem
cum uolucrem insequitur curuis trepidam unguibus urgens,
230   illa ubi fata uidet uitae, suprema profusis
ora rigans lacrimis timidum declinat humoque
occultat peritura caput, se tali ope tutam
seruatamque putans, demum raptoris iniqui
praeda fit et tenues moriens diuerberat auras,
235   haud aliter rapitur Troiano ex Hectore cretus.
Turris erat cuius caelum fastigia adibant,
unde pater Priamus Troiam omnem ipsosque solebat
prospicere Argiuos et natum bella mouentem
horrenda et flammis hostes ferroque prementem.
240   Huc puer Astyanax tecto mittendus ab alto
ducitur infelix. Circum omnis fusa coibat
visendi pubes studio, populique ducesque.
Ille autem haud segni passu leto obuius ibat,
huc illuc spectans oculis similisque minanti,
245   intrepidamque aciem ostentans. Gemuere coacti
nec lacrimas tenuere animum ut uidere Pelasgi
ingentem et tenero praestantem in corpore formam.
Postquam ad supplicium uentum est sacrosque uocaret
fatidicus uates, ipse ultro e culmine summo
250   proiecit sese uitamque sub aëre liquit.
Fama uolans miseram complebat nuncia matrem,
missum alta e turri natum duroque rotatum
procubuisse solo. Tum palmis pectora tundens

dampened by tears? Put aside your father's purpose, forget your
heritage. Learn to endure. Why do your arms wrap themselves
around my neck? My son, why do you call on your mother again
and again, redoubling your cry in vain? Alas, alas, woe is me."

Such were the words she wailed through her tears. At this the 225
crowd, following the command of its leader, dragged Astyanax,
trembling, from his mother's embrace as he sheltered himself to
no avail in her lap and pleaded for help. As a hawk pursues a help-
less bird which, shivering at its assailant's hooked talons, when it
sees that the moment of doom has come, its features awash with a 230
final flow of tears, bends in fright and, though death approaches,
hides its head in the ground, hoping by such a ruse that it will be
safe and sound; at last it becomes the prey of its mightier ma-
rauder and, dying, flaps its wings against the gentle breeze: in sim-
ilar fashion the child born of Trojan Hector is snatched away. 235

There was a tower whose bastions stretched toward heaven.
From this vantage father Priam was accustomed to look out on the
whole of Troy, on the Greeks themselves, and on his son, setting
in motion dread battle and pursuing the foe with fire and sword.
Here they lead Astyanax, to hurl the unfortunate boy from the 240
lofty roof. All the young pour together in a crowd, eager to watch,
and with them the peoples and their leaders. He himself marched
to his death with sturdy step, casting his eyes in one direction,
then another, his glance without fear, as if almost to threaten. The 245
Greeks, under orders to pay witness, groaned, nor did they re-
strain their tears when they beheld the young boy's mighty spirit
and noble mien. When the time for punishment arrived and the
prophet-seer summoned the holy priests, on his own the boy
threw himself from the tower's height and abandoned his life un-
der the heavens. 250

Rumor the messenger sped the full news to the distraught
mother, that her son had been catapulted with a whirl from the
lofty tower and lay on the hard earth. Then, beating her breast

sparsa comas rapido fertur per moenia cursu,
255   Astyanacta petens. Quem postquam agnouit et ora
foedata auulsumque caput disiectaque uidit
membra, suum lacrimis testari et uoce dolorem
haud potuit primo. Demum miseranda solutos
suspiciens artus, quam primum farier ingens
260   concessit dolor, his percussit questibus auras:
'Talem ego te nate aspicio? Talemne parenti
seruasti afflictae tandem? Quis te mihi diuum
inuidit? Quis tantum ausus, quis, nate, deorum?
Quae tibi sidereos rapuit mors impia uultus
265   egregiumque decus formae? Et qui plurimus aurei
purpureus decor oris erat? Nunc tristia cerno
uulnera, uel potius toto unum in corpore uulnus.
Nunc cerno laceros artus taboque fluentes
eiectosque suis oculos e sedibus. O me
270   infelicem! O me miserandam! Talia, nate,
allaturus eras uiduae solacia matri?
Haec requies sperata? Hoc est solamen adempti
coniugis, euersae haec patriae mihi gaudia restant?
Quo dulces risus soliti admirataque uerba?
275   Et blandae uoces puerili ex ore cadentes?
Quo cari amplexus abiere et mutua nostris
oscula fixa genis toties? Quod sidus iniquum
eripuit te, nate, mihi, ne regna paterna
succedens sceptro regeres et magnus auitum
280   imperium augeres? Quotiens ignara precabar
uenturas belli laudes et splendida dextrae
facta tuae ultricesque manus. Proh caeca hominum mens!
Dii contra euertere omnem spemque ire sub auras
iusserunt. Nunc nec leges nec iura subactis

with her hands, with her hair swirling around her, she runs in a
rush along the walls, seeking out Astyanax. After she had recog-   255
nized him with his face mauled, and had seen his head ripped
from its body, his limbs scattered, for the first moment she was all
but unable to give vent to her sorrow with tears and lamentation.
At last, deserving pity as she stared at the dismembered body, as
soon as her overwhelming grief allowed her to speak she pierced
the air with these cries of grief: "Is this the way I must behold   260
you? Is this the spectacle that you have saved for your despairing
mother? What god begrudged you to me? Which of the denizens
of heaven, which, my child, had such daring? What wicked death
has snatched away your star-bright features and your handsome,
peerless charm? What was the measureless grace, the gold of your   265
features, the purple of your lips? Now I behold your bitter
wounds or rather the one wound which is your whole body. Now I
behold your limbs tattered and dripping with gore, your eyes
dashed from their sockets. O such unhappiness is mine! O I am
so much to be pitied! Were such the consolations, my son, that   270
you were to have brought to your widowed mother? Is this the re-
pose for which I hoped? Is this the solace for my husband's loss,
are these the joys that remain for my destroyed homeland? Where
has your usual sweet laughter gone and your skill with words, the
winning speech that flowed from your boyish lips? Where have   275
your loving embraces gone and the exchange of kisses planted so
often on both our cheeks? O my son, what unjust star has
snatched you from me, so that you may not inherit the scepter and
rule over the kingdom of your fathers and with your own grandeur
expand your ancestral ruling power? How often in my folly did I   280
pray for glory to come your way through battle, for the splendid
deeds of your right hand, for the force of your vengeance. O the
mind of man that works in darkness! The gods in their contrari-
ness have turned every hope upside-down and commanded its dis-
appearance into the air. Now you will bring neither laws nor rights

285 ulla feres populis, neque uiribus Hectora patrem
aequabis. Quantum tibi, nate, simillima imago
patris erat! Sic idem habitus, sic mens animusque!
Tune puer terror Graium, tune ille futurus
excidio et gentem ferro extincturus Achiuam!
290 At quoniam fueras puer et nondum integer aeui,
seruatum a Fatis rebar. Sed dira luisti
supplicia et poenas quae Laomedonta manebant:
Nil ueritum in diuos peccare, et culpa nepotes
criminis insontes tetigit. Nunc ite Pelasgi,
295 ite alacres! Tutum nunc scindite nauibus aequor!
O superum rex magne tonans, si tangeris ulla
erga homines pietate, nefas ulciscere tantum.
Nunc iaculare ignes Argiuasque obrue puppes.
Perde salo Danaos, qui me crudelia nati
300 fata mei et lacerum fecerunt cernere corpus.
Hi sunt praeterita fletus quos nocte ferebat
coniugis umbra nimis mihi cognita. Quas, mea proles,
nunc statuam busto pompas, quem mortis honorem
supremum ex more aut quae nunc solemnia iungam?
305 Tota incensa iacet rapidis urbs diruta flammis.
Et quo te reddam tumulo? Priuaberis igni.
Heu quid agam? Cui me sorti delegit acerba
fortuna? O, si qua est pietas, euellite quaeso
hanc animam et nati sociam demittite ad umbras!
310 Talibus implebat caelum lacrimansque gemensque.
At uero interea fusi per littora Graii
aptabant classem redituurasque aequora nauis
cogebant. Tum Pyrrhus ouans et certus eundi,
cui sors Andromachen dederat, non pauca querentem
315 auulsit genitricem a cari funere nati,
solatus multum miseram puppique locauit.

62

to defeated peoples, nor will you equal your father Hector in   285
prowess. O my son, how closely you resembled your father, so like
was your demeanor, so like your ways of thought and your cour-
age! Will you, though a boy, be the terror of the Greeks, will you
be the person to bring about their ruin and to obliterate the
Achaean race with the sword? But since you were only a boy and
had not yet reached the fullness of youth, I had considered you in-   290
violate by fate. But you paid the dreadful penalty, you suffered the
punishment that was due Laomedon. He had no misgivings about
committing a crime against the gods, and his wrongdoing has
touched his descendants, guiltless of the fault. On your way now,
Greeks, on your way with all haste! Plough a path now through
the waters made safe for your vessels! O Thunderer, mighty king   295
of the gods, if you are touched by any pity toward humans, avenge
this grievous wrong. Hurl now your fire bolts and overwhelm the
Argive ships. Destroy at sea the Danai who forced me to see the
cruel death of my son and to behold his body in shreds. These are   300
the sorrows which the shade I well recognized of my husband
brought to me during the night now past. Now, my child, what
cortege will I form for your burial, what final honor, due to cus-
tom, will I now offer for your death, what solemn rite? The whole
city lies in ruins from the fierce fires that are burning. In what   305
burial-mound will I place you? You will want for fire. Alas, what
will I do? For what fate has bitter fortune selected me? O, if you
have any pity, I beseech you, pluck out this life and send me as my
son's companion to the shades!"

With such tearful lamentation and moans she surfeited the   310
heavens. Meanwhile the Greeks assembled on the shore to outfit
their fleet. The seas urged the vessels to set out for their return.
Then Pyrrhus, to whom Andromache had fallen by lot, exulting
in the certainty of their going, tore the mother, still in the throes
of grief, from the corpse of her dear son, and, offering much com-   315
fort to the forlorn woman, placed her on board. Then all took

Inde omnes uentis tendentes uela secundis
cessere et patrias laeti petiere Mycenas.

FINIS.
PAPIAE MCCCCXXX IDIBUS JUNIIS.

their departure, stretching the sheets toward the favorable winds, and set joyful course for their homeland, Mycenae.

THE END.
PAVIA, JUNE 13, 1430

VELLUS AUREUM

Liber Primus

Egregium canere Aesonidam iuvenesque Pelasgos
institui, quos prima ratis maria alta secantes
Phasiacam advexit Colchon. Non longa movebo
terrarum et vasti vitata pericula ponti,
5   non repetam Peliae invidiam, libet horrida caeci
fata senis, libet obscenas tacuisse volucres,
quas Borea geniti Calaïs Zetusque fugarunt.
Praeterea, quantis affecta est Troia tellus
excidiis duro sub Laomedonte, silebo.
10   Vos quoque, Lemniades, animosa et mascula turba,
quis prius arma placent, mox conubialia iura,
te, blanda Hypsipyle, vel te, furiosa Polyxo,
transierim et quicquid, medias dum transfretat undas,
Argolica effecit magnum et memorabile pubes.
15   Sola autem, quae sunt Colchorum in litore gesta,
expediam, raptum Phrixeae pellis honorem,
vesanosque sequar Medeae ardentis amores.
Vos memorate, deae, veteresque resolvite causas
— res antiqua ingens et non obscura sub antris
20   Aoniis — ; quae me totiens Helicona moventem
iuvistis, vestro rursum succurrite vati!
     Iam longas emensa vias Argiva iuventus
attigerat portus et Aëtae moenia regis,
cum subito totam vulgatur fama per urbem
25   advenisse viros externi e partibus orbis;
visura ergo duces gens undique barbara fertur.
Nunc ingentem Argo securo pondere in ipsis

THE GOLDEN FLEECE

Book I

I have set for my task to sing of the excellent son of Aeson and the
young men of Greece whom, furrowing the seas' depths, the first
ship bore to Colchis on the Phasis river. I will not pursue the
many perils they escaped on land and on the broad ocean. I will
not review the envy of Pelias, I gladly leave unsaid the dreadful   5
destiny of the blind old man, gladly the obscene birds, which
Calais and Zetus, offspring of Boreas, put to flight. I will remain
silent as well about the massive destruction which the land of Troy
suffered under stubborn Laomedon. You also, women of Lemnos,
a spirited and mannish crowd, whose pleasure was first in weap-   10
onry, then in the rites of marriage, I should pass by, you, seductive
Hypsipyle, or you, fierce Polyxo, and whatever grand and worthy
of memory the youths of Greece accomplished, as they voyaged
through the midst of the waves. I will recount only deeds done
on the Colchian shore. I will pursue the stolen glory of Phrixus's   15
fleece and the frenzied passion of enflamed Medea. Give voice,
o goddesses, and broach the ancient sources — mighty is the affair,
hoary, and not lacking in renown in the grottoes of Aonia. You,
who have so often granted assistance as I scaled Helicon, lend   20
your bard aid once more.

Having already traversed the lengthy ways, the Greek youth
had reached the harbor and the bastions of king Aeëtes, when
suddenly a rumor ranges through the whole city that men have ar-
rived from distant parts of the earth. So the barbarian folk betake   25
themselves from everywhere about to cast their eyes on the heroes.
Now they are awed by the mighty Argo, its weight steadied confi-

perstantem mirantur aquis, nunc ipsa virorum
corpora florentesque annos formamque decusque,
30 et quos esse putent moresque habitusque deorum.
Ipse quoque insolitum rumorem Sole satus rex
miratus tantam dubitavit credere molem
per vastas rupes, rapidum volitasse per aequor.
Inde viros, avidus scitari et discere causas
35 eventusque viae, iubet ad se in tecta vocari.
    Olli adventabant laeti, quorum Aesone natus
primus paciferae ramum gestabat olivae;
post clari Aeacidae atque ingens Meleager et acres
Tyndaridae gemini geminique Aquilone creati
40 atque una Admetus praestans Idasque superbus
et Lynceus et, quem Pelias generarat, Acastus.
Tum solitus rabidos cithara mulcere leones
semideos inter reges convenerat Orpheus;
docti etiam vates, quos provida cura futuri
45 addiderat, senior Mopsus, sed puberis aevi
absorptus nondum vasto Amphiaraus hiatu,
quique incurvatas agilis Polyphemus aristas
securusque maris stantes percurreret undas,
inde Periclymenus, magnam cui magnus aquarum
50 vim rector dederat, fortisque Leodocus et, qui
progenitus fuerat forti ex Alcone, Phalerus,
tum Nestor senior nondum, tum magnus Oïleus,
Mercurioque Erytus simul et prognatus Echion,
Eurydamasque satus Ctimeno, satus atque Menoetheus
55 Actore, quos pariterque Arcas generarat Alëus,
Amphidamas Cepheusque, et, quem Eupolemeïa partu
edidit, Aethalides; hinc Lerni filius ibat
Iphiclus, Aesonidaeque ingentis avunculus, alter
Iphiclus, inde Phlias, Neptuni et bina propago
60 Erginus Ancaeusque simul, tum viribus ingens

dently in the very waves, now by the men's mighty bodies, in the springtime of their lives, their handsomeness and charm. Their behavior and bearing they consider to be those of gods. The king himself also, seed of the Sun, astonished at the unwonted report, hesitated to believe that such a mighty ship had sped between huge crags and through strong-rushing seas. Eager, then, to inquire further of the men, and to learn the occasion and the experiences of their journey, he orders that they be summoned to him at his palace. 30

35

Joyfully they made their entrance, with the son of Aeson at their head, bearing a branch of olive as sign of peace; after him the famous offspring of Aeacus and mighty Meleager, the eager Tyndarid twins and twins sprung from the North Wind, with them matchless Admetus and proud Idas, and Lynceus and Acastus whom Pelias had begotten. Orpheus, too, used to taming ravenous lions with his lyre, had come as ally among the half-immortal heroes. There were also learned seers whom prudent awareness of the time that lay ahead had added: aged Mopsus and Amphiaraus, young in years, not yet swallowed by the earth's gigantic maw, and nimble Polyphemus who could skim, and leave unbent, the tops of wheat blades and, scatheless, the sea's up-reaching waves; then Periclymenus, on whom the mighty controller of waters had bestowed vast strength, and brave Leodokos and Phalerus, who was descended from brave Alkon; then Nestor, not yet aged, then mighty Oileus, and Erytus and Echion with him, offspring of Mercury, and Eurydamas, seed of Ctimenos, and Menoetheus, seed of Actor, and Amphidamas and Cepheus whom Arcadian Aleus had begotten at one and the same time, and Aethalides to whom Eupolemeia had given birth; then came Iphiclus, the son of Lernus, and the uncle of the stalwart son of Aeson, another Iphiclus; next Phlias, and Erginus and with him Ancaeus, double scions of Neptune, then Laocoon, mighty in 40

45

50

55

60

Laocoon, dehinc Eurytion Butesque Coronusque
Amphionque simul, simul Asteriusque simulque
Asterion, post Augias, post Clytius atque
Iphitus, Euryto geniti, genitique Biante
65   egregii Talausque Ariusque; hinc cetera pubes.
      Tot tantique duces gressum intra tecta ferebant
regia, praesigni rex maiestate verendus
sceptra tenens sese sublimi in sede locarat.
Quos postquam circumspexit laetumque notavit
70   luminibus lustrans oculorum et frontis honestum
eximiumque decus specimenque insigne iuventae,
ingentesque animos ingenti in corpore vidit,
obstupuit tanto aspectu casuque virorum.
Tum, quibus advecti veniant, inquirit, ab oris,
75   unde genus, quae causa viae, quo cursus euntes
compulerit.
           Quaerentem illum facundus Iason
affatur placidoque has fundit pectore voces:
'Non alias sedes aliosve exquirere portus
venimus, hanc certo, bone rex, adnavimus urbem
80   proposito: Tua nos nostro vulgata sub orbe
fama per immensum pelagus, per longa coegit
ire loca et primam ventis committere navim.
Nos clarae bello gentes, nos inter eundum
et populi et magni socios voluere tyranni
85   in partem et regni foedus commune vocantes;
sed te, quem miro famae immortalis amore
per maria et scopulos petimus, te scilicet unum
et tua praetulimus oblatis litora regnis!
Quippe, nisi in nostris narrata est fabula terris,
90   rumor iit durae statui hic certamina pugnae,
quae victori amplam laudem pretiumque superbum
afferrent, pretium spectabile velleris aurei,

strength; after them Eurytion and Butes, Coronus and with him
Amphion, as well as Asterius together with Asterion; then
Augias, after him Clytius and Iphitus, offspring of Eurytus, and
Talaus and Arius, splendid offspring of Bias, then the rest of the
company.   65

While the heroes, so many and so great, were making entrance
inside the royal palace, the king, worthy of reverence in preemi-
nent majesty, had seated himself on his lofty throne, scepter in
hand. After he had surveyed them and took note, with his clear
eyes, of the extraordinary noble grace of their cheerful brows and   70
their youth's remarkable resplendence, and seen their vast courage
in their vast physique, he was astonished at the spectacle of the
men and at their circumstances. Whereupon he asks from what
shore they come in their travels, whence their race, what was the
reason for their voyage, whither their course had driven them on   75
their way.

To his inquiry Jason eloquently replies as he pours forth these
words from his calm heart: "We have come in search of no other
locale, no other harbor. We have set sail, good king, toward this
city in certainty of purpose: your reputation, broadcast through   80
our region, urged us to make our way through the measureless sea,
through place after place, and to entrust our ship, the first, to the
winds. As we traveled, races famed in war, both powerful peoples
and kings, have craved us as allies, summoning us to share in the
common compact of rule; but it is you whom, over seas and past   85
crags, we seek, out of singular love for undying repute, you alone,
be assured, and your shores we have preferred to realms tendered
us! For, unless a false tale is bruited in our lands, rumor has gone
forth that here hard-fought contests have been instituted which   90
bring to the victor fulsome praise and a prize in which to glory, the
remarkable prize of the golden fleece, on which, they say, Phrixus

quo quondam Phrixum dicunt trans aequora vectum:
Hunc equidem, modo sit tua non adversa voluntas,
95   hunc ausim nostris gestis bene rebus honorem
adicere atque ipsis virtutem ostendere factis.
Nec tibi vile putes titulis ascribere nostris
rem tantam: Non hac indigni laude feremur
nec nos degeneres spolio indecoresve querere.
100   Progeniti e regum sumus alto et sanguine divum;
Graia tulit tellus, quae tot generavit alumnos
illustres virtute: Pater mihi Thessalus Aeson,
Alcimede est genetrix.' Simul haec effatus et una
percurrens sociorum animos stirpesque docebat:
105   Nunc clarum Oeniden, nunc magnos nomine monstrans
Aeacidas simul et formosae pignora Ledae
et Boreae insignes gnatos et singula Graium
corpora, quos verbis memorans laudabat amicis.
Tum vestes, quas ferre, deis dum sacra ferebat,
110   assuerat patruus, gemmis auroque rigentes
gestamenque patris sceptrum dat munera regi.
    Ille, ut iam dudum iuvenis pendebat ab ore
Haemonii, non muneribus donisve movetur
textilibus, sed enim tacito sub corde volutans
115   fortunas casusque virum patriamque genusque
et dignas voces et magniloquentia verba
cunctantem Aesonidam tali est sermone secutus:
    'Haud ego vos humili genitos de stirpe, Pelasgi,
crediderim, quos tanta animi vis, tanta cupido
120   impulit has tentare vias, haec quaerere tecta;
nec vero prorsus gentem ignoramus Achivam,
virtutes laudesque virum: Sunt cognita nobis
vestra etiam, quae iam toto celebrantur in orbe
nomina. Quod totiens avida cum mente petivi
125   nosse aliquos gente e Danaum, nunc obtulit ultro

once traveled across the waters: for my part this honor, provided
your inclination is not averse, this honor I would dare to add to
our exploits well done, to manifest our courage through the ac-   95
complishment of new deeds. Please do not deem it insignificant
that we append such a feat to our exploits: we are not considered
unworthy of this praise nor should you worry that our race is infe-
rior and that we are unbecoming of the award. We are sprung
from the exalted blood of kings and gods; the land of Greece bore   100
us which produced so many offspring famed for courage: my fa-
ther is Aeson of Thessaly, Alcimede my mother." After these
words he reviewed in turn also the character and ancestry of his
comrades: pointing out by name now the famous son of Oeneus,
now the mighty offspring of Aeacus as well as the love-pledges of   105
beautiful Leda and the remarkable children of Boreas, and the
Greek warriors one by one, whom in his narration he praises with
affectionate words. Then he tenders as guest-presents to the king
robes, stiff with jewels and gold, which it was his uncle's custom to   110
don while he was making oblations to the gods, and a scepter, his
father's accouterment.

    Already now for some time rapt by the words of the young
Haemonian, the king is not moved by the offerings or the woven
gifts, but, pondering in the silence of his heart the destiny and ex-
periences of the heroes, their fatherland and ancestry, the merit of   115
their speech and their exalted words, he responded thus to the
waiting son of Aeson:

    "It would by no means have been my belief, Greeks, that you
were born from humble stock, you whom such force of character,
such ambition has driven to essay this voyage, to seek out this city;   120
nor is the Greek race altogether unknown to us, its courage and its
heroic exploits. We are even aware of your names which are now
extolled through the world's extent. Time of its own accord has
now offered us the unexpected—something I yearned for so often
with eager thoughts—to make the acquaintance of members of   125

insperata dies; ut vos laetusque libensque
accipio, o iuvenes, ut vos audire loquentes
amplectique simul iuvat et contingere dextras!
Dona quoque haud sperno, sed vos per si qua putatis
130   numina, per genitorem oro: Ne fidite, Grai,
posse capi haec vestra petitis quae vellera dextra!
Nullae hic humanae possunt obsistere vires;
sola Hecate, solae hic herbae cantusque deorum
militis instar agunt pugnam: Primum ardua colla
135   tollentes gemini flammato corpore tauri
occurrent, quibus Aetnaeo non segnior igne est
spiritus, infernis nec cederet ille caminis.
Esto autem taurorum acres exstinguier ignes,
quis non vipereo sub terram semine iacto
140   armigeros fratres mediis horrescet in arvis
nascentes capitique suo crudele minantes
exitium, quis demum asprum immanemque draconem
tuto adeat taetrum informem, cui lumina semper
insopita trucique ardescunt ignea visu?
145   Vos, lecti, moneo, o proceres, ne pergite tantum
praecipitare animas vestris et fidere dextris;
dum dubia est et causa recens, absistite tanto
congressu, fugite haec pretiosa pericula, quaeso!
Si vos tangit amor duris opponere bellis
150   magnarumque trahit praedulcis gloria rerum,
non deerunt pugnae, non monstra rebellia deerunt.
Ite alio, celebrem melius perquirite famam;
sin libeat nostris etiam consistere regnis,
accipio socios casusque amplector in omnes.'
155   Dixit et Aesonidam Gaetuli pelle leonis
et pharetra insigni donat, quae munera Phoebus
primaevis genitor dederat gestare sub annis;
prosequitur reliquos et in omnes munera fundit.

74

the Greek race. How happily, how willingly I receive you, young
friends, what delight I have as well in hearing you speak, embrac-
ing you, touching your hands! By no means do I despise your
gifts. Still I beseech you, by any gods you believe in, by your fa-
ther: do not be confident, o Greeks, that this fleece, which is your   130
goal, can be won by your force of hand! In this instance human
might has no chance of success. Only Hecate, only magic herbs
and incantations of the gods can here do battle in soldierly fash-
ion. First twin bulls, rearing their lofty necks, bodies ablaze, will   135
confront you (their breath is no more torpid than the fire of Etna,
nor would it concede anything to the furnaces of the underworld).
Be it, however, that the bulls' brisk flames are quenched, who,
since serpent's teeth are spread beneath the soil, will not stand in
terror of the armed brethren, coming to birth in the midst of the   140
fields and threatening a cruel finale to his life? Who, at the last,
can safely approach the savage monster of a dragon, repulsive, ugly,
whose sleepless, fiery eyes ever glow with pitiless gaze? I warn you,
chosen princes: do not be in such haste to throw your lives away   145
and to trust in your own ability; while the situation is still fresh
and unresolved, avoid such a confrontation; flee, I pray you, these
costly dangers! If yearning provokes you to face wars' harshness
and if honeyed repute from heroic deeds is your lure, there is no   150
absence of places for battle, none of monsters given to war. Betake
yourselves elsewhere, seek out a better reason to broadcast your
glory; but if it is also your pleasure to settle in our realm, I receive
and embrace you as allies, whatever circumstances are in the
offing."

His words concluded, Aeëtes presents the son of Aeson with   155
the pelt of a Gaetulian lion and a remarkable quiver, gifts which
his father, Phoebus, had bestowed on him in his youth to wear.
He recognizes the others and lavishes gifts on all.

Tum vero Danaos intra penetralia ducit,
160 interiora domus; tum magna palatia et altis
parietibus sublata auroque ardentia tecta
atque amplas manifestat opes monstratque suorum
caelatas ebore effigies et facta parentum:
Illic Sol pater eius erat, quem veste sub aurea
165 intonsumque comas et pubescentibus annis
et flavos rutilo cinctum diademate crines
cernere erat, stantem curru cum verbere in alto
alipedesque feros moderantem et lora tenentem,
caelo etiam legem vitamque et lumina toti
170 et mentem et fetus mundoque alimenta ferentem
temperiem lucemque astris; dehinc pronus in undas
occiduas ubi flectit equos, mox iussa sequentes
accurrunt celeres Horae solvuntque iugales
frenaque diripiunt, quae dente sonantia mandunt;
175 pascua deinde vocant, ibi molli gramine dulcis
ambrosiae pascuntur equi; roseum ille colorem
mutata induitur palla; tum caespite fessus
in viridi sedet agresti et modulatur avena.
Talibus atque aliis, quae circum plurima Solis
180 divina infabricata manu monimenta videbant,
affixi stabant iuvenes, sed dura laborum
dum fata et casus secum meditantur acerbos,
quos monitu rex Aeëtes memorarat amico—
sive boum flammas insopitumque draconem
185 terrigenas alto fratres seu pectore versant.
Ingentes ea vox et curas concipit acres
laetaque magnarum turbat spectacula rerum—
non secus ac quando silvas et pascua circum
convenere ferae, saltus mirantur apricos,
190 mirantur nitidos fontes fluviosque lacusque:

Thereafter the king escorts the Greeks within his dwelling's in-
nermost chambers; he discloses the palace's grandeur, its ceilings   160
blazing with gold, raised on lofty walls, and its extensive wealth.
He shows off the portraits of his ancestors, chased in ivory, and
their deeds. There to behold, in robe of gold, was his father, the
Sun, in the years of his youth, hair untrimmed and blonde locks   165
encircled by a glowing red diadem. He was standing on his lofty
chariot, controlling his winged-footed steeds with a whip and
holding the reins, bringing order to the heavens, life and light,
zest, fruitfulness and nourishment to the whole earth, measured   170
light to the stars. Then, when headlong he bends his horses into
the western waves, in obedience to his commands the swift Horae
rush to release the team and pull off the clanking bit which they
champ with their teeth. Then pasture beckons them; there the   175
horses feed on the soft fodder of sweet ambrosia. Changing dress
the Sun clothes himself in a roseate hue. Then, tired out, he takes
his seat on the grassy turf and makes music on a rustic pipe.

The young men stood awestruck by such and many other mon-
uments, that were made by the Sun's immortal hand, which they   180
saw around them, while they yet ponder to themselves the harsh
challenges that impend, about which king Aeëtes had forewarned
with friendly counsel—whether their thoughts deep in their
hearts turn to the fire-breathing bulls and the sleepless dragon or
to the earth-born brethren. His words elicit concerns oppressive   185
and bitter, and trouble the joyous grandeur before their eyes, even
as when creatures of the wild amid forests and meadows have
gathered together, they admire the sun-drenched glades, admire
the glistening springs and streams and pools; but if the chance   190

Quodsi audita canum vox forte perhorruit aures,
nec nitidos fontes iuvat aut invisere saltus.
   Interea largo completur regia luxu:
Longa manus famulorum intus, quos ardua tangit
195 cura domus, adolent ignes epulasque calentes,
Bacchumque Cereremque parant atque ordine mensas
disponunt, laeto strepit omnis curia motu.
Conveniunt senior rex una et Graia iuventus,
fundunturque manus lymphis ostroque superbo
200 discumbunt stratisque super de more tapetis.
Venerat et iussu cari Medea parentis:
Filia regis erat, spes sceptri et gloria magni,
nondum iuncta viro; fulgenti colla monili
ornaratque auro crines et texerat aurea
205 se palla, qua Sol patrem donaverat olim.
Mirum illi ingenium, magicos doctissima cantus,
herbarum et pariter lapidum cognoverat usum.
Ipsa sua aeripedes tauros fabricaverat arte,
vipereos etiam dentes saevumque draconem.
210 Quae postquam stetit ante patrem mensaeque paratos
externos vidit iuvenes, deiecit honestos
in terram subito vultus laetumque ruborem est
fassa genis; tum vero inter discumbere reges
rex gnatam iubet et consistere Iasone coram.
215 Inde ferunt epulas et munera larga Lyaei;
vescitur Aeëtes, pariter vescuntur Achivi.

Liber Secundus

At Venus aetherei iam dudum e culmine caeli
formosum Aesonidam spectans pubemque Pelasgam

baying of distant hounds has terrified their ears, they find no pleasure in the contemplation of glistening fountains or glades.

Meantime pomp in abundance fills the palace. Bands of servants, whose challenge was the dwelling's care, spread out within, foster fires to keep the banquet warm, procure wine and bread, and set the tables in order. The entire hall reechoed with joyous bustling. The aged king and the Greek youth meet together, their hands are washed with water, and they recline on august purple over which are strewn the customary coverlets. At her dear father's behest Medea had also come. She was the king's daughter, the hope and the glory of his mighty reign, not yet joined to a husband. She had bejeweled her throat with a gleaming necklace, had adorned her hair with gold and had clothed herself in a dress of gold which the Sun had once bestowed on her father. Her intelligence was astonishing, and, deeply schooled in magic charms, she had learned the manipulation of herbs as well as pebbles. By her artistry she herself had fashioned the brazen-footed bulls along with the serpent's teeth and the ferocious dragon. After she stood before her father and caught sight of the foreign young men attired for the meal, she forthwith lowered her eyes toward the ground in modesty and her cheeks blushed red for joy. Thereupon the king orders his daughter to take her place at table among the heroes and to take the spot next to Jason. Then they serve the courses and the plenteous gifts of Bacchus. Aeëtes commences to dine; the Greeks sup along with him.

195

200

205

210

215

Book II

But Venus, for a long time watching from the crest of heaven's sky the handsome son of Aeson and the Greek youths, was moved by

commota est pietate gravisque pericula casus
et sortem crudelem animo non pertulit aequo.
5   Nondum illa Argivas partes infensa premebat,
Tyndaridem nondum Phrygius raptarat adulter.
    Tum secum: 'Patiarne malis se pulcher Iason
obiectet tantis? Eane est clementia nostri
numinis? Ergo illum taurorum occurrere flammis
10   absumique sinam? Vigili ergo praeda draconi
is dabitur? Terraque satis tot ab hostibus unus
ille petetur? Ego patiar? Nec vivida virtus
nec me nobilitas nec me sua forma movebit?
Praeterea genus invisum numquamne licebit
15   ulcisci Solis stirpem, qui nuntius olim
haud timuit nostros claudo monstrare marito
concubitus dulces nostrosque et Martis amores?
Stat totam vexare domum saevosque calores
moliri et rapidis incendere pectora flammis.
20   Quocirca Medeam, ipso de sanguine natam,
quam primum Haemonii stringam magno hospitis igne:
Sola virum a tantis potis est servare periclis.'
    Ergo pharetratum diva his cum vocibus ultro
compellat gnatum: 'viden, o carissima proles,
25   magnanimum, nisi nos servamus, Iasona, quanto
nunc situs est sub dirarum discrimine rerum?
Vade age, nate, petas, inter convivia namque
Medeam invenies inter iuvenesque ducesque.
Nunc rem tempus agit: pharetra deprome sagittam
30   et tota vi intorque et corde reconde sub alto
virginis; Aesonidam, si tantum discat amare,
illa potest servare malis et solvere tantis.
I, celera, invisum Solisque ulciscere semen!
Ipsa etiam praesens adero viridemque iuventam

his piety and with an anxious mind she pondered their concerns, fraught with peril, and their cruel lot. (Not yet was she the harass- 5
ing enemy of the Greek forces; not yet had the Trojan adulterer carried off the daughter of Tyndareus).

Then to herself: "Shall I allow handsome Jason to be the victim of such evils? Is that the forbearance of our divine power? Will I, then, be party to his confronting the fire-breathing bulls and to his being wrenched away? Will he as a result be offered as prey to the 10
watchful dragon? Will he be alone the object of so many earth-be-gotten foes? Am I one to stand for this? Will neither the intensity of his bravery nor his noble bearing nor his comeliness affect me? Besides, will the chance never be mine to gain revenge on the hated line begotten of the Sun, who some while ago had no hesita- 15
tion in pointedly telling my lame husband of our sweet concourse and our amours with Mars? It is my decision to bring turmoil to the house, to stoke the embers of ferocity and set ablaze their hearts with a rush of flame. And so, as soon as possible, I will en- 20
gird Medea, sprung from this very blood, with a mighty fire for her Greek guest. She alone has the power to save him from such great dangers."

Thence the goddess following out her will accosts with these words her quiver-bearing son: "Do you see, my dearest child, in what a dread juncture of events high-souled Jason is now placed, 25
unless we save him? Go now, my son, and seek Medea out: you will discover her in the festivity's midst, in the midst of the youth-ful heroes. Now opportunity urges the matter on: snatch an arrow from your quiver, shoot it with all your force and bury it deeply into the maiden's heart; if she can but learn to love, she can save 30
the son of Aeson, and release him from his enormous woes. Take wing and hasten to extract vengeance from the hated offspring of the Sun. I myself will also be there at your side and will enhance

35 perpetuumque viri laeta sub fronte decorem
 et dulcem aspectum decus atque insigne iuvabo.'
  Nulla mora, exsequitur genetricis iussa Cupido.
 Virgo, ubi praevalidos concepit corde furores
 insuetosque ignes hausit, non amplius ullas
40 illa dapes, Bacchi non munera suavia curat:
 Tantum illam teneri flammata Cupidinis arma
 stringunt et caeco languentem vulnere carpunt—
 haud aliter, quam si pascentem in valle virenti
 et sapidas avidis tondentem dentibus herbas
45 forte venenata venator harundine dammam
 percussit, non illa herbas, non gramina curat,
 fixa sibi tantum letali in vulnere mens est:
 Tale Cupidineae vulnus Medea sagittae
 intus alit; solum miratur Iasona, solum
50 optat et insano paulatim ardescit amore.
 Nunc faciem illius, nunc pectus et ora tuetur,
 nunc umeros ambasque manus et eburnea colla
 sidereosque oculos et totum denique corpus,
 nunc hac, nunc illac intento lumine lustrat.
55 Dumque refert, quibus est nuper iactatus in alto,
 terribiles rerum facies durosque labores,
 sive sua eloquitur vel avorum facta suorum
 et mores et virtutes telluris Achivae,
 pendet et illa avidis voces atque auribus haurit
60 admirans animumque viri casusque sequaces
 magnumque et dulce eloquium consultaque verba
 et genus et patriam, mores cultusque locorum:
 Uritur et saevo torquetur Phasias igni.
 Non illi curae cantus plaususque virorum,
65 non citharae et laeti fremitus per tecta frequentes;
 infelicem illam maior nam cura premebat.

82

the freshness of the hero's youth, the enduring charm of his joyous   35
features, the sweetness of his visage and his unparalleled grace."

    In a twinkling Cupid proceeds to the execution of his mother's
commands. Once the girl conceived in her heart the intensity of
madness and drank in the unwonted flames, she gives no further
thought to food or to the pleasant gifts of Bacchus, so much does   40
the kindled weaponry of tender Cupid tighten her in its grip and
consume her, lovesick as she is, with a hidden wound: it's as if a
hunter with poisoned arrow has chanced to strike a doe, pasturing   45
in a green valley and greedily browsing the savory grasses: she gives
no thought to grasses, none to the greensward, so much is her
mind fixed upon the deadly wound. Such is the wound of Love's
arrow that Medea nourishes within. Jason alone mesmerizes her,
she desires only him and bit by bit is engulfed by mad love's   50
flames. Now she stares at his face, now at his chest and mouth,
now here, now there, she surveys intently his shoulders, his two
hands and ivory neck, his eyes like stars and finally his whole
frame. And while he tells of the hideous experiences by which he
was recently tossed on the deep and his hard times of trial, or   55
when he details his deeds or those of his ancestors, and the cus-
toms and merits of the land of Greece, she hangs on his words
and absorbs them with eager ears, awestruck at his courage, the
mischances that dog him, the sweet grandeur of his speech and el-   60
egance of word, his heritage and homeland and the customs ob-
served in each place. The girl from Phasis is aflame and racked by
fire's ferocity. No concern to her the songs and the audience's re-
sponse, the lyre and the happy roar reverberating through the pal-   65
ace, for a greater care was burdening the unlucky girl.

Postquam vescendi finis finisque loquendi,
secedunt Grai proceres multum ardua secum
fata revolventes et voces regis amaras.
70   Tum sic intrepidus socios compellat Iason:
'Quo nos crudelis casus, quo dira malorum
tantorum ignaros tulerit fortuna, videtis;
at potius statui caput obiectare periclis,
qualiacumque ea sint, et duro occumbere leto,
75   quam repetisse domum turpi terrore metuque;
dicamur simusque ignavi fabula vulgi?
Spero autem, si qua est virtutis gratia nostrae,
latura auxilium nostris pia numina coeptis.'
Talibus Aesonides mortem praeconcipit altam
80   dedignans miserae superesse cupidine vitae —
qualis, ubi in silvam venandi ductus amore
nobilitate animi praestans magnaque canis vi
ingentem et longe vidit maioribus aprum
viribus excellentem, illi sua conscia virtus
85   dat stimulos, pudet ingenuum cor cedere, et ultro
congreditur pulchroque mori in discrimine mavult.
Virgo autem thalami secreta in parte sedebat
multa gemens validosque agitans insana furores:
Iamque peregrinum iuvenem miseratur opemque
90   afferre et carum proponit prodere patrem
externasque sequi patriasque relinquere sedes.
Vile sibi est natale solum, sibi vile paternum
et studium et nomen: Tantum sibi Thessalis ora est
dulcis et Haemonius tantum sibi dulcis Iason!
95   Vidit ab excelso caram Sol vertice prolem
incensam flammis graviter Venerisque superbam
infensae mentem atque odium vetus intellexit.
Indoluit meditansque diu, qua virginis ignes
exstinxisse via posset, sic Pallada demum

After an end had come to eating, an end to conversation, the Greek princes withdraw to ponder deeply the challenges of destiny and the king's bitter pronouncements.

Then, unperturbed, Jason thus challenges his comrades: "You 70 behold whither our cruel lot and the dread adversity of evil piled on evil has brought us in our ignorance. Still I have decided to hazard my life to the dangers, whatsoever they are, and to fall prey to a harsh death rather than to return home in an ignoble, fearful manner. Are we to be labeled cowards and made a tale of by the 75 common people? It is my trust, however, that, if there is any thanks for our courage, the gods in their pity will bring their help to what we have begun."

With such words the son of Aeson envisions a valiant death, disdaining to survive out of desire for wretched life: as when a 80 hound, excelling in nobility of mind and in vigor of limb, tempted into the forest out of desire for the hunt, has sighted from afar a stalwart boar, transcendent for his surpassing strength; knowledge of his courage goads him on, his gallant heart is ashamed to yield, of his own accord he closes in and prefers to meet death in a glori- 85 ous contest.

The girl, meanwhile, was sitting in a sequestered part of her chamber, groaning deeply and in wildness of mind exciting her frenzy's force; immediately she pities the foreign youth and makes up her mind to offer him help and betray her dear father as well as 90 to abandon her home and to seek alien lands. Her native soil seems worthless to her, worthless the support and reputation of her father. Only the shore of Thessaly seems sweet to her and only Jason of Haemonia seems sweet!

The Sun from his lofty vantage saw how deeply his dear prog- 95 eny flared with love's flame, and he recognized the hostility of Venus's proud spirit and her ancient hatred. Sorrow filled him and, after pondering at length how he might quench the girl's passion,

100 alloquitur: 'Te, diva, unam pro sanguine nostro
divorum ex omni numero poscoque rogoque:
Medeam insidiis Veneris gnatique potentis
obsequio gravibus torqueri — en, aspice — flammis!
Tantum illa immortale odium sub pectore gestat,
105 tantum illa insontes perstat punire nepotes!
Nescius at vero non sum, quam fida tuorum
sacrorum fuerit cultrix atque omne per aevum
te virgo observaverit haec; quam scilicet ob rem
te curam gerere et misereri ardentis alumnae,
110 diva, decet. Tu sola potes contemnere tectas
et blandas Veneris fraudes, tu sola sagittas
despicere auratas caecique Cupidinis arcus
Vulcanumque tuo potuisti arcere cubili!
Praeterea pater omnipotens te prae omnibus unam
115 diligit exauditque volens tua vota libensque:
Perge patremque roga! Si patrem forte rogaris,
forte pater praestabit opem — vel, si qua supersit,
perge alia et succurre via.' Nec plura locutus.
      Tum dea: 'Me talem dignum est assumere curam.'
120 Dixit et ante Iovem simul astitit atque ita fatur:
'Magne parens, si nata tuo de vertice tantum,
si sine matre fui, da carae munera gnatae
haud indigna: Meam liceat, pater optime, alumnam
Aeëta genitore satam servare furentem,
125 quam pharetratus Amor nil dignam vulnere tali
flammifera incautam transfixit harundine nuper.
Fac puer immitis quae fecit vulnera curet,
fac revocet flammas et amaros sanet amores!
Si iubeas, genitor, nimirum iussa facesset.'
130   Dixerat, orantique pater dedit oscula gnatae;
talia deinde refert: 'Nulla est res ardua tantum,
tam dura ac perdifficilis, quam pro te ego, gnata,

he thus at last addresses Pallas: "You alone, o goddess, from the   100
whole assembly of the gods, I call upon in prayer on behalf of my
offspring. Watch, behold for yourself, how Medea, through the
wiles of Venus and the allegiance of her powerful son, is tortured
by formidable flames! So massive is the undying hatred she carries
in her heart, so obdurate is she to punish my guiltless descen-   105
dants! I also remain fully aware of how faithful an adherent of
your rites the girl has been and how she has honored you at every
stage of her life. Wherefore it is unquestionably fitting, goddess, to
pay heed and pity your passion-driven devotee. You alone are ca-
pable of disdaining Venus's subtle, seductive guile, you alone have   110
the power to scorn the gilded arrows and bow of unseen Cupid
and to bar Vulcan from your bedchamber! Besides, the almighty
father prefers you alone before everyone and gladly inclines a will-
ing ear to your prayers. Make haste and ask your father! Perhaps   115
if you ask your father, perhaps your father will grant aid. Or if
there is any other course available, hurry and take it." He spoke no
further.

The goddess in reply: "It is only right that I enter on such a
task." She spoke, and at once stood before Jupiter and addresses   120
him thus: "Mighty father, if I was born from your head alone, if I
lacked a mother, grant to your dear daughter a request fully wor-
thy of you. Grant me, best of fathers, the possibility of saving my
nursling, the raging daughter of Aeëtes, whom just now, while she
was unwary and undeserving of such a wound, the quivered Love-   125
god pierced with his smoldering arrow. See to it that the pitiless
boy cure the wounds he has made; make him summon back his
flames and heal the bitterness of love. If you were to give the order,
father, he would no doubt follow it through."

When her words of prayer were finished, the father kissed his   130
daughter. He then thus replies: "No task is so venturesome, none
so hard and bristling with challenge that, my daughter, I would re-

efficere aut ulla ratione subire recusem.
Tu modo, quorumcumque capax est nostra potestas,
135   posce: Feres, quaecumque mihi concedere fas est.
Ius ego et imperium superos sum nactus in omnes,
sed tamen ille suo totum deus aliger arcu,
qui caelum et pariter totum qui territat orbem,
ille quoque, et non infitiar, me territat, unus
140   me premit et capiti nostro ferus ille Cupido
imperat et quas vult leges et foedera ponit
devincitque manus et duris colla catenis.
Illum ego flammatis miscentem bella sagittis
temnentemque, meum si fulmen ab aethere mittam,
145   horresco; longe teloque ac viribus impar
illi ego cedo uni victus: De fortibus ille
quippe viris, de semideis de disque triumphat!
At quia de nostro tantum capite orta fuisti
nec tibi conceptae corrupta et foeda libido
150   affuit, idcirco crudum contemnere gnatum
matris Acidaliae potes et servare cubile
intactum; nunc, si quod habes, aliunde petendum est
auxilium et magno studio curaque ferendum.'
    Iuppiter haec. Tanto stupefacta est diva virago
155   affatu; dehinc illa leves delapsa per auras
Colchon adit magnique aedes atque atria regis
intrat et annosae faciem vestemque parentis
induitur baculoque infirmos sustinet artus
fitque Trophe, nutrix Medeae et callida custos.
160   Atque ubi maerentem graviter lacrimisque madentem
singultusque acres ducentem agnovit alumnam,
secretas tandem causas narrare coegit.
His ergo coepit verbis Medea profari:
    'Cara, pudet, nutrix, nostri vesana fateri
165   vota et praerapidos flammati pectoris ignes;

fuse on any pretext to accomplish or take on for you. Do you only
ask for whatever our power is capable. You will take as yours what-
ever it is right for me to bestow. I myself have laid claim to com-   135
manding rule over all the gods on high. But nevertheless that
winged god, who with his bow brings terror to the whole of the
heavens as well as to the whole terrestrial orb, he, I will not deny
it, also terrifies me, he alone, that wild Cupid, holds me in thrall   140
and rules my existence. He lays down the laws and limits that he
desires, and tightly binds our hands and neck with heavy chains. I
live in dread of him as he brews battles with his flaming arrows
and scorns me, even when I hurl my thunderbolt from on high.
Far out-classed in armament and in strength, I, even I, yield to   145
him alone. You can see how he triumphs over the heroes, over
demigods and over gods. But since only you were sprung from our
head, nor did the taint of foul lust share in your conceiving, on
this account you have the power to disdain the savage child of his   150
Acidalian mother and to keep chaste your bedchamber. As for
now, you must seek help elsewhere, if any is available, and it must
be brought to bear with abundant energy and will."

These were Jupiter's words. The warrior goddess was taken
aback by such a response. Then, slipping through the nimble   155
breezes, she approaches Colchis and enters the hallway of the
mighty king's palace. She dons the features and clothing of an aged
foster-mother and supports her weakened limbs with a cane, to
become Trophe, nurse and astute guardian of Medea. And when
she recognized her devotee in the depths of mourning, drenched
with tears and sighing bitterly, she compelled her at last to explain   160
the reasons which she had kept to herself. And so with these
words Medea began to speak:

"Dear nurse, shame overcomes me to confess the maddened
prayers and wild fires in my flame-engulfed breast. I had not ex-   165

nec porro tanta hac affligi peste malorum
speravi nec tam duris succumbere poenis.
Sed me nescio quis torquet deus et mea saevo
flammarum exagitans aestu praecordia versat
170   sollicitisque angit curis carpitque premitque.
Vidistin proceres, Grais quos nuper ab oris
hospitio advectos genitor suscepit amico?
Quis vultus, quae forma viris! Quo pectore, qua vi
praestant, et quanta est laeto facundia in ore!
175   Unde ortos sese narrant, quot tristia passos
quotve horrenda ausos! Quorum lectissimus unus
et forma et virtute omnes excellit Iason.
Quantum illi sedet egregius decor oris et altae
maiestatis honos facundae et gratia linguae!
180   Quam nisi de dira conceptam tigride talis
non moveat, non ingenti perstringat amore?
Quae, nisi ferrea sit, tuto spectare cadentem
hunc talem et nulla poterit pietate moveri?
Certe ego tunc rabidas vincam feritate leaenas,
185   hunc si flammivomis moriturum occurrere tauris
terrigenisque sinam populis vastoque draconi!
At mihi non ea mens nec ea est sententia tantum
crudelis, iuvenem pereuntem ut cernere possim
simque ego causa necis, quae vitam afferre necemque
190   sola potis sum, sola viro concedere palmam.
Ergo libet servare meum incautumque monere
Aesonidam: Revocabo artes divamque triformem
et, quo sint subigenda modo quaecumque, docebo.
Sed tamen ille prius praestabit iura fidemque,
195   et face legitima iungemur et omine certo.
Ipsum illum sequar Argolicas regina per urbes,
quaque ibo, forsan clari reddentur honores.
Nec me autem fallit, quam taetrum immaneque factum

pected until a later time to be afflicted with this pernicious disease
nor to yield to such harsh torture. But some god or other tor-
ments me, twists my inner self, embroiling it in a ferocious swirl of
fire, strangles me, rends me, weighs me down with troubling cares.   170
Have you seen the princes, recently arrived by ship from the
shores of Greece, whom our father has received in hospitality and
friendship? What features, what a handsome appearance is theirs!
With what mettle, what courage they stand out, how refined the
eloquence that flows from their glad lips! They tell the tale of their   175
origins, of how many sufferings they have endured, of the horrors
they have dared! One of them, Jason, surpasses all in excellence of
beauty and nobility. Of what extraordinarily graceful features he is
possessed, what dignity in his lofty bearing and how attractive his
eloquence of speech! Whom, unless the offspring of a dread ti-   180
gress, would such a one not move, not constrain, with a mighty
love? Who, unless fashioned of iron, would be able to watch from
a safe vantage while someone like him succumbs, and not be
touched by pity? For sure I would then surpass gnashing lionesses   185
in savagery if I would allow him to die while confronting the
flame-spewing bulls and the earth-born tribe and the enormous
dragon! But that is not my nature, nor is my disposition so cruel
that I could behold the youth perishing and I be the reason for his
death — I who alone am able to extend him life and death, alone
grant the hero victory. It is my wish, therefore, to keep the fool-   190
hardy son of Aeson as mine and to caution him: I will summon
once more my arts and the goddess of triple shape, and I will teach
him how each adventure needs be approached. Nevertheless, be-
fore this occurs, he will furnish pledges of faith, and we will be
joined in a union legal and approved by heaven. He is the one I   195
will follow as queen through the cities of Argos, and wherever I
will make my way, worthy honors will perchance be offered me. I
have no illusions how ugly and monstrous a deed I propose, with

aggrediar, quanto dulces maerore parentes
200   afficiam, quos sim patriae latura dolores;
sed rapido feror igne, nec est tolerabile nostrum
hoc quodcumque malum est: Patrem patriosque penates
deserere est animus, dum tantum munere nostro
servatus sibi me iungat formosus Iason.'
205   Finierat lacrimans, contra sic diva locuta est:
'Tantane te, dulce o pignus, dementia cepit,
tanta animi nox, ut caeco succumbere amori
externoque sinas te demulcerier igni,
quae puram tibi servasti mentemque pudicam
210   hactenus et sine labe tuam, sine crimine vitam?
Non te tangit amor, non te reverentia cari
patris? An oblita es patriae, nec te ulla remordet
cura? Tuum poteris sic corrupisse pudorem,
corrupisse tuam, qua tangis sidera, famam?
215   Praemeditare, precor, voces quascumque futuras!
Quid de te Colchos, quid de te Graecia dicet,
quid populi et reges? Quae de te infamia surget?
Quanto dedecori fies? Quis gentium in ore
sermo erit ob tantum facinus? Quid sentiet ipse
220   Aesonides, quid cara parens patruusque paterque?
Tene putas, proprios quam deseruisse parentes
tam turpi norit facto, securus amabit?
Forsitan et mediis meritam te merget in undis!
Aut esto Haemonium detur tibi cernere litus,
225   forte domo miseram te pellet, et altera coniunx,
quam tu — pro demens — servaris, Iasona habebit!
Tunc nec erit genitor nec erunt fraterque sororque,
non genetrix, ad quos ausis despecta reverti.
Quare age, dum nova res et adhuc medicabilis exstat,
230   tute tibi succurre tuis et consule rebus!
Blanda quidem Veneris, sed dira et caeca cupido est,

what sadness I will afflict my dear parents, what sorrows I will
bring my homeland. But I am consumed by a devouring fire, nor   200
is my wretched condition endurable whatever form it takes. It is
my decision to abandon my father and his gods, provided only
handsome Jason, once he has been saved by my favor, join me to
himself in marriage."

Tears brought her words to an end. Thus the goddess spoke in   205
response: "O my dear charge, has such madness seized you, such
inner darkness, that you allow yourself to yield to blind love and
grow molten in flames for a world not your own, you who hitherto
have kept your mind pure and chaste, and your life without taint,   210
without reproach? Does no affection, no reverence for your be-
loved father touch you? Have you forgotten your homeland, does
no remorse gnaw at you? Are you so capable of sullying your chas-
tity, of sullying the repute by which you touch the stars? Ponder,
I beseech you, while the time is yours, the gossip that will be   215
your lot! What will Colchos, what will Greece, what will peoples
and their rulers whisper about you? What notoriety will develop
around you? What a massive disgrace will be your lot? What tat-
tle will be in every mouth because of such a misdeed? What will
the son of Aeson himself feel, what your dear mother, your uncle   220
and your father? Do you believe that he will cherish you without
fail once he knows that you have abandoned your very parents in
such an ugly fashion? Perhaps he will even plunge you, and de-
servedly so, into the midst of the waves! Or imagine that you
will be allowed to cast eyes on the Haemonian shore: it could be   225
that he will force you from his house, poor creature, and that a
different wife, whom you will serve as slave — such fury is on the
loose! — will possess Jason! At that time no father will be yours,
neither brother, nor sister, nor mother, to whom you might dare to
return in your scorned state. So act now, while the matter remains
fresh and capable of cure. Give a care to yourself and take thought   230
for your affairs! The lust that Venus sponsors, seductive though it

93

quae meditando alitur viresque acquirit et ultro
sese offert validosque ignes, ubi perstiterit mens,
concipit: Haec non fomento nec viribus ullis,
235   sed sola pellenda fuga est; hunc ilicet ergo
tolle animo fugiens, quem qui sit Iasona nescis!
Exue te has molles melioresque indue curas:
Si te conubio sociare et vivere voto
communi sanctoque voles: Quot te, aspice, reges,
240   quot cupiunt optantque duces! Tibi delige quemvis
e tanta procerum turba! Sine Thessalus hospes
te sine vela petat — vel, si contendere malit,
oppetat, ut mavult! —, ne, si illum forte sequaris,
te fallat ventisque simul det vela fidemque.'
245   Tali pulsa Venus sermone furorque recessit
virgineus — veluti, pluviis cum turbidus Auster
complevit totumque atra caligine caelum,
si contra adverso veniens occurrat ab orbe,
dispellit Boreas nubes pluviumque, serenat
250   aëra restituitque iubar spectabile terris.
Tum dea se, postquam cupidos sanasse furores
cognovit, levibus fugiens immiscuit auris.
Virgo autem, ut falsa nutricis imagine captam
se vidit certisque agnovit Pallada signis
255   cedentem, †placida sic illam voce secuta est:
'Mene ergo ignaram, diva o Tritonia, passa es
incautamque monere tuis et fallere verbis?
Mirabar, qui tantus erat splendorque decorque,
quae tibi iudicii integritas, quae copia fandi;
260   mirabar, quae tanta tuis sapientia dictis
maiestasque inerat! Quanto me lumine dudum
compleri et facilem tua me ad consulta moveri,
percipiebam animo. Nunc te faciemque tuumque

is, is also dread and dark. It finds nourishment in reflection and
gains strength. Its advent is spontaneous, and, once the mind stays
committed, it harbors powerful fire. No poultices, no physical
force, can drive it forth, but only flight. By flight, therefore, expel   235
him from your mind, and quickly, too. You are ignorant of who
this Jason is! Shed these corrupting concerns and clothe yourself
in better thoughts. If it is your wish to ally yourself in marriage
and live according to a shared, holy vow, cast a glance at the num-
ber of kings, the number of heroes for whom you are the object of
eager desire! Choose anyone you want from such a throng of no-   240
bles! Let your Thessalian guest set sail without you, or, if he pre-
fers to face the challenge, let him meet his end, as he prefers, lest,
if you chance to follow after him, he deceive you and offer at once
sails, and good faith, to the breezes."

Routed by such an harangue Love's girlish madness waned, as   245
when the swollen south wind has filled up the whole heavens with
rain and pitchy dusk: if the north wind, emanating from the
world's opposite reach, should clash against him, he scatters the
clouds and rain, calms the air and restores to earth's view the radi-
ance of the sun.   250

Then the goddess, after finding that she has cured lust's mad-
ness, mingled herself in flight in the nimble breezes. The girl,
however, when she perceived that she had been duped by the fake
image of her nurse and recognized the sure evidence of Pallas as
she withdraws, addressed her with an emotionless voice: 255

"Did you allow yourself, o goddess of Tritonis, to offer warning
to me, ignorant and unwary, and to cozen me with your words? I
was already awestruck at your prodigious splendor and grace, at
the probity of your judgment, at your eloquence. I was awestruck
by the vast wisdom and grandeur inherent in your words! My   260
mind grasped that I was for some time now filled with your bril-
liance and was easily affected by your advice. Now I recognize you
and your face and your immortal features. Is it thus, my Pallas,

divinum agnosco vultum. Sic me, o mea Pallas,
265   alloqueris, sic me illudis? Quo proripis aut quo,
diva, fugis? Cur te a nostris complexibus arces?'

Liber Tertius

Haec dum Pallas agit, magnam contra Aeolus iram
concipit et sceptrum, dextra quod forte gerebat,
quassans bis terque horrifico se murmure miscet;
iam pridemque sibi invisum exsecratur amaris
5   Aeëtam dictis et verba inimica profundit,
multa minans multo irarum succenditur aestu:
Quippe illum cari torquet vindicta nepotis,
quem rex incautum vita privarat avarus.
Inde suo pariter de sanguine natus Iason
10   haud parvos addit stimulos cogitque vereri.
Atque, ut erat mixtimque metu turbatus et ira,
continuo Zephyrum vocat ad se ac talia mandat:
    'Iunonem pete caelestes et curre per auras
atque illi haec mea verba refer. Scit se mihi namque,
15   quodcumque in ventos habeo, ius omne dedisse
imperiumque et ob id sua me mandata secutum
semper et hanc eius patriam rexisse furentem
arbitrio. Nunc per, si qua est mihi gratia secum,
illam oro, ut nostra Aesonidae de stirpe creato
20   praestet opem, cui nunc ingens sub Colchide terra
imminet exitium. Memini, dum per mare vastum
vela daret, quotiens tunc auxiliabar eunti,
mulcebam quotiens fluctus Austrosque ruentes!
Nunc vero extra undas frustrata potentia nostra est.
25   Haec praeter referes regis sanctissima facta

that you lecture me, thus that you beguile me? Whither do you
snatch yourself away or whither flee, goddess? Why do you shun   265
my embrace?"

Book III

While these affairs occupy Pallas, Aeolus was smitten with a burst
of opposing anger, and, shaking twice and yet again the scepter
which he chanced to carry in his right hand, he bestirs himself
with an horrendous roar. In bitter language he curses Aeëtes, who
had long since been an object of his hatred, and spews forth hos-   5
tile words. As his threats mount he is engulfed in a blaze of anger:
vengeance for his dear grandson tightens him in its grip whom,
while heedless, that greedy king had deprived of life. Moreover the
fact that Jason was also sprung from his blood goaded him relent-
lessly and compounded his worry. Unhinged by this melding of   10
anxiousness and anger, he forthwith summons Zephyrus and
commands him thus:

"Hasten through heaven's breezes to find Juno and carry her
these words from me. For she knows that she bestowed whatever
jurisdiction and ruling power I possess over the winds, and on this   15
account I have ever obeyed her dictates and reigned over this
seething land at her direction. Now, if she holds a residue of
thanks toward me, I pray her to lend aid to the son of Aeson,
sprung from our stock, over whom a huge disaster looms in the
land of Colchis. I remember how often then I aided his progress,   20
as he was sailing over the broad sea, how often I calmed the waves
and rushing south winds! But in his present circumstances, out-
side the waves, my power avails not at all. You will call her atten-
tion, as well, to the 'most righteous' deeds of king Aeëtes. So   25

Aeëtae, quem tam caecus tamque improbus auri
traxit amor, Phrixum ut, quamvis gener ille sibi esset—
ille neposque mihi—, tamen obtruncarit et aureo
vellere, quo vectus longum tranaverat aequor,
30   vitalique illum pariter spoliaverit aura.
Scit porro Iuno haec radiantia vellera munus
esse suum, scit se, dum tristia facta novercae
effugeret, Phrixo per matrem haec dona dedisse;
scit, quales patri furias immiserit et quas
35   ob taetrum scelus indignans conceperit iras.
Rem se igitur dignam faciet, si regis iniqui
factum atrox premat auratam pecudemque revellat
Aesonidamque meum iuvet hoc et munere donet.'
Sic ait, et celeri Zephyrus secat aëra cursu
40   fertque refertque utrimque sonos et iussa facessit.
At regina deum pro talibus excita dictis
Irim ad Chalciopen de summo mittit Olympo—
Medeae illa soror Phrixi et praedivitis olim
uxor erat—; iubet, ut patrem contra asperet illam,
45   a quo eius cecidit crudeli funere coniunx,
commoneatque suam succendere amore sororem,
quo pendat patris meritas iniuria poenas.
Illa volat ducitque per arcum mille colores.
Interea alloquitur Venerem Saturnia Iuno:
50   'Nos iustus, Cytherea, dolor, nos iusta decensque
Colchorum contra regem vindicta lacessit.
Cuique sua in promptu causa est: Ego maxima certe
atque indigna tuli, sed quos tu provida gnatae
intuleras, cerne, ut Pallas sanarit amores!
55   Nosque igitur diva vinci patiemur ab una?
Si libeat perstasque tuis insistere coeptis,
polliceor tecum hunc partiri et ferre laborem:

blind, so immoral a passion for gold attracted him that, although
Phrixus was his son-in-law, and my grandson too, nevertheless he
had him beheaded, and despoiled him in one blow both of the
golden fleece, carried on which he had traversed the sea's length,
and of life's breath. Furthermore Juno knows that this brilliant   30
fleece was a present from herself, she knows that she had bestowed
this gift — while he was escaping the malevolent deeds of his step-
mother — on Phrixus through his mother. She knows what mad-
ness she had visited upon his father and what wrath she had con-
ceived in her indignation over his ugly crime. Therefore she will   35
accomplish a deed worthy of herself if she avenges the dreadful act
of the evil king and snatches back the pelt of gold, helping my de-
scendant, the son of Aeson, and granting him this gift."

These were his words, and Zephyrus shears the air in his swift
descent; his wind whistles in reverberation on either side as he car-
ries out Aeolus's commands.   40

Thereupon the queen of the gods, roused by such words, sends
Iris from the peak of Olympus to Chalciope — she the sister of
Medea and once the wife of wealthy Phrixus. Her orders are that
she should incite Medea against their father, at whose hands her
husband was killed by a cruel doom, and remind her to keep her   45
sister's love afire so that her father pay deserved penalty for his
wrong. Iris wings her way and paints her rainbow with a thousand
hues.

Meanwhile Saturnian Juno addresses Venus: "Child of Cythera,
righteous resentment, a righteous and appropriate vendetta spurs   50
me against the king of the Colchians. We each have a ready rea-
son. No doubt I myself have suffered the greatest indignities, but
you, too, should watch how Pallas cures the passion which you
providently brought upon your daughter. And will we thus allow
ourselves to be overcome by a single goddess? If it pleases you and   55
you stand firmly committed to your enterprise, I give my promise
to share in undertaking this effort. I myself, whose province is

Ibo ego, conubiis quae praesideo atque Hymenaeis,
Medeamque pio subolis dulcique replebo
60   coniugii desiderio; tu, diva, decorem
Aeolidaeque simul splendorem afflare memento,
qualemcumque potes, quo rursum regia virgo
externi iuvenis magno incendatur amore!
Sic revocare suas invita Pallade flammas,
65   sumere sic poenas inimico a rege licebit!'

    Talibus assensit Venus et laetata recepit
vim maiorem animo—ceu, cum canis impetit acri
dente feram, si latrantum succurrere quemquam
viderit, exsultat cordique audacia crescit.

70   Et iam contigerat Iunonis nuntia Colchon:
Nox erat et tenebrae terras et sidera caelum
spargebant; ergo ut Iunonia iussa sequatur,
Chalciopen placida mulcentem membra quiete
excitat et verbis compellat talibus Iris:

75   'Me coniunx Iovis has iussit tibi promere voces:
Praedixere tuo poscenti oracula divum
Aeetae genitori olim de sanguine magni
Hippotadae fore, qui regnum subverteret eius.
Ille autem interpres divinae vocis iniquus,
80   ille tuum prognatum ipsa de stirpe maritum,
Phrixum, crudeli atque indigna morte peremit.
At non Phrixus erat, quem sancta oracla ferebant,
sed novus hospes adhuc, non intellectus Iason,
ipsa etiam cretus de stirpe: Hunc quippe futurum
85   excidio magno regis responsa volebant.
Quare sume animos patremque ulciscere cari
coniugis exstinctorem et, quae statuere severo
iudicio fata, exsequere hanc et suscipe laudem!
Quod fieri ut possit, verbis hortare sororem,
90   ut, quae sola potest iuvenem defendere Graium,

marriage and the nuptial ceremony, will be on my way to restore
Medea's yearning, dutiful and touching, for children and marriage.
You, goddess, have a mind to breathe into the scion of Aeolus 60
grace and luster of the sort you have in your power, so that the
royal maiden may again be inflamed by a mighty love for the for-
eign youth. Thus the possibility will be ours to ignite her flames
again, even against the will of Pallas, thus to exact punishment
from the mendacious king!" 65

Venus nods in approval and, happiness restored, strengthened
her mind's conviction, as a hound, in pursuit of a sharp-toothed
beast, if it notices another from the pack running to its aid, takes
courage, and boldness flowers in its heart.

And now Juno's messenger had reached Colchos. Night was 70
falling, and darkness was clothing the earth and stars the heavens.
The time was ripe to execute Juno's orders: Iris wakes Chalciope,
her body refreshed from the calm of sleep, and accosts her thus:

"The wife of Jupiter has commanded me to address you with 75
these words: some time ago, in answer to his request, the oracles
of the gods predicted to your father that someone from the line of
the mighty son of Hippotes would destroy his kingdom. But he,
evil interpreter as he was of heaven's utterance, killed your hus-
band, Phrixus, descended from that very line, in a cruel and un- 80
worthy death. But it was not Phrixus who was the subject of the
hallowed oracles but Jason, a new guest hitherto unknown, like-
wise sprung from the same line. The responses, rather, pointed
to him as about to be the king's mighty bane. So summon your 85
courage and take vengeance on your father who did away with
your dear husband; execute what the fates' judgment has gravely
affirmed and make yours the praise due. In order for this to be
able to happen, with urgency address your sister — she alone has
the ability to defend the Greek youth — that she bring him aid and 90

auxilium ferat et casus miseretur acerbos!
Proinde illi suade tamque acres incute flammas,
ut mitem Aesonidam sub Thessala regna sequatur,
ut patrem crudelem una patriamque relinquat!
95   Multa subinde manent illum monimenta malorum.
Iusserunt sic fata, iubet sic regia Iuno.'
Dixit et aufugit per quem descenderat arcum.

      His dictis magis incaluit vetus ira dolorque
Chalciopes: Veluti, quando calcaribus urget
100 miles equum volitantem ultro, vis altior illi
succrescit, superat se cursu atque ardet anhelo —
non secus haec: Stat dilecti mors coniugis atra
fixa animo, magnaque in patrem exaestuat ira.
Hac illac fertur meditans membrisque quietem
105 denegat, in varias se dividit anxia partes.

      Nox ruit interea, et roseis Aurora quadrigis
provehitur lustratque ardenti lampade terras.
Rex iterum proceres aulae in penetralibus altae
Argolicos gnatamque una ad convivia poscit.
110 Ergo ibat magnum ad genitorem filia dudum
plena dea Iunone acrique cupidine tacta
coniugii; simul Aeolides, cui diva creatrix
divinum late afflarat specimenque decusque:
Non illi Bacchus, non illi certet Apollo!
115 Verum ubi sidereum iuvenis mirata decorem est,
substitit et subito correpta Aeëtias arsit
excussitque almam de tota Pallada mente.
Ac velut, externi cum taurum bucula saltus
vidit et incaluit, licet illi flamma recedat
120 absenti, tamen, ut rursus conspexit amatum
forte marem, recipit vires amor inque calescit:
Sic incensa igitur virgo maerensque gemensque

take pity on the bitterness of his misfortunes! Encourage her fur-
ther and instill in her flames of such sharpness that she follow the
gentle son of Aeson to his Thessalian kingdom, and that she leave
behind her cruel father together with her homeland! Many re-
minders of his evildoing shortly await him. Thus the fates have   95
commanded, thus royal Juno commands." Words finished, she
took flight along the rainbow by which she had descended.

Chalciope's long-standing wrath and resentment were warmed
all the more by these words: just as when a soldier incites with his
spurs a horse already hurtling along of his own volition, a further   100
strength swells within him, he surpasses himself and burns with
breathless haste: so Chalciope. The dark death of her beloved hus-
band remains fixed in her mind, and she boils with intense wrath
against her father. Her ponderings carry her hither and yon, and
deny peace to her limbs. Her disquiet tears her now in one direc-
tion, now in another.   105

Meanwhile night falls away, and Dawn is carried abroad on ro-
seate chariot and spreads light around the earth with gleaming
torch. Once again the king summons the Greek heroes together
with his daughter to a banquet in the great hall's inner sanctum.
In response his daughter made her way to her mighty father, she   110
for sometime now filled with the goddess Juno and prodded by re-
lentless longing for marriage. Likewise the scion of Aeolus, over
whom the goddess of begetting had amply breathed both comeli-
ness and grace worthy of a god. Bacchus could not vie with him,
nor could Apollo! And when the daughter of Aeëtes paused, in
stunned admiration of the youth's glistening grace, she was sud-   115
denly engulfed in flames and expelled Pallas, who cherished her,
completely from her mind. And just as when a young cow is aglow
after sighting a steer from a meadow not her own, though the
flame lessen in his absence, nevertheless when she has chanced to
lay eyes again on her beloved bull, her love recovers its strength   120
and radiates anew: thus the maiden, heart afire, with sorrowing

secretos repetit thalamos; dehinc turbine mentis
sicut erat magno atque gravi compulsa furore,
125   Chalciopen tali compellat voce sororem:
'Audi, cara soror, patiens me nostra loquentem
arcana et miserae potius succurre sorori!
Excrucior, nostris et se novus ossibus ardor
implicat; ardentes carpit mihi flamma medullas,
130   nec soleo tales poenas talesve calores
ferre. Quis hic nostram tantum premit advena mentem!
Qua forma, qua virtute est, quo praeditus ille
eloquio! Quibus ortus avis! Quis splendor ab eius
ore fluit! Non divinus decor ille videtur?
135   Non facies digna illa deo, non coniuge dignus
regina Iunone? Iovine simillimus ille?
At certe ille mihi miros incussit amores,
et volui, fateor namque, his obsistere; sed me
concitat ardentem vis maior et undique cogit.
140   Iam mihi dulce nihil possim sperare sine illo,
non requiem, non ullam ausim sperare salutem!
Decrevi—et mentem ne quaere refellere nostram—
actutum, soror, Haemonio succurrere regi.
Illum ego monstra—bonus quid enim peccavit Iason?—
145   artibus infabricata meis superare docebo.
Non adeo crudele mihi ingeniumve protervum est,
ut per me Aesonides viridi exstinguatur in aevo!
Ille, ubi me certo sociam stabilique ligarit
conubio, patrias secum traducet in oras.
150   Ipsa equidem durum—sic stat sententia—patrem,
has etiam sedes et regna paterna relinquam;
sed te, oro, huic accinge, soror dilecta, labori:
Vade virumque ad me interea, dum nigra silet nox,
duc tempusque aptum furare: Ego foedera secum
155   percutiam firmaque sibi me lege dicabo.'

moan returns to her remote chamber. Then, swept up as she was
by her mind's mighty whirlwind and its oppressive madness, she
thus addresses her sister Chalciope: "Give ear, devoted sister, and   125
allow me to voice my secret. Lend help, I beg you, to your lovesick
sister! I am tortured, and a new flame entwines itself amid my
bones. The fire grasps at my burning marrow. I am not accus-
tomed to endure such suffering, such hell-fire. Who is this out-   130
sider who has so enslaved my mind! With what presence, what
nobility, what eloquence is he endowed! From what ancestry he is
sprung! What brilliance pours from his features! Does not his
grace appear god-like? Are not his features worthy of a god, is he
not worthy of queen Juno as wife? Is he not most like Jupiter? He   135
has inspired in me for sure a love to marvel at, and—I admit it to
you—it was my desire to stand firm against it. But a mightier
force stirs me afire, and drives me this way and that. Already I am
incapable of expecting anything sweet without him nor would I   140
dare to hope for any peace of mind, any salvation. I have made my
decision—don't attempt to reverse my thinking—forthwith, sister
mine, to lend help to the Haemonian king. I myself will be his
teacher—for of what malfeasance is good Jason guilty?—to over-
come the monsters wrought by my arts. My nature is neither so   145
cruel nor so fierce as to be the means of annihilating Jason in the
prime of youth! When he has bound me as his partner in the sure,
enduring alliance of matrimony, he will carry me with him to his
paternal shores. I myself—and my decision remains unshaken—
will leave behind our hard-hearted father, along with this dwelling   150
and the kingdom of our forefathers. But, I pray you, beloved sister,
gird yourself for this effort. Go now and, in night's dark silence,
grasping in stealth the appropriate moment, lead the man to me. I
will enter into compact with him and proclaim myself his in the
firmness of law."   155

  Haec virgo; tum Chalciope, quam iussa premebant
Iunonis simul et saevi vindicta parentis,
olli ita respondit: 'Si te, soror optima, movit
huius amor, licet externo sit ab orbe profectus,
160 haud miror; blandam quem posse movere Dionen
eximiam vel Iunonem vel Pallada duram
crediderim: Tanta egregiae praestantia formae,
tantus inest illi virtutis splendor et oris
tantus honos! Nec damno tuam mentemve refello.
165 Perge, soror, quo te impellunt tua vota trahuntque!
Mitis et auxilio est tali haud indignus Iason
et qui te in magnas, si se tibi iunxerit, urbes,
in longas te ducet opes. Ibi laetior aër
plusque apti mores cultusque animique virorum
170 et melior pater et nulla de caede suorum
conspersus: Nescis nostri crudelia patris
facta? Suamne illum scis exstinxisse parentem
et dulcem generum? Ne cetera tristia narrem.
Idyiam liceat matrem, Medea, relinquas,
175 Alcimeden socrum invenies instarque parentis.
Effuge regna, ubi nec fas est nec iura nec ullus
iustitiae et pietatis amor, fuge barbara tecta,
horribiles caedes et avaras desere terras!
Quaere alias sedes, ubi recta et sancta fides est,
180 iusque bonumque piumque, et ubi clementia regnat!
Quas laudes, quos tota, putas, tibi fundet honores
Graecia? Quo plausu, quanto excipiere triumpho,
quo coetu populorum et qua iuvenumque senumque
et nuruum et matrum festa occurrente caterva!
185 Ergo age, servatrix generosae pubis Achivae,
prosequere, ut coepisti animo! Me cura laborque
iste petit: Pergo et iuvenem — mora nulla — Pelasgum
ante tuos statuam vultus.' Sic illa locuta est.

These were the girl's words. Then Chalciope, whom Juno's
commands, as well as vengeance for her father's harshness, urged
on, gave her answer thus: "If, best of sisters, this man's love stirs
you, though he have set sail from a distant part of the globe, I am
in no way taken aback. I would believe that he could stir soft Ve-   160
nus or lofty Juno or even stony Pallas. Such is the excellence of his
handsome beauty, such the brilliance of his courage, such the grace
of his features! Nor do I condemn or argue with your inclination.
Make haste, my sister, whither your prayers push and tug you!   165
Gentle Jason is in every way worthy of such help. If he joins him-
self with you, he will lead you in a journey toward great cities and
toward abundant wealth. There the climate is more salubrious,
men's customs, their habits and ways of thinking are more fitting.
There dwells a better father, one unstained with the blood of his   170
kin. Do you remain ignorant of our father's cruel deeds? Do you
realize that he put to death his own father and his sweet son-in-
law? I'll not detail the rest of his evil. Medea, though you abandon
your mother Idyia, you will discover in Alcimede, your mother-in-
law, the equivalent of a parent. Take flight from this realm where   175
there are neither rights nor laws nor any devotion to justice or pi-
ety. Escape this brutish house and leave behind murder most foul
and a land of greed. Seek a spot elsewhere where true faith is re-
vered and righteousness is deemed good and worshipful, where
forbearance holds sway. Are you giving thought to the praises, to   180
the honors that the whole of Greece will shower on you? With
what applause, with what a triumphal cortege you will be received,
with what a throng of people, with what a festive crowd—the
young, the old, newly-weds, matrons—running to greet you! So, I
urge you, savior of the noble youth of Greece, persevere in your   185
initial thoughts. My effort is devoted to your behalf: I set out
without delay and will bring the Greek youth face to face with

Sic animum longe maiori incendit amore—
190 qualis congestas, tacitus quibus incubat ignis,
aura solet rapida stipulas accendere flamma.
  Tum maestum Venus his affatur Iasona verbis:
'Pro te ego, si nescis, dudum Cytherea laboro.
Medeam, quippe una tibi quae ferre salutem
195 quaeve potest quodcumque libet, flagrantibus ussi
ignibus in mirumque modum te ardere coegi:
Te solum cupit, in solo te virgo moratur!
Et nunc illa tibi tacita sub nocte sororem
colloquium ad commune vocans transmittit et ultro
200 spondet opem poscitque torum poscitque sub oras
transferri Argolicas. Ito et, quaecumque rogarit,
efficito! Nostrum hoc opus est, tibi munere nostro
parta salus.' Dixit tenuesque effugit in auras.
Talibus haud aliter maerore levatus Iason,
205 quam torrentem aestum, quem sicca incenderat aestas,
mitigat aëreis resolutus nubibus imber.
Mox sequitur iuvenis divam haec et verba profatur:
  'O dea, quae meritis pro tantis digna rependam
dona? Quibus celebrem, quibus aut te ad sidera tollam
210 laudibus? O placidum et clemens, o dulce piumque
numen et o nostros casus dea mitis iniquos
et duram sortem miserata! O si mihi detur
sub patrium litus, Graias remeare sub urbes,
quot summos, quales reddam tibi victor honores!
215 Quae tibi marmoreis delubra aurata columnis
constituam! Quae dona altis pendere iubebo
fixa tholis! Quam multa tuas ante occidet aras
victima!' Sic ait ille, fores cum nuntia pulsat
Chalciope; et postquam iuvenem data copia verbis
220 compellare, refert dilectae iussa sororis.

you." Such were her words. Thus she inflames her mind with a far
greater love, like a breeze that is wont to set aflame with quick   190
flash a heap of stubble in which fire quietly broods.

Then with these words Venus speaks to Jason in his grimness:
"In case you were unaware, I, goddess of Cythera, have for a long
time been at work on your behalf. Medea, who alone, we are sure,
can procure your safety or whatever she wishes, I have set afire
with raging flames and compelled to burn most extraordinarily.   195
The maiden yearns for you alone, her thoughts dwell only on you!
And now in the quiet of the night she dispatches her sister to
summon you to talk together, and of her goodwill promises help
and asks for the marriage bed and to be taken to the shores of   200
Greece. Make haste and bring to fruition whatever she asks. This
is my doing. Your salvation comes into being as my gift." Words
finished, she took flight through the gossamer breezes. As a result
of her words Jason is relieved of his gloom, just as rain, released
from lofty clouds, brings relief to raging heat set aglow by sum-
mer's drought. Forthwith the youth follows the goddess and utters   205
these words:

"O goddess, with what offerings, worthy of such generosity, can
I repay you? With what praises should I honor you or elevate you
to the stars? O divine power, calming and kind, gracious and pi-
ous, o gentle goddess who has taken pity on our unjust misfortune   210
and our hard lot! O, if it will be granted me to return to the shore
of my homeland and to the cities of Greece, how many honors,
numberless and without peer, will I in victory bestow upon you!
What gilded shrines with pillars of marble will I raise up for you!
What offerings will I order nailed and hung beneath their high   215
roofs! How many a victim will fall before your altars!" Such were
his words when Chalciope the messenger knocked at the door.
And after she was offered the opportunity to have words with the
youth, she conveys the commands of her beloved sister.   220

Olli dicta placent, unaque in nocte silenti
incedunt tacito passu — ceu turba luporum,
quos inimica dies pallentis noctis in umbra
praedae avidos iubet ire, canum ne irrumpat euntes
225   custodumve invisa cohors — et iam ipsa furentis
virginis intrarant tecta arcanosque recessus:
Hic atrum nemus, hic fuerant sacrata Dianae
tergeminae delubra, suos ubi dicere cantus
infernosque ciere deos Medea solebat.
230   Postquam illa optatum conspexit Iasona, tali est
orsa sono: 'Tene, o Graium pulcherrime, tandem
aspicere et tuto licet has adiungere dextras
inque vicem capere et secretas reddere voces?
O quotiens, mea flamma, meae spes unica vitae,
235   o quotiens ego te lacrimas miserata profudi!
Quot pro te gemitus et quot suspiria rupi
horrendos volvens casus, quibus, o nimium audax,
obiectare animam statuisti! At, ni mea servet
te manus, haud dubito, sortem experieris amaram.
240   Verum ego, quae tanta haec fabricare pericula novi,
ne dubita, faxo, ut subigas atque omnia victor
exsuperes. Non hic enses, sed carmina divum,
non arma hic, sed tantum herbae et medicamina possunt!
Tu solus tanti pretium mihi muneris esto!
245   Non regna Argolicasve urbes, non aurea tecta
ingentes vel opes — sat enim praedives abundat
his genitor —, sed te, Aesonida mitissime, solum
coniugiique fidem posco. Me foedere certo
iunge tibi et taedas praesenti numine firma!
250   Te sequar et terras ultro comitabor in omnes.'
His dictis sic respondit laetatus Iason:
'O virgo, decus et nostrae spes una salutis,
quas tibi ego tali laudes pro munere dicam?

Her words give him pleasure and together, in the midst of
night's silence, they make their way with quiet step—like a pack of
wolves whom the hostile light of day forces to go on their way, rav-
enous for prey, during the twilight's shade so that the hated throng
of dogs or keepers does not burst in on their pursuit—and now   225
they make their way into the very dwelling of the love-mad maid
and its hidden retreat. Here was a black grove, here the shrines
consecrated to triple-twinned Diana, where Medea was wont to
utter her incantations and to elicit gods from the world below.

After she had cast eyes on Jason, her heart's desire, she intoned   230
her first words: "O handsomest of Greeks, am I allowed at last to
behold you, and safely to join hands with you and to exchange
words in private, each in turn? O how often, my flame, the single
hope of my being, o how often have I poured out tears in pity for   235
you! How many groans and how many sighs have burst from me
on your behalf as I pondered the fearful challenges to which in
your rash daring you have decided to expose your life! For, unless
my hand saves you, I have little doubt that a bitter lot will be
yours to suffer. But have no doubt that I, who have the skill to   240
manufacture such dangers as these, will see to it that in victory
you win the day and carry all before you. Power here lies not with
swords but with the gods' incantations, not with weapons, but
only with herbs and medicinals! You alone are worth the value of
such a gift on my part! I ask not for the kingdoms and cities of
Greece, nor for gilded palaces or wealth piled on wealth. My father   245
already overflows with a satiety of this wealth. I ask, o most gentle
son of Aeson, only for you and for your trust in marriage. Join me
to yourself in assured compact, and confirm the wedding ritual in
heaven's presence. I will follow you and be your willing companion
in every land."   250

Rejoicing, Jason answered her words thus: "O maiden, our
glory and our one hope of salvation, what praises can I sing on
your behalf for such a gift? What thanks worthy of you, what re-

Quas dignas grates, quae debita praemia solvam?
255   Non, si mille mihi linguas totidemque dedisset
ora deus, dignis sequerer te laudibus umquam,
nec, mihi si constent totidem mentesque manusque,
par possim officium praestare paresque referre
hisce vices meritis; sed, dum mihi vita superstes,
260   tantorum numquam immemorem ingratumve bonorum
cognosces; tu nostra quies nostrumque levamen
semper eris, tu consilium, tu nostra potestas
unica! Nullus honos sine te mihi, nulla petetur
gloria; te sociam pariter dominamque sub omnes
265   accipio casus teque unam affusus adoro,
nulla meo nisi tu iungetur nupta cubili!
Iuro per hanc, fidei in pignus quam porrigo, dextram
perque Hecaten, cuius praesentes tangimus aras,
Iunonis per sacra, toris quod numen amicum est,
270   per Solem iuro et Venerem, per, si mihi restat
ulla salus, per spes reditus: Tu sola futura es
Aesonidae coniunx! Me dura absorbeat optem
terra prius, quam te fallam promissaque rumpam!'
Haec ait et lacrimas media inter verba profundit.
275   Dehinc vero cantus magici et medicaminis usum
et, quibus exsuperanda modis sint singula, discit.
Secedit laeta socios et fronte revisit
et faustos casus et divum munera narrat.
Dant laudes dis inque vicem laetantur Achivi.

Liber Quartus

Viderat haec dudum magno Tritonia Pallas
cum gemitu, demum lacrimis ingressa profusis

wards that are your due, can I offer? Not if a god had furnished
me with a thousand tongues and a thousand mouths would I ever   255
bring to fullness praises worthy of you, nor, if a like number of
lives and hands were under my control, would I have the capability
of granting you like devotion, of bringing you recompense equal to
what you now deserve. But, as long as life remains to me, you will
never find me to be forgetful of, or ungrateful for, such generosity.   260
You will always be our rest and comfort, you our counselor, our
singular source of power! No honor, no glory will be my quest
without you; I take you as my companion as well as my mistress in
all circumstances, I prostrate myself before you in worship, no one   265
except you will be the bride united with me on the bed of mar-
riage. I swear by this right hand, which I stretch forth as a pledge
of faith, by Hecate, whose epiphanic altars we touch, by the rites
of Juno, since her godhead befriends the marriage couch; I swear
by the Sun and by Venus, by my salvation, if any is to be mine, by   270
my hope of return: you alone are to be the wife of the son of
Aeson! I would wish the hard earth to engulf me before I will de-
ceive you and break my promises!" Thus he speaks and pours
forth tears in the midst of his words.

Then he learns the use of magic incantation and of drugs and   275
in what ways each difficulty could be surmounted. With happy
mien he withdraws and returns to his comrades and tells them of
the propitious events and the gifts of the gods. The Greeks in
their turn offer praises to the gods, and rejoice.

Book IV

Tritonian Pallas had for a while beheld these events with great
sighing. At last, making her way bathed in tears, she appeared

ante Iovem tristes visa est effundere questus:
'Quid mirum, si me solam tot numina vincunt,
5   si pellax Cytherea in me simul et tua coniunx
coniurant! Sed tu, genitor, rex aequus ubique es?
Mene ergo haec sufferre sines? Haec praemia nostrae
virginitatis erunt?' Dicentem et plura parantem
effari gnatam placidis pater occupat ultro
10   vocibus: 'Has, quaeso, lacrimas, hos mitte dolores,
filia: Non nostrum est vestras absolvere lites!
Sed breve tempus erit, quo circum moenia Troiae
Iunonem et Venerem simul exercere furentes
irarum flammas odia atque aeterna videbis.
15   Tunc fautrix tibi Iuno tuam causamque iuvabit.
Quas deinde in pulchro Latio et Laurentibus arvis
accendent inimicitias litesque movebunt,
conspicies; tunc praesentes solabere casus.
Nunc cursum sine fata suum et sua iura sequantur!'
20   Haec pater omnipotens; rutilum iubar interea Sol
extulerat totum radiisque impleverat orbem.
Tum regem Aeolides sociis comitatus adibat
exposcens pugnamque sibi concedier orans.
Rex, quamquam audaci placidis obsistere verbis
25   conatur iuveni memorans, quibus ille periclis
et cui se sorti moriturum obiectet iniquae,
vota tamen sequitur desideriumque precantis
conceditque locum pugnae. Mox laetus Iason
magnum ad certamen turba comitante Pelasga,
30   quodque fuit Marti sacrum, procedit in arvum.
Conveniunt omnes passim Colchique sequuntur
visuri certare virum: Vicina frequenti
concursu implentur iuga. Rex in milibus ipse
constitit et sceptro gravis et venerabilis aevo.

before Jupiter with a flood of sad complaints: "What a wonder, if so many divinities overwhelm me alone, if the seductress from Cythera and your spouse conspire against me! But you, father, lord of justice, where are you to be found? Is this therefore what you will suffer me to endure? Will this be the recompense for leading a virginal life?" While she was still speaking and readying to say more, father of his own accord interrupts daughter with words of calm: "No more tears, I pray you child, no more of these bouts of woe. It is not my task to resolve the strife that has come your way. The time will soon be upon us when around the walls of Troy you will see Juno, and Venus as well, wielding the frenzied fires of wrath and of undying hatred. Then Juno will be your partisan and will lend aid to your cause. You will see what hostility they will then ignite, what a conflict they will set in motion in beautiful Latium and the Laurentian fields. Then you will gain consolation for your present trials. At the moment let fate follow its rightful course!"

These were the almighty father's words. Meanwhile the Sun had raised his crimson brilliance and filled the whole earth with his rays. Then the descendant of Aeolus in the company of his comrades approached the king, begging, beseeching that he be granted the opportunity to do battle. The king attempts to thwart the youth's boldness with words of calm, reminding him to what dangers and to what a treacherous destiny he was subjecting himself as he verged on death. Nevertheless he supports his petitioner's prayerful desire, and grants a setting for the combat. Soon Jason, accompanied by a throng of Greeks, joyfully makes his way toward the mighty contest, onto a field that was sacred to Mars. All converge from everywhere about, and the Colchians follow, prepared to see the hero enter the fray. The nearby slopes are filled with the massing crowd. Amid the thousands the king himself, august with his scepter and venerable with age, took his place.

35   Et iam tempus erat, cum saeva concitus ira
terribilique hastam praetendens cuspide Mavors
infremuit 'tantum' et 'quis' ait 'nos tendere contra
audeat et loca sacra, diu quae numine nostro
respicimus, quis tantum audax evertere tentet?
40   Haud impune quidem, si quid mea dextera possit!'
     Agnovit longe Martem Cytherea gravique
inflammatum ira placido sic pectore mulcet:
'Quis furor hic, o dulce meum sacrumque iuvamen,
noster amor pariterque pudor? Sunt debita nostri
45   concubitus, sunt haec exstinctae praemia famae?
Quo ruis? Hanc igitur Vulcania retia solvunt
mercedem? Soleone tuos ego sola furores
obvia et armorum rapidos compescere motus
et requiem bellis animoque imponere pacem?
50   Et nunc nulla mihi prorsus sit gratia tecum,
quae dudum poenas inimici e sanguine Solis
quaero et communem vindictam persequor? An te
effugit illa vetus pudibundi iniuria facti?
Haec tela, hoc potius dextra quin abice ferrum
55   et sine me hanc hodie invisam stirpemque domumque
ulciscar!' Sic fata olli dedit oscula dulci
complexumque sinu fovit; iamque ossibus ignem
Bellipotens haurire et iam mitescere sensim
incipit. Interea pugnae se Thessalus heros
60   obicit intrepidaque ciet certamina dextra.
     Tum gemini Stygium tauri ore et naribus ignem
efflantes taetro vultu occurrere frementes
horrisonisque locum late mugitibus omnem
implerunt. Timuit tanto perterrita visu
65   Graia cohors, ipse haud metuens satus Aesone tutum
ultro offert pectus duplicesque ad sidera palmas
extollens humili divos sic voce precatur:

At last the time was at hand, when Mars, stirred to savage an- 35
ger and stretching forth his spear with its menacing point, roared:
"Who could possess such daring as to confront us, and who
would be so bold as to bring violence to a sacred spot which we
have long overseen with our divine majesty? Retribution there will
certainly be, if my right hand has any power!" 40

The goddess of Cythera from afar gave ear to Mars, and with
calm heart thus soothes him, inflamed as he was with grievous an-
ger: "What is this madness, my sweet, my blessed delight, at once
my love and my disgrace? Is this the recompense due me for our
love-making, this, for my darkened reputation? Whither are you 45
dashing? Is this indeed the reward that Vulcan's nets let loose?
Am I the only one who confronts your rages and restrains your
rushing movement to arms, imposing calm on conflict and peace
on fury? Are you now offering absolutely no kindness to me who 50
for some time has been seeking punishment from the blood of our
enemy, the Sun, and been pursuing our common vengeance? Has
the long-standing insult done me from our moment of immodesty
escaped you? Rather, instead, throw away these spears, this sword,
from your right hand, and allow me on this day to take vengeance 55
on this hated house and its progeny!" After these words, she
kissed her dear one and soothed him in her bosom's embrace. And
now the war-god begins to absorb her passion in his bones and bit
by bit, now, to grow gentle. In the meantime, the Thessalian hero
thrusts himself into battle and with fearless hand sets the contests
going. 60

Then the twin bulls, breathing hell's fire from mouth and nos-
trils, their faces hideous, ran rumbling toward him, and filled the
area's full sweep with dreadful bellowing. The Greek squadron
stood terrified with fright at such a prospect. The son of Aeson,
without fear for his safety, willingly himself faces the danger and, 65
raising both his palms toward the stars, prays to the gods with
suppliant voice: "You, sire of the world and of humankind, and

'Te, rerum atque hominum pater, et te, maxima Iuno,
teque voco, Cytherea, et te, Gradive, vocantem
70   dique deaeque audite omnes, quicumque vel altos
incolitis caelos, quicumque vel ultima Ditis
regna: Favete, oro, et tantis succurrite coeptis!
Mille feram vestris ingentia munera templis,
mille manu hac vestrae recalescent caedibus arae!'
75   Sic ait et sacro adiutus medicamine saevos
congreditur mollitque boves: Nunc cornibus ille
praefixis solido aere manus iniectat utrasque,
nunc placida attractat demulcens pectora dextra,
nunc premit et curvo pressos supponit aratro
80   cogit et insuetos producere vomere sulcos.
Obstupuere novo aspectu populusque paterque
percussique animis omnes; sed Achaica pubes
exsultans laetum clamorem ad sidera tollit
hortaturque additque animos. Ille impiger instat
85   vipereis cultos et campos dentibus implet
semina letali spargens perfusa veneno.
Nec mora, cum multam — dictu mirabile — gentem
feta venenato genitam de semine tellus
parturiit simul et radiantibus induit armis.
90   Hi, postquam lato solum videre sub arvo
Aesonidam, strictis subito se comminus hastis
in iuvenem vertere, animos vertere furentes.
Percussit socios timor ingens; ipsaque facti
conscia, ut agnovit tot in unum grandinis instar
95   corruere armatos hostes, expalluit amens
Medea et magicas, quas ante iniecerat, artes
advocat atque iterum cantus et carmina dicit.
Ille autem intrepidus venientia in agmina durum
proiecit silicem, quem sacrum et mite futuri
100   tutamen dederat virgo haud ignara pericli.

you, mightiest Juno, and you, goddess of Cythera, I address, and
you, Mars the Strider: do you hear, gods and goddesses all, who-
soever dwell either in the lofty heavens or in the nethermost   70
realms of Dis: look with favor, I beseech you, and grant me help in
my vast enterprise. I will bring a thousand massive offerings to
your temples, a thousand of your altars will feel the warmth of
sacrifices presented by this hand of ours."

  Thus he speaks and, aided by the magic ointment, approaches   75
the bulls and tames their savagery. Now he thrusts each of his
hands onto their horns, peaked with solid bronze, now he draws
them toward him, gently stroking their chests with his right hand.
Now he bends their knees and yokes them, bent, to the curved
plow and compels them to fashion unwonted furrows with the   80
share. Both people and king were stunned by the novel sight. The
minds of all were thunderstruck. But the young Greeks, exultant,
raise a shout of gladness to the stars. Their encouragement in-
creases his will's purpose. Energetically he presses on and fills the
newly-plowed fields with dragon's teeth, strewing seeds saturated 85
with deadly poison. In a flash, the pregnant earth — astonishing to
tell — gave birth to a populous race, born from the poisoned seed,
and clothed them as well in gleaming weapons. After they had
sighted Aeson's son alone upon the broad field, of a sudden ready- 90
ing their spears, they turned themselves and the energy of their
rage against the youth, face to face. A mighty fear struck his com-
rades. Medea herself, aware of the peril, frantic when she saw so
many armed foes, like a shower of hail, rushing against this one
man, grew pale. She calls upon the magic arts which she had pre- 95
viously applied, and once again utters chants and spells. Fearless,
he in his turn hurled against the oncoming ranks the hard flint
which the maiden, well aware of his imminent danger, had given
him as hallowed, soothing talisman. They turned upon themselves 100

Bellum illi inter se feraliaque arma paresque
convertere acies et se exstinxere cruento
Marte. Velut quondam Boeotia moenia circum
— nondum moenia erant — cum natus Agenore saevum
105 saevior ingentem stravitque ingentior anguem
vipereosque iniecit humi pro semine dentes:
Haud aliter quam nunc gravida e tellure creatos
tunc adolesse viros perhibent armataque fratrum
corpora civilique simul se Marte petisse
110 confossosque suis pariter cecidisse sub armis.
     Ultimus ecce labor: vastum superare draconem,
custodem auratae pellis, cui lumina somni
nescia, cui totum squamis atque unguibus horret
corpus et uncatis atrum eiectantia virus
115 dentibus ora fremunt et sibila dira trilingui
fauce movent. Hunc Lethaeo iam victor Iason
conspersit suco et faciles ter carmine dicto
induxit somnos optataque vellera tutus
apprendit tanto laetus factoque superbus.
120   Concurrunt ulnis et complexantur amicis
victorem Aesonidam socii dulcique fruuntur
colloquio et dextrae dextras coniungere gaudent.
Ipse etiam, magno quamquam rex Aëta tenetur
maerore et captum pecudis tristatur honorem,
125 dissimulat tamen et vultum faciemque serenat
Aesoniumque hilari iuvenem regesque Pelasgos
excipit ore ferens placidas e pectore voces
commendatque virum et gentem commendat Achivam.
Tum vero divos et divum templa revisit
130 effunditque preces et vota exsolvit Iason.
     Iamque sub Hesperii descendens gurgitis undas
Sol fessis properabat equis; sed tristior alto
corde novos casus gemitusque fovebat amaros.

war's deadly weapons and in matched battle-lines massacred each
other in bloody strife. Just as once upon a time, around the
Boeotian walls which were not yet walls, when the son of Agenor
laid low a fierce, gigantic serpent, himself more fierce and gigantic,   105
and strewed the earth with dragon's teeth as if they were seed: they
say that, no differently from this present situation, the offspring
engendered from the teeming earth grew to manhood and that the
brothers, their bodies now armed, forthwith sought each other out
in civil strife and then and there fell to the ground, transfixed by
their own weapons.   110

Here was the final task: to overcome the huge dragon, guardian
of the golden fleece, whose eyes know no sleep, whose whole body
bristles with scales and claws, whose mouths roar as they spew
black bile through hooked teeth and give vent to hideous hissing   115
from triple-tongued jaws. Already victorious, Jason sprinkled it
with liquid of Lethe and, after thrice chanting a spell, enveloped it
with easy sleep and safely grasped his target, the fleece, in happy
pride at his impressive deed.

His comrades stream together and clasp the conquering son of   120
Jason in friendly embrace. They delight in his sweet conversation
and rejoice as they join hands with hands. Even king Aeëtes him-
self, though great gloom grips him as he mourns for the plundered
glory of the fleece, nevertheless hides his feelings. He keeps his
face and features calm, and, uttering words of gentleness from his   125
heart, welcomes the young offspring of Aeson and the Greek
princes with happy demeanor. He congratulates the hero, congrat-
ulates the people of Greece. Then Jason visits again the gods in
their temples. He pours forth prayers and fulfills his vows.   130

And now the Sun, with weary steeds hastening his descent be-
neath the waves of the western sea, was ruefully pondering recent
events in his heart's depth and nursing bitter groans. The reason

Quem pater Oceanus — neque enim se causa latebat —
135   ut vidit fronte haud laeta tacitumque dolorem
percepit, verbis sic indignantibus ultro
compellat: 'Tune es — te per tua lumina quaeso —
egregii Aeëtae genitor, quem filia quondam
nostra tibi enixa est? Scis — nec te scire negabis —
140   insignem gnati pietatem et fortia facta,
qui propriam saeva genetricem exstinguere dextra
haud timuit! Nec matris amor nec sanguinis illum
gratia nec nostri, si qua est, reverentia movit!
An curare hominum res et mortalia divos
145   facta putas? Memoresne boni rerisne malive
tutarine bonos et castigare nocentes?
Tarda licet movet ira deos — en, denique poenas,
quas meruit, tuus Aeëtes luit; at mala certe
longe illum maiora manent!' Sic fatus, et atris
150   umida iam caelum nox texere coeperat umbris.
    Graia autem turba et pariter Titania neptis
versabant variis inter se pectora curis,
quo tuti invisa possent abscedere terra.
Demum, ut nox illis abeuntibus atra favebat,
155   discedunt taciti tecta atque inimica relinquunt.
Interea admonitus secreto in litore Tiphys
munibat navim ventis et vela parabat.
    At Medea fugam facilem meditata nefandum
mente parat facinus nec prodita regna patremque
160   contenta est: Audet fraterno sanguine sese
polluere et teneros crudeli barbara dextra
Absyrti lacerare artus, quem callida secum
duxerat ob tam immane scelus, nec dulcis iniquam
germani sanguis subit aut infantia mentem.
165   Quippe rata est, si se fugientem aequorque petentem
infensus pater et pubem insequeretur Achivam,

was plain to father Ocean when he saw him, with brow much
troubled and understood the sorrow that he kept to himself. He   135
addresses him on the spot with these resentful words: "Are you — I
ask you through your very rays — the sire of glorious Aeëtes whom
our daughter [Perse] once bore to you? You know — nor will you
deny your knowledge — the extraordinary piety of your offspring
and his brave deeds. He had no fear of taking the life of his   140
mother with his fierce right hand! Neither love of his mother, nor
goodwill owed kinship, nor respect due to me, if any there is, have
moved him! Do you suppose that the gods give thought to the
affairs and deeds of mortal men? Do you believe that, mindful of   145
good and evil, they cherish the upright and chasten the guilty?
Though anger is slow to move the gods, watch: finally your Aeëtes
pays the penalty he deserves. Far greater evils are his sure destiny!"
Thus he spoke, as dewy night began to weave the heavens with
dark shadows.   150

The Greek troop and with them the Sun's granddaughter were
pondering at heart their sundry cares: how they could withdraw in
safety from the now hated land. At last, with black night assisting
their departure, they take their leave in silence and abandon the
dwellings of their enemies. Meanwhile Tiphys, forewarned, was   155
outfitting the ship on a secluded beach and readying its sails for
the winds.

But Medea, her thoughts on easy escape, not content to betray
fatherland and father, contrives an abominable deed. She dares to
pollute herself with Absyrtus's blood and barbarously with cruel   160
right hand to rend her brother's tender limbs. Anticipating in her
wiliness a criminal act of such monstrosity, she had brought him
with her, nor did the fact that he was her sweet, young brother en-
ter into her evil planning. For she thought that if her father,   165
turned enemy, were to follow her and the Greek youth as she seeks

frustrarique mora atque illum vitare furentem
divulso cari et disiecto corpore gnati,
quo tanto offensus visuque infractus acerbo
170   sisteret et sese genitor tardaret euntem.
Ergo audax parvum turpisque venefica fratrem
apprendit laeva cervicique applicat ensem.
Quem postquam gemitu et lacrimis sua fata querentem
insontesque manus et mollia brachia vidit
175   tendentem taetrumque suae et crudele sororis,
quo poterat, facinus miseranda voce ferentem,
continuit subito ferrum iuguloque pepercit,
atque animo pietas et amor fraternus inhaesit.
     Sensit et, horrendis ut erat praecincta colubris,
180   Tisiphone e tristi sociarum sede suarum
prosilit et stridens Medeae ante evolat ora
deque suis geminos abrumpens crinibus angues
illius in faciem mittit; dehinc talia fatur:
'Quae te vana novae traxit pietatis imago?
185   Quid trepidas? Talem tibi tunc assumere mentem
debueras, cum raptus honos versaeque potentis
immensae genitoris opes, cum iura deosque
laesisti atque omnem exstinxti furiosa pudorem!
Tunc pietas haec te decuit! Nunc, omnia quando
190   turbasti et regnum et miseri decus omne parentis,
quid dubitas sceleri scelus addere? An, ut tua saevus
scissa pater latos dispergat membra per agros,
exspectas, et, quam parvo de fratre cruentam
horrescis, sumat de te patris impia mortem
195   dextera? Pelle levem magno hunc de corde timorem!
Aude, age, namque potes caede hac sperare salutem!'
     Sic fata atque avidum tepido sub pectore liquit
conceptaeque auxit dirum feritatis amorem.
Non secus ac, si forte acrem sit nactus in ima

the open water in flight, she might baffle him by delay and elude
his rage by tearing apart and scattering the body of his dear son.
Thus the father, pained and broken by such a grievous sight,
would halt and slow his journey. So the emboldened sorceress   170
foully grasps her small brother with her left hand and presses her
sword on his neck. But when she saw him lamenting his fate with
tearful groans, stretching forth his blameless hands and tender
arms, and, with whatever strength his pitiable voice could muster,
proclaiming the ugly cruelty of his sister's deed, she suddenly held   175
her weapon back and spared his throat. Duty and love for her
brother were still deep in her soul.

   Tisiphone took note and, girded with her grisly snakes, leapt
from the gloomy abode of her fellow Furies. Shrieking she flies be-   180
fore the countenance of Medea and hurls at her face twin serpents
torn from her hair. Only then does she speak: "What hollow im-
age of new-found piety has won you over? Why are you shaking?
You ought to have adopted such a stance at the time when the   185
honor due your powerful father was wrenched from him and his
vast resources subverted, when you wronged laws and gods, and
in your wildness stifled all feelings of shame! This piety would
have been becoming to you then! Now, since you have confounded
everything—both the sovereignty and every grace owed your   190
wretched sire—why hesitate to pile crime on crime? Or are you
waiting for your father savagely to scatter across the fields' breadth
your limbs which he has ripped apart, and for a father's impious
right hand to claim from you the bloody death at which you shud-
der in the case of your little brother? Banish this flimsy fear from
your 'noble' heart! Come now, take courage, for from this murder   195
you can hope for salvation!"

   With these words she lodged in Medea's lukewarm breast a
dire, passionate eagerness for the savagery that she had devised.
No differently than if deep in a valley a hound has chanced to en-

200   valle canis dubiusne feram petat, ocius autem
         hortatus doctique impulsus voce magistri
         congrediturque audetque ingentem et colligit iram:
         Tali impulsa igitur rursum Medea furore
         corripit et ferrum germani in viscera condit
205   cervicemque secat medios et dividit artus
         inque Tomitana fugiens tellure relinquit.
            Venerat antiqui rumor genitoris ad aures
         gnatam aufugisse et Graium peregrina secutam
         hospitia: Extemplo casu turbatus amaro
210   purpureum, quo indutus erat, discindit amictum
         et pectus pugnis ferit et rabido ungue capillos
         vellit et, ut capiti diadema illustre gerebat,
         et sceptrum dextra labi sinit; armaque demum,
         arma virosque vocat gnatamque ducesque Pelasgos
215   insequitur multaque ruit comitante caterva.
            Iamque propinquabat, facinus cum apparuit atrox:
         avulsum gnati caput et lacerata pudendis
         vulneribus membra atque atro squalentia tabo.
         Quod postquam agnovit scelus immensumque recepit
220   perculso infelix genitor sub corde dolorem,
         continuit pressitque gradum: Non amplius olli,
         quae fuerat, fugientem hostem comprendere cura est,
         cura sibi tantum laceri est in funere gnati.
         Ceu, cum rapta acri cursu sua pignora tigris
225   raptoremque petit, si quemquam offendit apertis
         gnatorum, studio fugiens quem liquerat arvis
         venator, commota suo se sanguine sistit
         illa, simul certant pietas materna furorque;
         interea tutus raptor fugit: Haud secus Aëtae
230   contigit. Ingentem demum laxare dolorem
         cui postquam licuit, tales dedit ore querelas:
         'O mea, gnate, quies, quondam o mea magna voluptas,

counter a fierce beast of the wild and is in doubt whether to pur-   200
sue it, goaded to action by the urgent voice of his skilled trainer,
he builds up a huge anger and rushes with daring to confront the
foe: so Medea, spurred by such madness, rouses herself and buries
her sword in her brother's entrails. She beheads him and divides
his limbs in halves, and, during her flight, abandons them in the   205
land of Tomis.

Rumor had reached the ears of her aged father that his daugh-
ter had absconded and had heeded the invitation of the Greeks to
make for a foreign soil. Bewildered by this bitter turn of fate,
straightway he tears his purple robe and beats his chest with his   210
fists He plucks out his hair with furious finger. The brilliant dia-
dem which he was wearing he lets slip from his head and his scep-
ter from his right hand. At last he calls for arms, arms and men.
He sets out in pursuit of his daughter and the Greek heroes, and
rushes forth, accompanied by a large retinue.   215

He was even now drawing near, when the dreadful crime be-
came apparent: the head of his son ripped off, his limbs shredded
with shameful wounds and dripping with dark gore. After the un-
fortunate father had comprehended the crime and absorbed the
surge of grief in his stricken heart, he brought his steps to a halt.   220
No longer, as before, does he give thought to capturing his fleeing
foe. His only consideration is the burial of the remnants of his
son. Just as when a tigress gives quick chase after her stolen young
and their thief, if she comes upon any of her offspring which the   225
hunter in his eagerness for flight has abandoned in an open field,
in her consternation she stops in their blood—rage and a mother's
piety vie with each other—meanwhile the predator flees safely
away: just such happened with Aeëtes. After he was at last able to   230
let flow the enormity of his grief, he voiced these laments: "O son,
once my serenity, once my grand delight, now the grief and cruel

nunc lassi dolor et speculum crudele parentis!
O qualem aspicere, o qualem te, parve, tueri,
235 gnate, datum est! O dulce caput dulcesque lacerti,
deliciae o nostrae quondam, nostri inclita regni
et patriae spes una tuae, quis funere tali,
quis superum mihi te rapuit? Sed numina divum
quid queror? Illa tua—nec enim soror!—illa scelesta est,
240 quae tantis me teque malis affecit iniqua!
Quodsi qua est vestra, o superi, pietasque fidesque,
adnuite his precibus: Misero quanta omnia patri
attulit, illa luat depulsa a coniuge caro!
Ut fratrem, proprios perimat sic impia gnatos,
245 quosque tulit patri gemitus, ferat illa marito!
At demum maria et terras caelumque pererrans
exsul, egens, despecta, sua se caede cruentet!'
    Fundebat pater haec lacrimans, quem deinde frequentes
collapsum excipiunt famuli. Iam navita tutam
250 solverat abscedens inimico a litore puppim,
iamque ibat patrios victor portusque petebat
Aesonides laetique nova cum coniuge Grai.

PAPIAE KAL. SEPTEMBRIS MCCCCXXXI

reflection of your careworn father, what is this self, what this sight
of you, my youthful scion, that has been given me to behold? O
sweet head, o sweet limbs, once the object in which I took delight,   235
the one glorious hope of our kingdom and your fatherland, which
of the gods, which snatched you from me in such a death? But
why should I complain about the gods' powers? She is the crimi-
nal, she—for she is no longer your sister—who in her wickedness
afflicted me and you with such ills! But if, O gods, piety and trust   240
are yours, nod approval to these prayers: the full extent of the bur-
den which she imposed on her piteous father, may she herself
suffer when sent away by her dear husband. As she did her
brother, so may the impious creature slay her own offspring. The
lamentations which she brought her father, may she bring to her   245
husband. And in the end, after she has roamed sea and earth and
sky as a fugitive, needy and despised, may she bring a bloody death
upon herself!"

This was the outpouring of the weeping father whose servants,
thronging about, caught him as he collapsed. Now the sailor had
safely unmoored his ship as he parted from the shore of his enemy.   250
Now the victorious son of Aeson, with his new wife, and the re-
joicing Greeks were on their way, their goal the harbors of their
homeland.

PAVIA, SEPTEMBER 1, 1431

ANTONIAS

[Carmen Dedicatorium]

Ad sanctissimum summumque pontificem
Eugenium papam quartum

Eugeni, ductor populi custosque fidelis,
    quae legis haec nostri dona laboris habe.
Saepius his fessam mentem mulcere licebit,
    saepius et curas his recreare tuas.
5   Non hic ficta leges ueterum mendacia uatum:
    Tu sacer et sacra dignus es historia.
Hic Antoniaden (titulum si scire libelli
    cura sit), hic diuum persequar acta patrum.
Digne pater, qui iustitia cultuque fideque
10   et populis et diis principibusque places,
digne pater, longis ne te nunc laudibus ornem,
    laus prior haec ingens splendidiorque tua est,
scilicet infestis quod tandem euasit ab undis
    te duce clauigeri naufraga cymba Dei.
15   Qui Saluatoris uestigia sancta secutus,
    tot casus nosti, totque pericla pati.

ANTONIAD

[Dedicatory Poem]

To the most holy, supreme pontiff
Pope Eugenius IV

Eugenius, captain and faithful guardian of your people, please accept these gifts, won with our toil, to read. These may more than once bring solace to your weary mind, may more than once bring refreshment from your cares. Here you will not read the false- 5
hoods of poets of old. Your holiness is worthy of a holy history. Should you wish to know the title of our little book: here I will pursue the story of Antony, here the deeds of the God-like fathers. Worthy father, who gratify peoples, saints and princes by your jus- 10
tice, civility and faith, worthy father, lest I adorn you now with lengthy praises, this is the paramount, this the more spectacular of your glories, that, under your leadership, the foundering bark of God, bearer of the keys, has for certain at last escaped from hostile seas. You, who have followed in the holy footsteps of the Sav- 15
ior, you have learned to withstand any number of disasters and perils.

Liber Primus

Non hic Pegasides, non ficta et inania Musae
nomina, non prisco numen de more uocarim,
Phoebe, tuum, neque enim regum nunc tristia bella
aut ueterem falsumque Iouem turbamue deorum
5   incertam lususque leues pompasque tumentes
ordiri est animus; nunc te, sate uirgine, te nunc
certe Deus, nunc mortales, tua munera, diuos
angelicos dicam in terris hominesque beatos.
Ergo, dei magni soboles, pande optime nostris
10 uela secunda Iesu placidusque adlabere coeptis.
Et tu, care Deo, ueterum sanctissime patrum
Antoni, cuius miro succensus amore
accingor facta Aoniis celebrare Camoenis,
nosce pium desiderium et succurre uocanti.
15   At non cuncta sequi rerum diuina tuarum
gesta uelim. Quis enim uerbis se singula posse
crediderit benefacta tuae comprehendere uitae?
Non referam quibus infernos superaueris hostes
uiribus, aspectuque truces quo pectore formas
20 horrendasque acies pugnasque exceperis acres;
insidiasque astusque et uerbera saeua tacebo.
Non celebres rarasque tuarum exponere dotes
uirtutum stabilemque animi uultusque tenorem
aggrediar: non quas animas, quae corpora sancto
25 iuueris auxilio, non quae uentura resoluens
iudicio uerus uates praeuideris alto,
non quos insignes cunctis uulgatus in oris
et populis et principibus ueneraris honores,
quodque sub aeterno mansurum tempore nomen
30 quaesieris, non mille tuae quae sancta iuuentae,

Book I

I would not here call upon the tribe of Pegasus, not on counter-
feit and vapid labels for the Muse, not, following ancient custom,
on your divine power, o Phoebus. Nor is it in any way my inten-
tion now to take as my start the baleful wars of kings, or a false Ju-
piter of old, or the elusive throng of gods, life's fleeting follies and
prideful parades. My subject will be now You, born of a virgin,   5
You, assuredly God, now mortals, your gifts, the angels of God on
earth, men worthy to be blessed. Therefore Jesus, most glorious
offspring of the mighty God, spread favorable sails for our endeav-
ors and grant calm seas. And Antony, you who are dear to God,   10
holiest of the ancient fathers, because I burn with a wondrous love
to gird myself and with the Muses of Aonia to tell of your deeds,
attend to my pious wish and lend me aid as I call upon you.

   Yet I would not wish to trace all the holy deeds you have ac-
complished. For who would imagine that he could embrace in   15
words every one of your life's noble undertakings? I will not tell of
the resilience by which you vanquished the Infernal enemies, with
what firmness you confronted savage shapes, dread battle lines and
bitter combats. I will remain silent about the treachery, the guile   20
and the savage scourges. I will not attempt to expound the special
endowment of virtues for which you are famed, and your steady
guidance of mind and mien, nor what souls, what bodies you
aided with your saintly help, nor what future events you foresaw as   25
a true prophet and revealed from your profound good judgment,
nor the excellent honors, known through all the earth, for which
you are venerated by both common people and their lords, nor the
reputation, to endure for eternity, which was your goal, nor the   30
thousand holy accomplishments which remain to us of your youth

longaeuae pariterque extant monumenta senectae.
Verum quo magni monitu imperioque Tonantis
accesti loca uasta situque horrentia longo
sacrum ingressus iter diui sacra limina Pauli
35   expediam primamque heremum primosque recessus.
Haec operis tantum nostri, haec est summa laboris.
        Creuerat et, quamuis heremique humilisque sacelli
cultor, honorato totum compleuerat orbem
nomine, confectus iam longo Antonius aeuo,
40   quo non consilio maior, quo purior alter
non foret, integriorue Deiue ardentior alter,
qui conculcarit, qui profligauerit, et se
castigans alta uirtute subegerit omnem
uim sensumque, et tot mira ratione rebelles
45   infestosque animi motus, tot dura furentis,
tam crebra infensi superarit proelia saecli,
caelestem humano ducens sub corpore uitam.
        Ergo pater senior dum secum tempora forsan
praeterita et uarios uoluit casusque uicesque,
50   ecce noua in sanctam uenit meditatio mentem.
Namque pio uersare animo, uastaeque parentem
cultoremque heremi primum se credere coepit.
quod Pater omnipotens de summo ut uidit Olympo,
haud errare uirum passus, subito agmina cogit
55   caelestum, et laetus sic alta e sede profatur:
'Felices uos o nostri pars fida cohortes,
proposito quae nos quondam meliore secutae,
aeterna et meritis coepistis debita uestris
praemia iam gaudere. Metus et ponere fas est
60   antiquos. Sedet ecce animo, semperque sedebit
illa dies, qua diuorum pulcherrimus olim
intumuit, ualida incendens tristique supernos
seditione choros, qua magno turbine miscens

or, further, of your long-lived old age. Rather I will relate how, through the commanding imperative of the Thunderer, you made your way to the desert's broad expanse, drear from length of desolation, as you set out on the holy journey to the hallowed threshold of blessed Paul, to the first hermitage and the first retreat: this 35 alone is the sum of our task, this the sum of our efforts.

He had grown old and, although his dwelling was the desert and a lowly chapel, Antony, now spent from the lengthy passage of years, had fulfilled life's round with honored name. There never would be another his superior in counsel or in purity, none more 40 whole of heart or more devoted to God. With self-discipline, he crushed, he overthrew, such was his virtue's extent, in self-mortification he annihilated every willful feeling. And, with reasoning at which to marvel, he vanquished many a contrary and destructive impulse in many a difficult conflict stemming from a maddened, 45 ruinous era. He led a saintly life in a human body.

And so, while the aged father chanced to be turning over within himself times gone by and their motley twists and turns, to his astonishment a new notion entered his thoughts for consideration. For, as his pious mind started to ponder these ideas, he began to 50 believe that he was the first elder to dwell in the desert's breadth. When the almighty Father observed this from the heights of Olympus, not suffering him to remain in error, of a sudden he summons the heavenly hosts and in happiness addresses them from his lofty throne: "O fortunate squadron, Our loyal contin- 55 gent who once upon a time followed Us and Our loftier purpose, you have begun now to enjoy the everlasting rewards due your merits. Now it is right to put aside ancient fears. Yet, consider how that day remains, and always will remain, deep-seated in the 60 mind on which some time ago the most beautiful of God's creatures puffed himself up, rousing the celestial choirs toward rebel-

innumero aethereas spoliauit numine sedes.

65 Non impune autem iusta et nos tangimur ira.
Nunc ille et populus, nunc ille miserrimus omnis
ultrices luit aeterno sub carcere poenas.
Nunc uero satis est medio fera proelia caelo
Conciuisse. At, quas etiam mortalibus imas

70 tradidimus terras, longa asperitate fatigat
bellorum. Quin arte rudes primosque parentes
transgredier nostros iussus prauoque maloque
concilio et monitis est exhortatus iniquis,
praemetuens et, quos illi suffecimus, aegra

75 mente ferens homines ad nostra haec regna uocari.
At ualuere doli multum et nocuere, fatebor,
humani donec generis commotus amore
demisi et proprium terreno pondere gnatum
uestiui, qui nostra libens mandata secutus

80 factus homo est, et martyrio tristique litatus
supplicio, ueteres sublimi sanguine culpas
purgauit, stirpemque hominum caelestibus oris
restituens, tetri rapuit de faucibus Orci.
Sic cassae antiqui fraudes iacuere draconis.

85 Necdum autem sedata sitis rabiesque nocendi est.
Quippe acuens qui se nunc luridiore ueneno,
inuidiaque ardens maiore erumpit in omnes
audaces scelerum hortatus, ius omne bonumque
proterit et rapida inuoluit uertigine terras.

90 Quoque nihil grauius fueritque dolentius unquam,
dum fallit ueterum sub relligione deorum
mortales, nostri tentat pia numina gnati
uertere, et emeritos fidei melioris honores.
Et uertet, nisi nostra modum sapientia ponat.

95 At sperate, animis atque haec aduertite laetis
quae dicam. Surgent celebres sanctique nepotes,

lion strong and dire. As he embroiled the seats of heaven in a great
whirlwind, he pillaged them of untold divinity. But punishment   65
lies in store: even We are touched by righteous anger. Now he and
his adherents, now he, worst of all, pays vengeance's full requital in
a prison ever to endure. Now it is enough to have stirred up wild
battles in the midst of heaven. But he still wears down the earth
below, which We handed over to mortals, with the long bitterness   70
of warring. He even drove the first parents, by means of the per-
verse wickedness of his counsel and of his malevolent persuasion,
in their innocence to transgress Our edicts. He lived in fear, and it
rankled in his mind, that humankind, whom We had elected in
his place, was destined to share in this, Our kingdom. But, I will   75
confess it, his wiles had much force and did much harm, until,
moved by love for the human race, I clothed My own Son with
earth's weight and sent Him down thither. Willingly He followed
Our orders. He was made man and, sacrificed as a martyr's sad   80
offering, He cleansed the old guilt through His noble blood. He
snatched mankind from the noisome jaws of Orcus and restored it
to the shores of heaven. Thus the deceits of the ancient serpent lay
useless. Yet the thirsty madness of his will to harm is not yet
slaked. Indeed, sharpening his bite, with venom now ghastlier   85
still and aflame with envy yet expanding, he attacks everyone, urg-
ing the bold on to crime. He treads upon every right that's good
and envelops the earth in a fierce maelstrom. And—there could
never be anything more grievous or painful—while he beguiles   90
mortal men with belief in the ancient gods, he attempts to pervert
the holy will of Our Son and the honors won for a better faith.
And he will bend Him unless Our wisdom puts a stop to him.
But be of good hope and attend with joyous thoughts to what I   95
have to say. Progeny renowned for their sanctity will arise, an ex-

eximius monachorum atque illustrissimus ordo,
qui summa uirtute polos et sidera tangent,
qui nostrum augebunt nomen, qui pectore forti
100   obicient sese contra bella aspera, contra
insidias, stimulos calcabuntque hostis amaros
antiqui, nostro atque gerent sub nomine quidquid
optarint, sistent fluuios, montesque mouebunt,
imperio cogent imbres noctemque diemque,
105   curabunt aegras mentes et corpora morbis
absoluent, animas ueterisque ad lumina uitae
restituent, nostro efficient quaecunque potenti
auxilio et nostra freti pietate uocarint.
Hi quanto augebunt olim terrasque iuuabunt
110   praesidio! Longis demumque laboribus actis
cernere erit quanto decorabunt lumine caelos,
quanto illustrabunt sedes splendore beatas,
in patriam magno iussi remeare triumpho.
Ecce autem caput et tantorum causa bonorum,
115   natus in Eois Aegypti Antonius oris,
quali ille integritate et quali pectore pollet,
quanta ille infernum tulit inuictissimus agmen
uirtute, horrendis caesus fractusque flagellis.
Quam longa, en cerno, simili se turba sequetur
120   exemplo, nec nunc percurrere singula nostri est
consilii, magnum est atque admirabile quidquid
uenturum longa sub posteritate tacemus.
Interea ignarum, qui se interiora latentis
se primum ratus est heremi secreta subisse,
125   stat carumque monere senem. Namque optimus alter
et prior et multis se longe antiquior annis
solus agit uasto iam pridem obscurus in antro
Paulus, Thebanis quondam sub finibus ortus,

traordinary and illustrious order of monks. They will touch the
heavens and the stars with their pinnacle of virtue. They will en-
hance Our fame and face bitter fighting and treachery with a bold
heart. They will trample beneath their feet the bitter barbs of Our   100
old enemy and under Our authority they will accomplish whatever
they desire. They will halt streams and move mountains. They
will marshal rain on command both night and day. They will cure
sick minds and rid bodies of disease. They will restore souls to the   105
brightness of the life of old. Relying on the power of Our help and
on Our piety they will accomplish whatever they ask. Under what
firm protection will they then nourish and foster the earth! And
with their lengthy labors at last completed, it will be time to be-   110
hold with what grand glow they will grace the seats of heaven,
with what brilliance will they illumine the dwellings of the blessed
when directed to return to the Father's home in mighty triumph.
Take notice of the source and stimulus of these great blessings:
Antony, born in the eastern reaches of Egypt, with what integrity,   115
with what worthiness he flourishes, with what courage, though
slashed and rent by dread scourges, he withstood the Infernal
army with never a loss. Lo! I behold how extensive is the crowd
that will emulate him as model. It is not our present plan to ex-   120
pand upon the details. We will keep silent about whatever great
and admirable will occur in the long future ahead. Meanwhile I
have in mind to rebuke the dear ancient who, in ignorance, has
considered that he was the first to enter the sequestered spots for
withdrawal in the remote desert. For there is another, the best of   125
men and far older by many years. He, Paul, born long ago within
the territory of Thebes, has lived alone for many a year, hidden
within a huge cave; he is worthy now of his generation's accolade,

iam saecli fama, iam caeli dignus honore.
130　Illum adeat uisatque senex senis ora iubeto.'
　　　　Haec diuum pater, et toti mira addita caelo est
laetitia, haud aliter quam Graium si quis amicas
uel Danaum ductor placida dum uoce cateruas
hortatur, magno innumeram cum robore gentem
135　uenturam auxilio, multa ardua corpora narret.
Laetantur speque ingenti complentur ouantes.
Tum uocat et caelo Gabrielem mittit ab alto,
utque ferat sancto quae sint facienda parenti
nuntiet et quaenam sua sit sententia mandat.
140　Ille uolat, tacitaque uirum sub nocte quieti
dum seruit, uerbis inuadit talibus ultro:
'Haec tibi de summa caeli fero nuntius arce,
Antoni: mandat diuumque hominumque creator
ut, quae sacra colit Paulus locaque abdita, poscas
145　accelerans. Hominem nulli iam nomine notum,
praestantemque incredibili uirtute uidebis.
Non tu, ut rere, prior desertae occulta subisti.
Claustra heremi prior ille, annis et grandior ille.
I, certum, pater almus, iter tibi pandet eunti.'
150　Sic ait, in tenues fugiensque relabitur auras.
At sacer, aetherei uoluens ingentia secum
iussa patris, noctem quam primum Antonius atram
dispelli, nitidum uiditque rubescere caelum,
haud mora carpit iter iussum, baculoque seniles
155　sustentans artus graditur, per quae horrida nescit
deserta, et quorum fidens sub numine tendit,
caelicolas mitis caeli regemque precatur.

now of the honor of heaven. See to it that the old man comes to
visit him and to cast eyes on his elder's features."   130

　　These were the words of the Father of the heavenly hosts, and a
wondrous joy enhanced the whole of heaven. It was as if some
leader of the Greeks or of the Trojans, while he prompts his
friendly troops with measured voice, tells of a numberless people
with many a stalwart body coming with great strength to their aid.   135
They rejoice and in their happiness are filled with boundless hope.
Then He beckons Gabriel and speeds him from the lofty heavens
to tell the saintly father what he must do and commands him to
be messenger of His judgment. He takes flight and, when he   140
comes upon the man, at peace in night's silence, without ado he
addresses him thus: "A messenger from heaven's highest citadel, I
bring these words, Antony: the Creator of immortals and of hu-
mankind bids that you hasten to seek out the remote, holy spot
which Paul inhabits. You will witness a man known to no one now   145
by name and excelling in unparalleled virtue. Though it is your
belief, you were not the first to choose the hidden places of
the desert. The sahara's cloister was his, first, and he is older in
years. On your way, good father. A sure route will lie open for
your journey." After these words he takes flight, gliding into the   150
thin breezes. But blessed Antony ponders to himself the imposing
mandates of the heavenly Father, and as soon as he sees black
night scattered and the sky glimmer with red, with no delay he
presses on his route, as he was bidden. He supports his aged limbs
on his staff as he goes through the dread desert of which he is ig-   155
norant. He prays to the kindly heaven-dwellers and the King of
heaven, trusting in whose divine will he makes his way.

Liber Secundus

Interea infelix horrendi rector Auerni
conuocat infernos, et amaro pectore coetus
alloquitur, tristi fundens has ore querelas:
'Hae nostrae en, socii, uires, haec gloria nostri,
5   hoc regni decus? Ingenio taline nocemus?
Calliditas haec nostra, hi sunt astusque dolique?
Hae frustratae artes, heu, cassa infractaque nostri
consilii uis et nostrorum illusa laborum!
Quid primos astu captos peccasse parentes,
10   quid prodest miseros tot inde luisse nepotes
facta patrum propria, si uitam morte redemit
omnipotens, proprio si crimine sanguine lauit?
Haud Dominum seruos tantum exarsisse putassem,
ut pro se morti caput ultro offerret acerbae.
15   Nunc quod cum magno cogor meminisse dolore,
cedimus, atque ipsis uicti a mortalibus omnes,
per terras longe abiecti indecoresque fugamur.
Nec nostrae insidiae, nec, quis saeuire solemus,
ingentes stimuli, nec bella ingentia possunt.
20   Cernitis, ut reliquos taceam, quo robore nostras
sustinuit pugnas, quam mente Antonius aequa
nostra flagella tulit, qua ui nos ille fatigat
nunc miseros, quibus excruciat nunc ille flagellis.
Et nunc caelesti iussu uastissima fertur
25   per deserta petens Paulum non dispare cultu,
non uita inferiore hominem, sed cognita nulli est
fama latentis adhuc. Vereor, nec uana uereri
causa monet, ne, si placidis se amplectier ulnis,
inque uicem fari et dextras contingere detur,

Book II

Meanwhile the ill-starred ruler of dread Avernus calls together the inhabitants of Hell, and addresses the assembly in harshness of heart, spewing these complaints from embittered lips: "Comrades, is what you see our strength? Is this our glory? Is this the honor our rule can claim? With such genius what harm do we wreak? Is 5 this our cleverness, these our wiles and our deceits? Alas, this art- istry of ours is stymied, and the force of our wisdom and of our travails vain, broken, only a dream! What does it profit us that the first parents committed sin when enmeshed in our intrigue? What good is it that as a result so many of their descendants paid a pen- 10 alty for their forebears' misdeeds if the Almighty redeemed their lives through His own death, if He washes away their crime with His own blood? I would not have thought that the Lord felt so passionately about His servants that He would willingly offer His life on their behalf in a bitter death. Now we are giving way—I am compelled to remember it to my great sorrow—and, van- 15 quished by mortals themselves, in humiliation and disgrace we are all put to flight to realms far distant. Neither our plottings nor the mighty goads with which we were wont to show our rage, nor our grand forays into war have any power. To be silent about the rest, you see with what inner fortitude Antony has withstood our at- 20 tacks, with what equanimity he has borne our scourgings, with what power he wears us down, poor creatures that we now are, with what scourges he tortures us! And now, under dictates from heaven, he makes his way through the vastness of the desert to find Paul, a man of like devotion and no less character, but be- 25 cause of his sequestered life his reputation is known to none. I fear, and good reason warns me to fear, that, if opportunity comes for them to enclose each other in tender embrace, to speak each in turn, and to clasp hand with hand, the meeting of the aged fathers

30   in nostra annosi iungant se damna parentes.
     Quocirca quid consilii capiamque sequarque
     haud scio; nota hominum uita et constantia nota est;
     sat mihi sit tanti uos admonuisse pericli.
     Si qua uia est, uos ite, malisque obsistite uestris.'
35   Dixerat, et magno cuncti infremuere tumultu,
     perculsi affatu tanto: uelut improba quando
     praedonum manus insidiis loca tuta uiasque
     perturbat, foedusque ruens conspirat in unum;
     si ualidam sese contra uidet ire uirum uim,
40   tristatur, metuitque nouis iam uiribus impar.
         Et iam consensu cunctorum emissus ab ima
     sede Satan, caeli inuisas conscenderat auras.
     Continuo horrendam effigiem, qua fallere sanctum
     ac terrere uirum, spe multum aggressus inani est,
45   induit—os informe hominis, pectusque manusque,
     cetera equum—tali mentitus imagine, qualem
     centauris docti tribuere immanibus olim,
     dum multa exornant, dum fingunt plurima uates.
     Iam medium peragrarat iter, libransque regebat
50   ardentes Sol altus equos, ubi se obtulit horrens
     forma uiro. Stetit et paulum conterritus haesit.
     Deinde Dei auxilio tutans se Antonius, ultro
     occupat: 'Heus tu, oro an quisquam sub finibus istis
     uir carusque Deoque placens latet incola forsan?'
55   Ille nihil contra, namque id diuina uetabant
     iussa, ausus tentare uirumue illudere uerbis,
     sed blandas rigido uoces e pectore, quamuis
     non intellectas, fudit dextraque cupitum
     protensa monstrauit iter; per deinde patentes
60   effusus cursu campos, mirabile uisu,
     ex oculis Geticae diffugit harundinis instar.

spells ruin for us. So I have no idea what plan I'll seize upon and 30
follow. Their lives we know well. We know their steadfastness.
May it be enough for me to have forewarned you of this great
threat. If there is any way, hurry and block the mischief that por-
tends." After his words were finished the whole throng shouted 35
with a mighty roar, stricken by such an outburst: just as when an
ignoble band of robbers by their subterfuge brings trouble to
places and roadways ordinarily safe, and hastens, as one, to swear
in compact; if it sees a man marching mightily against it, it grows
anxious and fears now to be unequal to the new force. 40

And now by universal agreement Satan was sent forth from his
Infernal post and had climbed to the hated upper air. Forthwith, a
prey to empty hope, he adopted a hideous shape with which he at-
tempted to deceive and frighten the holy old man — the mal-
formed visage, the chest and hands of a human, for the rest a 45
horse — mimicking the fictive image such as once upon a time was
attributed to huge Centaurs by learned poets who were about their
work of embellishing much, inventing still more. And now the
lofty sun had gained the midpoint of his journey and drove his
burning horses in tandem, when the dreadful shape advanced be- 50
fore the saint. He halted and, terrified for a moment, he hesitated.
Then, shielding himself with God's aid, Antony seized the occa-
sion on his own: "Tell me please, I ask you, is there by chance
some man dwelling in these parts who is both dear and pleasing to
God?" There was nothing from the creature in response, for the 55
dicta of heaven forbade that he dare put that man to the test or
deceive him with words. But he spouts forth seductive sounds
from his hardened chest, though they could not be understood,
and with his right hand stretched out he pointed toward the de-
sired path. Then, sped on his way through the wide-extending
fields, he fled from sight — it was a marvel to witness — like a Getic 60
arrow.

Obstupuit pater admirans casumque uirumque.
Tum, se commendans superis superumque parenti,
progreditur. Nec longa mora est: ecce altera monstri
65   saxosam conuallem inter se forma bicornis
humana effigie, sed aduncis naribus offert
quae capram media parte inferiore figurat.
Hanc palmae fetus, quasi pacis signa, ferentem
ut uidit, primum ille Dei se numine firmat.
70   Tum qui sit, quoue ex genere, aut quis casibus actus
adueniat, fari hortatur. Sic semiuir illum
hortantem placido supplex est ore secutus:
'Ne dubita, non uana oculos decepit imago
nostra tuos, pater, o magnis carissime diuis,
75   et mortalis ego, et mortali ex sanguine cretus,
et tacita haec habito, quae nunc deserta pererras.
Sum numero ex illorum olim quos caeca uetustas
admirata deos, satyros, faunosque uocauit.
Legatum tibi me sociorum turba meorum
80   transmittit: pater, unanimes te, diue, precamur,
communem ut dominum pro nostra orare salute
digneris; scimus siquidem certumque fatemur:
namque omnem fama illius penetrauit in orbem,
quanta homines pietate et quanto exarsit amore,
85   pro quis et se hominem nasci, natumque necari
tam dira passus morte est.'
                         Nec plura locutus
conticuit; stabat defixo Antonius ore,
iam dudum mirans et uultum et uerba loquentis.
Dum tantosque animo affatus casusque uolutat,
90   ingenti prae laetitia longum ille profusis
emanans lacrimis praedulcibus ora rigabat,
ac ueluti redeunte nouo cum germinat anno,
arridetque omnis reuirescens frondibus arbos,

The father was spellbound in astonishment at both the event and the monster. Then, commending himself to the dwellers in heaven and to their Father, he continues on his way. Scarcely a delay and, lo, another strange specter, with human form but twin-horned and with hooked nose, presents itself amid a rocky glen. A goat gave shape to the lower part of its middle. When Antony saw that it carried palm shoots as a sign of peace, he first confirms his resolve under God's will. Then he presses him to tell who he is, what his race and what chanced to bring him there. At his urging the half-man thus replied with a suppliant's calm voice: "Cast doubt away, father, beloved of the great saints. Ours is not an empty image that has deceived your eyes. I also am mortal and sprung from mortal blood. I too dwell in this silent desert which you now roam. I am of that troop whom the awestruck ancient world blindly labeled gods, satyrs and fauns. The mass of my com-rades sends me forth as legate to you. One and all we beseech you, hallowed father, that you deign to pray to our mutual Lord for our salvation. Indeed we know and we confess it a certainty, for His repute has made its way throughout the whole world, with what piety, with what love He has burned for men on whose behalf He allowed Himself to be born a human and then His Son be put to so dreadful a death."

Words finished he fell silent. Antony stood with steady glance, for a long time now, long lost in wonder at the speaker's demeanor and at his words. While he was pondering the import of his utter-ance and the situation before him, from a surge of joy he damp-ened his cheeks with a continued burst of weeping, a flood of the sweetest tears, just as, when a tree begins to bud when the new year returns, it smiles as its foliage grows green all over with fresh

65

70

75

80

85

90

tunc largus laetis aperit se e uitibus humor,
95   tunc omnis lacrimans lucentes parturit arbos.
Dehinc baculo terram pulsans: 'Heu, quae impia uanis',
inquit, 'Alexandrina deis gens construis aras!
Heu, quae caelestes falsis exsoluis honores
numinibus, gens infelix, quae temnere uerum
100   saluatorem audes hominum quem bellua mitis
fassa ultro est et opem precibus uenerata poposcit!'
Talia conquestus senior, ceu forsitan audent
cum serui in dominum, paret cui fida canum uis.
Necdum finis erat uerbis, uolucri pede quando
105   cornigerum se animal tollens per deuia fugit.

Liber Tertius

Longa peragrabat sanctus deserta uiator
et iam bis radiis Sol illustrauerat orbem
et bis nox tenebras induxerat humida terris.
Iam quid agat, iam quo uertat uir se optimus ergo
5   ignarus, quae spes tantum restabat, ad altum
intendens caelum palmas extendit utrasque
per totam insomnis noctem longasque profundit
cum gemitu lacrimisque preces, caelestia poscens
auxilia. Et nondum roseis prouecta quadrigis
10   linquebat solitum Tithoni Aurora cubile,
cum per pallentis dubiae ire crepuscula noctis
cernit anhelantem propius montisque petentem
vicini uacua antra lupam, quam deinde secutus
actutum pater est oculis uestigia fixis
15   obseruans, demumque feram abscessisse ubi sensit,
speluncae stetit ante aditus, paulumque moratus,

life. Then lavish sap flows from the flourishing vines, then every
tree begets a flood of gleaming tears. Thereupon, striking the   95
ground with his staff, he says: "Alas for you, pagan people of Alex-
andria, who rear altars to empty gods, woe to you, unfortunate
folk, who pay to made-up spirits honors due the saints in heaven,
who dare to despise the true Savior of mankind to whom a gentle   100
beast willingly confessed belief and reverently asked for His help
with prayer." Such were the old man's sorrowful complaints, as it
were, perhaps, when slaves grow restive against their master whose
hounds obey with the strength of loyalty. He had not yet put an
end to his words when the horned creature took to its heels and
fled through the thickets at a quick pace.   105

Book III

The saintly wayfarer was travelling through the desert's length,
and now the sun had twice illuminated the earth with its rays, and
twice damp night had swathed the land in shade. This best of
men, unsure of what now he should do, of where now to turn, of
what hope yet remained, glanced, therefore, at the heavens above   5
and stretched forth both his hands. Sleepless, he pours forth
prayer after prayer the whole night through, with moans and tears
begging for succor from heaven. And not yet had Aurora, drawn
on a roseate chariot, left her wonted bedchamber of Tithonus   10
when, through the gloaming of the wan, withdrawing night he
spies not far off a mother wolf making her way, panting, as she
seeks out the empty cave of a nearby mountain. The father then
followed her forthwith, tracking her footprints intently. When he
noticed that she had eventually made her way out of view, he   15

atque introspiciens caecis nil uidit in umbris.
Suspenso mox se fert intra limina passu
progrediens, simul intentis atque auribus omnem
20 luminibusque locum explorans, tum forsitan atram
per noctem tremulum lumen splendescere uidit.
Quo uiso properare et iam sperare quietem
incertaeque uiae melius confidere coepit,
non secus ac si quando, sitis quem torquet anhela,
25 sollicito ceruus gressu dubioque per umbras
siluarum ingentes per camposque anxius errat
ignarusque locorum ignotas quaeritat undas.
Tunc si forte sonum crepitantum et murmur aquarum
auditum agnorint aures, laetatur et acri
30 iam uolitat pede, iam liquidi spem concipit amnis.
Sic pater. At magno dum membra senilia demum
uisendi desiderio studioque fatigat,
accelerans lapidem caeca sub nocte iacentem
incidit obiectuque pedis se offendit amaro
35 ingentemque dedit strepitum, quo concitus altae
uir mentis, dum forte Deo uacat, ostia Paulus
accurrens claudit, solido et munimine firmat.
Ut solet in uasto si quis regit aequore nauim,
cum tonitru horrendo primum strepere aera sentit,
40 colligere et uelis ualidos aptare rudentes
fortius et cura maiore incumbere remis
et si quid desit naui succurrere egenti.
Utque aper audita, dum saltibus errat apricis,
uoce canum subito latebrarum se obice tutans,
45 frondosa aut silua, secreto aut conditur antro.
    Tum bonus ante fores clausas senioris amici
multa diu placido fundens Antonius ore,
perstitit obsecrans aditum: 'Per si qua tibi,' inquit,
'est pietas, miserere, oro, pater optime. Nosti

stood before the entrance of the cavern. After a brief pause, he
peered inside and saw nothing in the black shadows. Soon with
hesitant step he makes his way forward across the threshold, his
ears all alert and eyes glancing around the whole expanse. Then he   20
chanced to spy a quivering light glimmering through the dusky
gloom. After he had seen this, he hastened along, beginning now
to hope for an end to his efforts and to put greater confidence in a
journey that remained uncertain. He was like a stag whom gasping
thirst tortures: with troubled, tentative step he roams in worry   25
through the deep forest shade and along the fields. Ignorant of the
region, he goes in search of liquid he knows not where. Then, if
by chance his ears catch the trickling sound of water's plash, he re-
joices. Now his hastening feet gain speed, now he imagines the
hope of a clear stream. Thus father Antony. But while he was tir-   30
ing his ancient limbs from yearning and from striving to see some-
thing at last, as he hurries along in night's blackness he comes up
against a rock lying before him. He struck the offending barrier
hard with his foot and gave a loud cry. Roused by this, while he   35
chanced to be at prayer to God, Paul, a man of wisdom, hastens to
close the portal and to secure it with a firm bar. So if someone is
steering a ship on the broad sea, when he first feels the air rumble
with the dread of thunder, he is accustomed to pull together the
sturdy sheets and to fit them boldly to the sails. He leans on the   40
oars with greater insistence and lends whatever help his ship may
still need. So a boar, while it ranges the sun-drenched glades, if it
hears the barking of hounds, immediately seeking safety for itself
in a secure hiding place, buries itself either in a leafy wood or a
withdrawn hollow.   45

   Then good Antony stood for a long time before the closed
doorway of his elder friend, pouring forth a flow of pleas from his
mouth and asking gently for admittance: "If you have any pity,
best of fathers," he says, "I beg you, have mercy on me. You are

50 qui ueniam, quae causa uiae, quis missus ab oris.
    Si tibi nulla mei cura est, tua namque, fatebor,
    haud mereor, pater, ora tuos uultusque tueri,
    tantorum at saltem tibi sit cura ulla laborum.
    Concedesne feris aditus hominique negabis
55 qui per tot te dura petit discrimina, per tot
    incertasque grauesque uias aestusque furentes?
    Pande fores, pater: hinc nusquam discedere fixum
    propositum est, ubi uiuentem contempseris, at me
    extinctum certe excipies condesque sepulchro.'
60 Talia persistens lacrimis fundebat obortis.
    Cui sic ille refert paucis: 'Per totne labores
    uenisti nostro conspectu admittier optans?
    Nunc moriturum autem te, ni admittare minaris,
    impetrantne minis alii?' Sic fatus est. Olli
65 arridens dextra postes patefecit amica
    suscepitque hominem sanctum sanctissimus hospes,
    inque ruens eius complexum atque oscula iungens,
    sic prior aggreditur: 'Quem tu, o carissime, tanta,
    Antoni, cura tantoque labore petisti,
70 ecce ego nunc longa marcens aetate rigensque
    canitie inculta membrisque trementibus et iam
    parua mora est lacerum putensque horrensque cadauer.'
        Haec senior, simul intra heremi penetralia diuum
    eximio flagrans hominem ducebat amore.
75 Vestibulum hic ingens intus, cui desuper altos
    palma uetus ramos caelo fundebat aperto.
    Quodque inter nitidis oriens purissimus undis
    se circum uiridante solo fons lene fluebat.
    Inde per exesum loca errant ibi plurima montem
80 atque intus uastae incudes et multa fabrilis
    materiae instrumenta quibus iam certa uetusque
    historia est: illo percussa numismata furtim

aware of who I am, of what was the reason for my journey, from   50
where I was sent. If you have no concern for me—for, allow me to
speak from the heart, I do not at all deserve to glimpse the features
of your face—yet at least show some interest in the enormous tri-
als I have undergone. Will you allow entrance to animals but deny
it to a man who seeks you out through so many harsh hazards, so   55
many unsure, dangerous pathways and heat's constant seething?
Open your doors, father. I remain firm in my purpose never to de-
part from here. Though you have despised me while I was still
alive, yet you will take me in for sure when I have died and will
bury me in a tomb." Remaining where he was he let free a contin-   60
ued flood of tears. This was the brief reply to him: "Have you
made your way through so many times of trial, desirous of being
admitted to our sight? And now you threaten that your death is
imminent unless are allowed entrance. Do others gain success
through intimidation?" Speaking these words with a smile, he laid
open the door for him with the hand of friendship, and the holiest   65
of hosts received his holy guest. Rushing into his embrace and
kissing him, he is the first to speak: "Look at me, dearest Antony,
whom you have sought out with such trouble and such suffering,
look at me, withered and stiffened from my length of years, my   70
white hair unkempt and my limbs shaking. And in a short time
now I'll be a corpse—falling apart, decaying, dreadful."

As the elder spoke, with a display of the warmest affection he
led the holy man within the hermitage's inner sanctum. This had
an expansive entranceway over which an ancient palm tree show-   75
ered lofty branches against the open sky. In its midst the purest
of fountains arose from gleaming waters and spread a soft flow
around the tree on the verdant earth. From there they wander
through the vast spaces of the hollowed mountain. Within were
huge anvils and the many tools of the smithy's trade. These had a   80
history as old as it was certain: coins were struck there in secret at

tempore, quo iunctus Cleopatra Antonius olim est.
Huc igitur sese uix pubescentibus annis
85   contulerat fugiens odia infensissima Paulus,
quae Decius studiis et Vallerianus iniquis,
infandae binae pestes, immania monstra,
contra exercebant Christum Christique fideles
cultores. Et iam prope centum, haud cognitus unquam,
90   hic latitans, mirum dictu, transegerat annos.
Ipsa ministrarat uestitum palma cibumque.

    Tale intra hospitium laeta cum fronte receptus,
tale intra penetrale senex Aegyptius ibat,
ingentesque Deo laudes pro munere tanto
95   fundebat. Vitrei tum uero in margine fontis
multa recensentes fessi sedere parentes,
nunc annos casusque suos narrabat uterque,
nunc hominum studia et mores, nunc saeua potentum
imperia et regum Furias. Nunc, si qua nefandae
100   relligionis adhuc starent monumenta, rogabat.
Hic miserans uerbis ille exponebat amicis.
Quales, diuersis si qui iunguntur ab oris,
militiae assueti duros tolerare labores,
congaudent, uarioque simul sermone fruentes,
105   magnorum heroum casus et bella recensent.

    Haec inter, sedisse alta super arbore coruum
suspectant plaudentem alis atque ore ferentem
flauentis micam Cereris, quam deinde uolatu
se coram leni posuit: miratus uterque
110   substitit, his Paulus prior est tunc uocibus usus:
'Nunc te, nunc quanta es nosco, o dilecte Deo uir,
uirtute et quanta diuae integritudine uitae.
Iam bis sex actis hoc munus ab alite lustris
dimidium excepi: nunc te adueniente benignus
115   integra dona Deus ferri caelestia iussit,

the time, long ago, when Antony was married to Cleopatra. It was
here that Paul, scarcely even a youth, betook himself, in flight
from the loathsome hatred which Decius and Valerian, unspeak-   85
able banes, two towering monsters, with zealous evil unleashed
against Christ and the faithful worshippers of Christ. And now —
a wonder to tell — he had passed nearly a hundred years here in
hiding, scarcely known to anyone. The palm itself had served him   90
for clothing and food.

Welcomed with happy countenance inside such a hostelry, in-
side such a shrine, Antony, the old man of Egypt, made his way,
and gave voice to a flood of praises to the Lord for such a gift.
Then the two exhausted fathers sat by the edge of the glassy foun- 95
tain, passing many matters in review. Each spoke now of the story
of his adventures over the years, now of the inclinations and habits
of mankind, now of the harsh autocracy of maddened kings in
power. Now he asked if any memories still remained of paganism's
curse. The other in pity gave reply with kindly words. They were   100
like men schooled to endure the trials of soldiering. They rejoice
when they come together from different parts and, while finding
pleasure in varied conversation together, they recount the exploits
and battles of mighty heroes.   105

During their talk, they catch sight of a crow, flapping its wings
as it settled on the lofty tree and carrying in its beak a piece of
golden bread which in gentle glide it then deposited near them.
The two paused in astonishment. It was the turn of Paul to speak   110
first: "O man beloved of God, now, now I perceive how great your
virtue is and how great the integrity of your holy life. For sixty
years already I have received the blessing of this half-loaf from the
winged creature that you see. Now with your arrival God in His
beneficence has ordered that the heavenly gift be whole and entire, 115

dona suum quae longum in te testentur amorem.
Ergo haec omnipotens quae nobis munera mittit
tanta, libens sume atque tua tu diuide dextra.'
'Immo', ait ille, 'tua est et uita et dignior aetas,
120   te potius partire decet.' Certamine tali
contendere diu patres et iam ibat in undas
occiduas Sol pronus equosque urgebat anhelos.
Tandem quisque sua — placuit sententia namque haec —
apprehendit dextra munus Cereale simulque
125   apprehensum leuiter partes diuisit in aequas.
Inde Deum summis tollentes laudibus ambo,
se pariter tenui uictu recreantque fouentque
et pariter liquidi libantes fontis amoenas
excipiunt undas, uigilem tum scilicet omnem
130   orantes noctemque Deo duxere uacantes.

Liber Quartus

Ecce rubens currum Sol matutinus agebat
et madidae in uiridi lucebant gramine guttae.
Tunc placido externum Paulus sermone parentem
compellat: 'Te, care, sub his regionibus, hospes,
5   esse olim certo scibam, quem maximus alti,
praesentis quando uitae suprema ueniret
laeta dies, uenturum ad me regnator Olympi est
pollicitus; nunc ecce animo flagrante cupitum
optatumque diu tempus, quo carcere tandem
10   soluar ab hoc abiens, aeternaque regna reuisam.
Tu missus qui uita meos ubi linqueret artus
contegere effossa uellesque recondere terra.
Tu repete ergo domum contextaque munera palli,

a gift which bears witness to His abiding love for you. Therefore please take with gladness this extraordinary present which the Almighty sends us, and divide it with your right hand." "Rather," the other responds, "your life and your age are the worthier. It befits instead you to do the dividing." Such was the protracted struggle   120 in which the fathers engaged as now the sun began to plunge toward the western waves and to quicken his panting horses on. This at last was the procedure agreed upon: each clutched the gift of bread in his right hand and, once grasped, partitioned it easily into equal shares. Then, glorifying God with exalted praises, to- 125 gether they find themselves refreshed and nourished from the meager fare, and together they drink the delicious waters which they pour from the clear fountain. We may be sure that they then spent the whole night awake, devoting themselves to God.   130

Book IV

Suddenly the morning's ruddy sun was spurring his chariot ahead and drops of dew were glinting on the green grass. Then Paul addressed his brother-guest with kindly speech: "I knew for sure, my dear visitor, that you would one day be with me in my dwelling here, you whom the almighty Ruler of lofty Olympus had prom- 5 ised me would come when the final happy day of my earthly existence arrived. Now, behold, this is the moment for which with burning mind I have yearned and prayed, day after day, the time when at last I will be released from this prison and, abandoning the earth, I would see again the eternal kingdom. You were sent   10 who would wish to cover over my limbs, when life had abandoned them, and to bury them where you had dug out the ground. Therefore go home in search of a woven mantle which bishop

quae tibi Athanasius praesul donauerat olim,
15   affer, ut extinctum sancto uelamine corpus
obuoluas.' Sic fatus erat, sic ille rogarat,
non quo cura sibi tectus nudusue iaceret
qui palmae intextis foliis tam paupere amictu
contentus sese tantum uestire solebat,
20   sed quo illum instantis mortis maerore leuaret
tantisper, patrias ratus est dimittere ad oras.
His pater auditis stupefactus pectore toto
constitit, admirans diuina Antonius ora
diuinasque eius uoces, quam spiritus esset
25   incensus, quam gnara sibi, quam plena Deo mens.
Tum ne desereret sese, lacrimansque gemensque,
et comitem exciperet, quaecunque ad fata, rogabat.
Contra ille: 'Hanc, te quaeso,' inquit, 'nunc exue curam
et te certa dies, suprema et meta laborum
30   fixa manet; nunc ad commune piumque tuorum
exemplum sociorum almae et uestigia uitae
te mundo—iam mitte preces—superesse necesse est.'
Amplius haud uerbis audens Antonius ullis
obniti, sancto primum fert oscula patri;
35   iussa uiri deinde exsequitur, senioque grauatos
exercet rursum gradiens artusque fatigat.

    Haec inter rex aetheriae sanctissimus aulae
caelestes uocat ad sese longo ordine turmas,
ut terrasque petant, utque atro e corpore soluant
40   felicemque animam Pauli alta ad sidera manda⟨n⟩t
ut laeto applausu, laeto ut comitentur honore.

    Et iam contigerat uir sanctus tecta domumque
optatam et patriis fessus consederat aruis.
Ecce duo, quos longaeuo sibi pectore fidos
45   et uita insignes delegerat ille ministros,
confectum excipiunt longarum mole uiarum,

Athanasius once gave you as a gift. Bring it so that you can clothe
this lifeless corpse in the holy wrap." He spoke thus and asked   15
such a favor not because he worried about whether he would lie
covered or naked, he who was content regularly to dress himself
only in a poor garment of woven palm leaves, but, so that he
might for the present relieve Antony from the sadness of impend-   20
ing death, he thought to send him off to the region of his fathers.
When he heard this, father Antony stood stunned in his whole
heart, in awe at Paul's announcement, at his words as if from
heaven, how on fire was his spirit, how self-aware his mind and
filled with God. Then, amid tears and lamentation, Antony   25
prayed that Paul not desert him and that he accept him as col-
league, whatever remained in store. In response Paul says: "Put
this care from you now, I beseech you. A fixed day and a firm, final
goal for your struggles awaits you also. Now cease your appeals. It   30
is necessary that you remain in the world as universal, holy model
for your comrades and as pattern for a nurturing life." Not daring
to object further, first Antony approaches the holy father to offer
kisses. Then he follows Paul's orders. He starts on his trek and   35
tires out his limbs, overwhelmed with old age, as he again presses
on his way.

Meanwhile the most holy King of the palace of heaven calls His
celestial squadrons to Him in a long rank that they might be
earthbound so as to release the fortunate soul of Paul from his
darkened body and to entrust it to the stars above, accompanying   40
it with joyous applause and joyous acclaim.

And now the holy man had reached the ancestral dwelling
which was his aim and, exhausted, had taken a seat amid its fields.
And, behold, two men, whom he had chosen as his servants for
their longstanding trust and their behavior beyond reproach, come   45

confectum et longo senio recreantque, parentem
conspectuque eius laeti amplexuque fruuntur,
quales forte diu qui non uidere magistrum
50   absentem, demum redeuntem agnoscere laeta
fronte canes et mulcere et contingere gaudent.
Non secus hi tum causa morae quae tanta requirunt,
quis latitans steteritque locis. Pauca ille locutus:
'Vidi hominem quo non est alter sanctior,' inquit,
55   'diuinum humano specimen sub pectore uidi.'
Talia dicentem sacra atque antistitis una
munera Athanasi secum deferre parantem,
ut quaenam tanta haec essent exponeret olli,
poscebant. Abiens senior, 'Ne quaerite, alumni,
60   cetera,' ait, 'neque enim praestat nunc cetera fari.'
Ergo ad grandaeuum citius tendebat amicum,
unum illum cupiens, unum illum, uita priusquam
linqueret aethereas et spiritus iret in auras,
complecti coram flagrans coramque tueri.
65   Postera iamque dies aderat breuis et uia eunti
restabat. Tunc forte oculos Antonius altos
sustollens, miro Paulum candore nitentem
plaudentes inter diuum longasque cateruas
uidit siderei scandentem ad culmina caeli.
70   Magnanimos tali Capitolia ad alta triumpho,
si minima aequare et summis componere fas est,
Romulidas uicto credas ex hoste redisse.
Tum lacrimans atroque incomptam in puluere foedans
canitiem, 'Cur, Paule,' inquit, 'me deseris, ut quid
75   me sine supremum uoluisti attingere finem
et sine me longos uitae finire labores?
Cur mihi te tam sera dies ostenderat, ut nunc
tam subita eriperet? Salue, o uenerande, Deoque
uiue ualeque pater.' Sic fatus, et ilicet acri

to meet their master, spent from the trials of his extended journey
and worn down with his length of age. Happy at the sight of him,
they enjoy his embrace and offer him refreshment, like hounds,
who have not seen their absent master for awhile, with happy grin   50
acknowledge that he has returned at long last, and they find plea-
sure in fawning upon him and rubbing against him. So they, in
their way, ask what was the reason for his great delay and where
he had stayed away in hiding. His answer was brief: " I saw a man
holier than any other," he says; " I saw the likeness of God in a hu-   55
man breast." While he was voicing these words and preparing to
take away with him the blessed gift of bishop Athanasius, they ask
that he explain what was his purpose with this great object. The
old man, as he departs, says: "Do not inquire further, my com-
rades; it is of no value to explain anything more just now." And so   60
he made his way as fast as he could to his ancient friend, yearning
eagerly to draw near him to contemplate him alone, him alone to
embrace before his life departed and his spirit set its course to the
breezes of heaven.

And now the next day was barely at hand with the journey still   65
ahead of him, when it chanced that Antony, raising his eyes aloft,
saw Paul, glimmering with an astonishing brightness and climbing
to the starry heights of heaven amid the crowded throng of ap-
plauding saints. With such a triumph you might believe that the   70
high-souled sons of Romulus — if it is proper to compare the least
with the foremost — returned to the lofty Capitolium, after the en-
emy was conquered. Then in tears, fouling his unkempt white hair
with dark dust, he says: "Paul, why do you abandon me, and why
is it your wish to reach the final goal without me and without me   75
to put an end to life's long labors? Why was the day that showed
you to me so near setting that now it snatches you so suddenly
from me? Hail and farewell, father, worthy of my devotion. Live
now with God." After these words, his mind aflame with love's

80 ardore incensus mentis reliquum omne cucurrit
    instar auis uolitantis iter, ceu quando sopora
    stertentes placidam capimus sub nocte quietem
    et nunc sistere, nunc agiles attollere plantas
    et passim longum ferri per inane uidemur.
85   Mox introgressus speluncam, tendere palmas
    inflexis genibus sublato et uertice uidit
    exanimum Pauli corpus, hunc uiuere primum
    credidit orabatque simul gressumque tenebat,
    quem postquam agnouit uitali lumine cassum,
90 proripuit subito, lacrimis atque oscula largis
    mixta gerens, et inexpletis complexibus haerens,
    ingentis gemitus dedit ingentisque ululatus.
    Ac demum sacro defuncti corpus amici,
    quem secum tulerat, circumuoluebat amictu
95 solemnesque illi cantus ex more ferebat
    supremosque simul mortis soluebat honores.
    Tum frustra terram, qua sancta reconderet ossa,
    effodere aggressus, neque enim quo id posset haberet,
    indoluit uarioque diu sub corde uolutans
100 quid faceret, staretne, domum tandemne rediret
    diuinumque patrem tumuli sine honore iacentem
    linqueret, ecce duo fusis per colla leones
    ex heremo interiore iubis decurrere cernit.
    Extimuit primo aspectu, tum lumina uertens
105 ad superos stetit, intrepidam mentemque recepit.
    Olli demissis animis et pectore miti,
    mira fides, petiere senis uenerabile corpus
    illiusque pedes circa accubuere frementes
    extinctumque prope humana pietate querentes.
110 Dehinc pedibus tantum terrae scalpuntque ruuntque
    certatim, quantum tumulo satis esset, et ipsum
    eximere⟨n⟩t cura patremque leuare⟨n⟩t egentem.

keen ardor, he ran the whole way like a bird on the wing: such is   80
the moment when, snoring during the drowsy night, we claim our
rest in sleep's calm, now we seem to stop still, now to lift our nim-
ble feet, now to be born along hither and yon through a vast void.

As soon as he entered the cave, he saw the lifeless body of Paul,   85
on his knees, hands outstretched and head raised. He believed at
first that he was still alive. At once he uttered a prayer and stood
where he was. Afterward, when he realized that the corpse lacked
life's light, he hurriedly rushed forward, offering kisses mixed with   90
many a tear, and, clinging in an embrace never to bring response,
he uttered groan upon groan, wail after wail. Finally he wrapped
the body of his lifeless friend in the holy shroud that he had car-
ried with him, and he performed for him the customary chants   95
and along with them completed the final rites for the dead. Then
he attempted in vain to turn over the ground in which he might
bury the bones of the saint. He grieved that he did not possess the
means to do so. While he was debating in his changing heart what
he should do, whether he should stay or at last return home and   100
abandon the saintly father to lie there without the honor of a
grave, lo, he sees two lions, manes flowing over their necks, come
on a run from the interior of the desert. He was at first fearful at
the sight. Then with his eyes turned to the heavenly beings above,
he regained his composure. It passes belief, but with gentle de-   105
meanor and mildness of heart they sought out the body of the old
man, worthy of veneration, and with a roar lay down by his feet,
wailing for the dead with piety all but human. Then they vie with
each other in rushing to scoop up enough earth with their paws to   110
make a burial mound, and to come to the help of the father in his
time of need and to relieve him of his worry. So it is when fields of

Sic quando aret holus, arent et prata, nec ullas
quas infundat habet terris sitientibus undas
115 agricola infelix, tunc si praelargus aquarum
exundet torrens, et riui et hiantia passim
prata fluunt laetis et egentes imbribus horti.
Continuo ad sanctum blando cum murmure patrem
ibant, deiecta ceruice manusque pedesque
120 lingebant, quales studium quos nutrit herile,
blandiri caudaque solent linguaque catelli.
Ille stupens quae tanta esset sub corde ferarum
cognitio, duplices tendebat ad aethera palmas,
extollens laudansque Dei admirabile munus,
125 proque bonis digna exsoluens quasi praemia tantis,
praecipuas pro se atque preces fundebat amicas.
Discessere ferae tandem, capit ille beatum
inclinans sese corpus tumuloque recondit.
Intextum at foliis palmarum, in pignus amoris
130 grande tulit, quem se reliquo sub tempore tantum
solemnes rarosque dies uestiuit amictum.
Tunc, ubi clara sequens tenebras Aurora fugauit,
discedit cupidusque domum sociosque reuisit
caelestemque hominem, facta et caelestia narrat.

FINIS

BONONIAE MCCCCXXXVII IV. IDUUS MARTII

crops are parched and meadows withered, when the wretched
farmer lacks any moisture with which he might drench his thirsty
lands: should a rushing torrent then bring floods of water, both   115
the streams and the gaping meadows and the gardens in need of
the nourishing liquid are everywhere aflow. Forthwith they made
their way with tender growl to the holy father and, necks lowered,
they lick his hands and his feet, like whelps whom a master's
efforts have reared are wont to fawn on him with tail and tongue.   120
Astonished that such understanding resided in the hearts of
beasts, he stretched both his hands to the heavens, extolling and
praising the miracle of God's gift. Offering the form of reward due
such beneficence, he poured forth special prayers of friendship for 125
Paul.

When the animals at last departed, bending over he grasps the
holy body and buries it in the grave. As a token of his deep love he
put on a cloak, woven from palm leaves. With this alone he   130
clothed himself for the rest of his life on days of special solemnity.
Then, when the subsequent morn's bright dawn had put the dark-
ness to flight, he departs and eagerly returns to his home and com-
rades, and tells them of the godlike man and his godlike deeds.

THE END

BOLOGNA, MARCH 12, 1437

Appendix

❦❧❦

Epigram on the *Golden Fleece*, from the first book of Vegio's *Libri Epigrammatum* (1439–43). The addressee is the poet Cambio Zambeccari (see Raffaele, p. 39; Brinton, p. 19). The text is taken from Vatican City, Biblioteca Apostolica Vaticana, MS Vat. lat. 1669, ff. 32v-33r.

In Vellus Aureum

Quid mihi sit, quaeris, Cambi. Scribuntur amores
    Medeaeque novum surgit amantis opus.
Quod seu Medeis seu ius dicatur Iason
    dignum materia nomen utrumque sua est.
Salve, velis Argo seu Vellus dicier Aureum.
    Convenient operi nomina et ipsa meo.

You ask, Cambio, what I am doing. Loves are the subject of my pen, and a new work, Medea in Love, is coming into being. But whether right lies on the side of Medea or on that of Jason, the repute of each is worthy of expression. Hail, whether you wish to be called Argo or Golden Fleece. The titles themselves will also suit my work.

Note on the Text

The Latin text of the Supplement to the Aeneid is based on the critical edition of Bernd Schneider, ed., *Das Aeneissupplement des Maffeo Vegio*, eingeleitet, nach den Handschriften herausgeben, übersetzt und mit einem Index versehen (Weinheim: Acta Humaniora, 1985).

The Latin text of the Golden Fleece is based on the critical edition of Reinhold F. Glei and Markus Köhler, eds., *Maffeo Vegio: Vellus Aureum — Das Goldene Vlies (1431), Einleitung, kritische Edition, Übersetzung*, Bochumer Altertumswissenschaftliches Colloquium, 38 (Trier: Wissenschaftler Verlag Trier, 1998).

Readers are referred to these excellent editions for discussion of the textual traditions of the two poems and full critical apparatus.

As neither the *Astyanax* nor the *Antoniad* has been edited in modern times, a provisional edition of these texts, based on a selection of early witnesses, has been prepared by James Hankins. For further information on the textual history of these works, readers may consult Shalimar Abigail O. Fojas and James Hankins, "A Checklist of Manuscripts and Early Editions containing Maffeo Vegio's *Astyanax* (1430) and *Antonias* (1436/7), with a note on the date of the *Antonias*," forthcoming in the journal *Scriptorium*.

The *Astyanax* survives in some 28 manuscripts and nine printed editions; the first edition was printed in Cagli in 1475, the last in Florence in 1724. The witnesses collated for the present edition (all of the fifteenth century) are as follows:

A1   Milan, Biblioteca Ambrosiana, D 5 sup.
A2   Milan, Biblioteca Ambrosiana, T 21 sup.
A3   Milan, Biblioteca Ambrosiana, M 26 sup.
E   El Escorial, Biblioteca, MS f II 12 (dated Bologna, 21
            December 1436)
F1   Florence, Biblioteca Nazionale Centrale, Naz. II IV 704
F2   Florence, Biblioteca Nazionale Centrale, Naz. II IX 4

F3 Florence, Biblioteca Nazionale Centrale, Naz. II IX 148

H London, British Library, Harl. 5198

L1 Florence, Biblioteca Laurenziana, Plut. XXXVIII, 38

L2 Florence, Biblioteca Laurenziana, Plut. XXXIX, 40

N Naples, Biblioteca Nazionale, IV F 18

V Vatican City, Biblioteca Apostolica Vaticana, Vat. lat. 1668

Ca The first edition, printed in Cagli (near Urbino) 'per
           Robertum de Fano et Bernardinum de Bergamo'.

Vegio's dedicatory poem to Marchettus is found printed at the end of the *Astyanax* in Cagli and subsequent imprints, but is omitted in the earliest manuscripts. The text given here follows the edition of Cagli.

The *Antoniad* is preserved in twelve fifteenth-century manuscripts and was printed eleven times between 1490 and 1677. For the present edition the following witnesses have been collated:

E   El Escorial, Biblioteca, MS f II 12, copied before 1443.
           A seventeenth-century hand (E^2) has made corrections,
           some of them possibly derived from L.

L   Lodi, Biblioteca Comunale Laudense, XXVIII A II, s. XV
           2/4, possibly the earliest manuscript.

V   Vatican City, Biblioteca Apostolica Vaticana, Vat. lat. 3600, s.
           XV med., apparently a presentation copy.

Three of the printed editions (Deventer 1490 and 1491, Lyons 1677) have been collated in their entirety but their variants represent later editorial tamperings with Vegio's text and have not been recorded here. Soundings have also been made in several other manuscripts (Vat. lat. 1669, an apograph of V; Vat. lat. 5163; and Rome, Biblioteca Casanatense 4563).

Spelling and punctuation have been modernized in accordance with the usual practice of this series.

James Hankins gratefully acknowledges the help of Virginia Brown and Michael Putnam, who read the texts of the *Astyanax* and *Antoniad* and offered numerous useful suggestions.

Notes to the Text

༺ঙঁঙ༻

ASTYANAX

Title: Mafei Vegii Laudensis Astianas incipit feliciter lege *V:* Maffei Vegii Laudensis Astianas incipit feliciter *F1 L2:* Maffei Vegii Laudensis de morte Astianatis carmen incipit *L2:* Astianas Vegii Laudensis *F2:* Astiancti mors per Manpheum Vegium e greco in Latinum traducta incipit feliciter *H:* Mafei Vegii Laudensis poete celeberrimi de morte Astyanactis opus iocundum et miserabile *Ca*   3 inulto] in alto *L1*   8 mortua *A2:* moratura *H*   11 facta *N*   13 cessus *A1:* torsus *L1*   15 Achaia *A1 A3 L1 Ca*   16 ferens aris et] referens aris *N*   18 dulces *A1 L1 N*   parensque *N*   22 stabat] stetit *L1*   24 eunt] erunt *L1 H:* erit *A1*   28 parva] parata *E*   31 Deflevit sparsos proprioque *corrected in V to* Sat flevit proprio sparsos, *perhaps a later redaction*   32 attendite *L1*   35 fortis *Ca*   37 Protendat *A2 H:* Portendant *F3:* Portentat *Ca*   neu] ne *Ca*   39 id] hunc *A1* libaret *H:* laborat *A1*   40 fide aut fraude *H*   44 nostris *A1*   45 erectae *Ca*   46 affari *Ca H*   52 casta *A1*   56 animos . . . paternos *H*   60 –que *om. H*   66 euertite] excindite *A1*   71 omnis *Ca*   75 est *om. Ca*   77 didici] vidi *F3*   81 eadem] cladem *F2:* tandem *Ca*   85 e] de *A1*   91 Miserae *F3*   99 despectus *A3 L1 L2 N:* depactus *F2 H*   102 toto de gente *A1 L1:* tanta *H*   106 ardentis] ingentis *Ca*   108 stabilesque *A3 F1 H L2 N*   114 Tuus] pius *s.s. F3 (but this may be a gloss on* Aeneas)   124 proeli *A3 F1 F2 F3 L2 N*   125 ubi *A3 F2 L1*   127 lacrimas . . . profudit] magno ingemuit perculsa dolore *F2 F3 L2 V, probably from an earlier redaction*   128 fugarat *A1 L1*   129 Tunc] Cum *H L1 N V:* Tum *H*   130 moueret *A1 F1*   131 insurgent *A1 A2 A3 N:* consurgere *H* hostis *Ca*   132 turbas *E L1 H*   141 Hunc] Nunc *A2 F3*   143 praeterrita *A1 F3*   149 mutabat] mittebat *L1*   153 ubere] utero *E* facta *Ca H*   154 Laertides dux] dux Laertius *after correction in V by a second hand* omnes *A1 L1 N*   157 di *A1*

171

164 cessoque *A2 N*   172 torquensque *H*: torquesque *Ca*
175 prorsusque per *Ca L1 H N*   178 fugeret *Ca*   huc *Ca*
182 omnia] omnia bella *Ca*   tamen *A1*   194 Hectorea *E*
195 summe *A2 F2 F3 L2 N* (*perhaps a variant spelling*)   196 at illum]
atque ut melior dux *Ca*   202 comisere *A1*: miserere *F3*: compatiare
A2 A3 Ca L1 N Ca   205 Vicisti *L1 F3*   porro] siquidem *N*   o *om.*
Ca H (*as demanded by prosody*)   212 quantoque quis *Ca*
215 dubiamque rerum *E*   219 proh] per *A1 F1 L1*   et nomina et
altum *Ca*   225 frementem *N*   229 sequitur *Ca*   234 fit et]
fuit *A1*   246 ut]et *A1 A2 A3 L1* 252 duroque] summoque *L1*
253 Tum] tamen *A2 A3*: Tunc *L1*   256 euulsumque *L1*   268 flu-
entis *Ca*   271 uiduae] miserae *L1*   276 nostris] matris *Ca*
279 sceptro] regno *L1*   auitum] initum *L1*   282 fata *A2 N*
283 spem atque *Ca*   289 ferro gentem *trans. Ca*   298 Nunc] Et
Ca ignis *Ca*   304 more] mole *A2*   309 nato *E*   312 naues *A1*
L1 N   315 funere] uulnere *F3*   *At end*: Ex Papia in ludis Julianis
MCCCCXXX *E*

THE GOLDEN FLEECE

BOOK II

226 quam] quem *Glei-Köhler*

ANTONIAD

DEDICATORY POEM

12 ingens] certe *E*

BOOK I

Title: Maphei uegii laudensis Anthoniados liber primus incipit *L*: incipit
feliciter *EV*   1 non] vos *EL*   2 vocarum *L*   4 verterem *L*
turbamue] turbamque *EL*   28 ueneratus *EL*   32 quo] quae *E*
47 duces *L*   56 o *om. L*   57 quondam] olim *EL*   68 Nunc]
Nec *EL*   73 consilio *EL*   85 satiata *EL*   87 omnis *L*
93 fideri (*sc. foederi*) *L*   94 uerteret *L*: euertet *E²*   119 se] illum

L, E²   126 se longe] longe illo *L, E²*   130 iubeto] uidebo *L*
135 uenturum *V*   147 subisti *LV, E²*: fuisti *E*

BOOK II

Title: INCIPIT SECVNDVS FELICITER *EV*: INCIPIT LIBER
SECVNDVS *L*   7 hae] heu *E*   8 elusa *EL*   10 inde]
deinde *EL*   16 a *om. L*   36 affatu] ad fatum *L*   68 fetus: *the
parallel passage in Jerome's Vita s. Pauli has* fructus   86 more *L*
95 lacrimas *E*

BOOK III

Title: INCIPIT LIBER TERTIVS *L*: INCIPIT TERTIVS
FELICITER *EV*   11 dubia *E*   29 acri] agri *L*   39 tonitru]
strepitu *EL*   44 cantum *L*   49 quo *LV*   60 abortis *E*: ab
ortis *L*   61 totue *L*   64 est] et *EL*   79 erant *E*
83 iunctus *following the source, Jerome's Vita s. Pauli:* functus *mss., edd.*
94 ingentisque *EL*   109 se coram leni] ante ipsos leui *L*: coram illis
leni *E²*

BOOK IV

Title: INCIPIT QUARTVS FELICITER *EV*: *om. L*   12 uellusque
V (?)   13 donum *V*   -que *om. L*   17 nudusne *E*   25 sibi]
illi *L*   33 haud] aut *L*   41 adplausu *E*: ad plausum *L*
46 molle *L*   47 confectam *V*   48 eius *E²L*: suo *EV*
62 *E²V give* se *for both instances of* illum   72 redire *L*   87 hunc]
se *V*   91 gerens] ferens *EL*   93 Ac] At *E*   98 enim quo id]
enim id quod *after correction in Vat. lat. 1669*   102 duos *L*
112 iuuaret *sic E*   egeret *L*   113 ullos *L (and before correction in E?)*
123 tendebat] mittebat *EL*   126 pro se] longe *L*   *Explicit:* DEO
GRATIAS AMEN. EXPLICIT LIBER QVARTVS FELICITER *V*:
Bononie MCCCCXXXVII IIIIa Iduus Martii Deo gratias amen *E*:
om. L

Notes to the Translation

࿊࿊࿊

BOOK XIII OF THE AENEID

1. Ardea in Latin means "heron." Vegio adopts the story from Ovid *Metamorphoses* 14.573–80.

2. Household gods.

3. In lines 519–20 Vegio adopts the etymological word-play that Virgil puts into Evander's mouth at *Aen* 8.322–23, connecting *Latium* and *latuisset,* Latium and "lurking."

4. That is to say, native god.

ASTYANAX

1. Possibly Marchetto Baldironi, mentioned in the correspondence of Antonio Beccadelli, "il Panormita", as the recipient of a letter dated Pavia, 1429. See Gianvito Resta, *L'Epistolario del Panormita, Studi per una edizione critica* (Messina: Università degli Studi di Messina, 1954), p. 209. Beccadelli also wrote a poem "Pro Marcetto ad Montienses," which is preserved in a number of fifteenth-century literary miscellanies.

Bibliography

❧❦❧

MODERN EDITIONS

Glei, Reinhold F. and Markus Köhler, eds. *Maffeo Vegio: Vellus Aureum —Das Goldene Vlies (1431): Einleitung, kritische Edition, Übersetzung*. Bochumer Altertumswissenschaftliches Colloquium, Band 38. Trier: Wissenschaftlicher Verlag, 1998.

Schneider, Bernd, ed. *Das Aeneissupplement des Maffeo Vegio*. Weinheim: Acta Humaniora, 1985.

For early modern editions, see the article of Fojas and Hankins cited below.

SELECTED MODERN STUDIES

Allen, Don Cameron. *Mysteriously Meant: The Rediscovery of Pagan Symbolism and Allegorical Interpretation in the Renaissance*. Baltimore, Maryland: The Johns Hopkins University Press, 1970.

Beale, S. "From Vocational Emulation to Addition: The 'Complementing' of Vergil by Mapheus Vegius and Dante." *Brown Classical Journal* 14 (2002): 43–52.

Blandford, D. "Virgil and Vegio." *Vergilius* 5 (1959): 29–31.

Bono, Barbara J. *Literary Transvaluation: From Vergilian Epic to Shakesperian Tragicomedy*. Berkeley, 1984.

Brinton, Anna Cox. *Mapheus Vegius and his Thirteenth Book of the Aeneid*. Stanford, 1930. Repr. New York, 1978. Repr. London, 2002.

Buckley, Emma. "'What happened next. . .:' Closure and Continuation in Virgil's Aeneid and the thirteenth book of Maffeo Vegio." M.Phil. Thesis, Cambridge University, 2002.

Duckworth, George. "Mapheus Vegius and Vergil's Aeneid: A Metrical Comparison." *Classical Philology*, 64 (1969): 1–6.

Fojas, Shalimar Abigail O., and James Hankins. "A Checklist of Manuscripts and Early Editions containing Maffeo Vegio's *Astyanax* (1430) and *Antonias* (1436/37), with a note on the date of the *Antonias.*" Forthcoming in *Scriptorium.*

Fragonard, Marie-Madeleine. "Le 'treizième livre' de l'Énéide." In René Martin ed., *Énée et Didon: naissance, fonctionnement et survie d'un mythe,* pp. 79–88. Paris, 1990.

Greene, Thomas M. *The Descent from Heaven. A Study in Epic Continuity.* New Haven, 1963. See especially pp. 107–12.

Hardie, Philip R. *The Epic Successors of Virgil: A Study in the Dynamics of a Tradition.* Cambridge, 1993.

Hijmans, Benjamin L. "Aeneia Virtus. Vegio's *Supplementum* to the Aeneid." *Classical Journal* 67 (1971–72): 144–55.

Kallendorf, Craig, "Maffeo Vegio's Book XIII and the Aeneid of Early Italian Humanism." In Anne Reynolds, ed., *Altro Polo: The Classical Continuum in Italian Thought and Letters.* Sydney, 1984.

—— *In Praise of Aeneas: Virgil and Epideictic Rhetoric in the Early Italian Renaissance.* Hanover, New Hampshire, 1989.

—— *Virgil and the Myth of Venice.* Oxford, 1999.

—— "Historicizing the 'Harvard School': Pessimistic Readings of the Aeneid in Italian Renaissance Scholarship." *Harvard Studies in Classical Philology* 99 (1999): 391–403.

Kallendorf, Craig, and Virginia Brown. "Maffeo Vegio's Book XIII to Virgil's Aeneid: A Checklist of Manuscripts." *Scriptorium* 44 (1990): 107–25.

Klecker, Elisabeth. *Dichtung über Dichtung: Homer und Vergil in lateinischen Gedichten italienischer Humanisten des 15. und 16. Jahrhunderts.* Wiener Studien, Beiheft 20. Vienna, 1994.

Lippincott, Kristin. "The neo-Latin historical epics of the north Italian courts: an examination of 'courtly culture' in the fifteenth century." *Renaissance Studies* 3.4 (1989): 415–28.

Maguinness, W. S. *The Thirteenth Book of the Aeneid.* Virgil Society Publications. London, 1957.

Minoia, M. *La Vita di Maffeo Vegio umanista lodigiano.* Lodi, 1896.

Putnam, Michael C. J. "The Loom of Latin." *Transactions of the American Philological Association* 131 (2001): 329–39.

Raffaele, Luigi. *Maffeo Vegio: Elenco delle opere, scritti inediti.* Bologna, 1909.

Schmidt, Paul Gerhard. "Neulateinische Supplemente zur Aeneis. Mit einer Edition der *Exsequiae Turni* des Jan van Foreest." In Josef Ijsewijn and Eckhardt Kessler, eds., *Acta Conventus Neo-Latini Lovaniensis. Proceedings of the First International Congress of Neo-Latin Studies. Louvain 23–28 August 1971*, pp. 517–555. Louvain-Munich, 1973.

Sottili, Agostino. "Zur Biographie Giuseppe Brivios und Maffeo Vegios." *Mittellateinisches Jahrbuch* 4 (1967): 219–42.

Suerbaum, Werner. "Hundert Jahre Vergil-Forschung: Eine systematische Arbeitsbibliographie mit besonderer Berücksichtigung der Aeneis," *Aufstieg und Niedergang der Romischen Welt* 2. 31. 1 (1980): 3–358. See p. 349 on Vegio.

Thomas, Richard. *Virgil and the Augustan Reception*. Cambridge, 2001.

Tudeau-Clayton, Margaret. "Supplementing the Aeneid in Early Modern England: Translation, Imitation, Commentary," *International Journal of the Classical Tradition* 4 (1998): 507–25.

Vignati, Bruno. *Maffeo Vegio umanista cristiano (1407–1458)*. Bergamo, 1959.

Zabughin, Vladimiro. *Vergilio nel Rinascimento Italiano da Dante a Torquato Tasso*. 2 vols. Bologna, 1921–23.

Index

References to the poems are by line number (and book number where appropriate), and are given in order of publication. References to the Introduction are by page number. S = *Supplementum*, As = *Astyanax*, GF = *Golden Fleece*, An = *Antoniad*.

Publication of this volume has been made possible by

The Myron and Sheila Gilmore Publication Fund at I Tatti
The Robert Lehman Endowment Fund
The Jean-François Malle Scholarly Programs and Publications Fund
The Andrew W. Mellon Scholarly Publications Fund
The Craig and Barbara Smyth Fund
for Scholarly Programs and Publications
The Lila Wallace–Reader's Digest Endowment Fund
The Malcolm Wiener Fund for Scholarly Programs and Publications